BULMERS OF HEREFORD

To All Participants
In The Bulmer Enterprise
Past, Present, And Future

L.P. WILKINSON

BULMERS OF HEREFORD

A CENTURY
OF CIDER-MAKING

Stay me with flagons; comfort me with apples.
The Song of Solomon, II.5

DAVID & CHARLES
NEWTON ABBOT LONDON NORTH POMFRET (VT)

British Library Cataloguing in Publication Data
Wilkinson, L.P.
Bulmers of Hereford: a century of cider-making.
1. Cider industry — England — Herefordshire
—History
I. Title
338.4'76632   HD9398.G73H/

ISBN 0-7153-9116-X

Printed in Great Britain by
Billings Ltd, Worcester
for David & Charles Publishers plc
Brunel House Newton Abbot Devon

Published in the United States of America
by David Charles Inc
North Pomfret Vermont 05053 USA

CONTENTS

EDITORIAL NOTE

Before his final illness in 1986 Patrick Wilkinson had prepared for the press all fourteen chapters of this book. He had been given access to all the company and family records, but the responsibility for the selection of material for those chapters, the statement of fact and the expression of opinions was his alone. He had drafted an epilogue bringing the history up to the date of writing, but this was not in finished form, and the epilogue which is published here, on a reduced scale, is an editorial addition to Patrick Wilkinson's text.

PREFACE

In recent times highly professional histories of industrial concerns, bristling with statistics, have so proliferated as to constitute a new genre. There is a regular Business History Newsletter, and a Dictionary of Business Biography is being prepared. We have had massive books such as Charles Wilson's *Unilever 1946-1965* (1968) and W.J. Reader's *Bowater: a History* (1981). These must be of a primary interest to the industrialist and the economic historian. Coming nearer, from the world of liquor, there has been *Greene King*, by Richard G. Wilson (1983).

This book has no such pretentions. Indeed the rather haphazard nature of the evidence available for the earlier part would have precluded such treatment. Primarily it is a history of the firm of Bulmer, composed for its centenary at its invitation; but it hopes to appeal to a wider, and therefore essentially diverse, readership – to the general reader, but naturally to certain classes in particular, e.g. to inhabitants of Hereford and the neighbouring counties, to people concerned with the drink trade and especially workers for Bulmers; to businessmen interested in the growth of industries; or to social historians. It is largely concerned with *people*, and celebrates the centenary in 1987 of a family enterprise begun by two brothers in their father's rectory orchard, which has so prospered that it has been for some 70 years the biggest cider business in the world, producing nearly half of the cider drunk in Britain, yet has managed not to lose its human identity.

For the first two, historical, chapters I read a number of old books, most of them kindly lent to me by my friend Mr Bertram Bulmer or his daughter, Miss Gillian Bulmer. I also profited considerably from an unpublished dissertation which earned a diploma for Mr P.R. Bowyer, R.I.B.A., from the Brighton Polytechnic, *A History of Cidermaking in England* (1977), and from Dr R.K. French's lively and attractively illustrated *The History and Virtues of Cider* (1982). For the early history of the firm Fred (E.F.) Bulmer's pamphlet *Early Days of Cidermaking* (1937), reprinted with notes by his second son Harold in 1980, is as indispensable as it is enjoyable. But it was no easy matter to recontruct the history of the firm from 1887 to 1919, when his brother Percy (H.P.) Bulmer died. The brothers decided things orally: there were no reports or minutes. The formation of the private company of H.P. Bulmer & Co. in 1918 did at least produce some regular documentation, tenuous though it was; but to conceive any continuous account I still had to rely on cuttings, particularly from the *Hereford Times*.

Fortunately however Fred Bulmer was a prolific letter-writer. His surviving letters, notably to his fiancée from 1897 to 1899, and to his lifelong friend from college days Nathaniel Wedd, have been available to me in typed copies through the good offices of Harold Bulmer, who also dug out and had typed such lists of sales, tonnage of apples etc. as survive from early days, besides several papers about his father which he composed himself. These materials, and other files, e.g. of advertisements, are to be found in the archives of the Cider Museum at Hereford. There is also a Bulmer Collection in the Hereford City Record Office (J 65, 1–1500) of documents relating to the family, again largely collected by Harold. Not until 1962 was there a house periodical. For the few years after that which are covered by this book the *Woodpecker News* has been valuable (would it had been sooner!), and for the Epilogue, *News Line*, its successor from 1975, appearing more frequently but more like a newspaper than a magazine. One other useful work should be mentioned here, Professor W.E. Minchinton's article 'The British Cider Industry since 1870' in the *National Westminister Bank Quarterly Review* for November 1975, 55–67.

After the First World War our story enters the period of living memory, including memory of the reminiscences which so enlivened Fred's conversation. And here I must explain how I, a retired Cambridge classical don, come to be writing this book. When I was a student at King's College, Cambridge, my teacher in classics, J.T. (later Sir John) Sheppard, took me for a memorable Hellenic Cruise for which we joined up with his friend Fred Bulmer and Harold, who was also reading classics at King's. From then until World War II Fred and his wife Sophie often invited me to their home, which became a second home to me, and even took me on a family trip to the Continent. So when I was asked to write this book I was glad of a chance to repay what I could of my gratitude to them and their children. To enable me to do so their eldest son Bertram and his wife Christine have opened their home near Hereford, Little Breinton, to me for regular visits without which I should not have been able to study the documentary material. My only qualifications were familiarity with the Bulmer family, ten of whom I have known as alumni of King's, and the experience of having written a somewhat analogous book about the college, *A Century of King's 1873-1972* (1981). About cider and about business I have had to pick up what I could, and rely on more qualified people to lighten my darkness and correct my errors.

CHAPTER ONE

HISTORY OF CIDER TO 1886
(with special reference to England)

The word 'cider' or 'cyder' has a long descent. From the Hebrew *shekar*, 'strong drink', comes the Christian Greek *sikera*, whence the Christian Latin *sicera*, later spelt *cisera*, and the French *cidre*. True cider consists of the fermented juice of particular breeds of cider apple, distinguished for their tannin content and generally lower acidity. These breeds are hardly ever good to eat; nor do eating apples generally yield good cider. The fibrous texture of cider apples facilitates the extraction of juice. On the Continent the chief areas of production are Normandy, Brittany and Maine, which account for more than 70% of the French supply. But from early times cider has been popular also in the Channel Isles, and in the Basque lands of northern Spain;[1] and it is produced in Belgium, Switzerland and Germany. It used also to be made in Eire, in Munster, and it is still drunk there.

In England there are two adjacent areas, divided by the Severn and the Bristol Channel, which produce slightly different kinds of liquor: the shires of Gloucester, Worcester and Hereford, with parts of Monmouth (Gwent), and those of Somerset and Devon, with parts of Dorset and Cornwall. (The drink produced in Norfolk and Kent is made largely with local eating apples.) These areas have a climate combining a fair amount of rain with a fair amount of sunshine. They are not, at least nowadays, really hot enough for vines. Both Herefordshire and Devon are remarkable for the character of soil they share, a deep clay loam of Old Red Sandstone.

A little true cider is produced in Canada, less still in the United States, where however the freshly pressed juice of eating apples is called 'sweet cider' (as distinct from fermented 'hard cider'), and unfermented apple juice preserved in can or bottle is popularly known as 'cider'. The alcoholic content of true cider varies between 3% and 8% by volume, as in beer. This is lower than that of wine, 8.5%–14%, because of lower sugar quantity in the fruit. If it goes above 8.7% it becomes liable to much higher duty. The best and soundest cider should contain 5%–7% of alcohol, with 8.5% as a maximum.

Liquor made from pears (Latin *piracium*, French *poire*, Old English *pirige*, English *perry*) is made by a similar process to cider, but presents more problems as to control of after-fermentation, prevention of deposits and cloudiness. It can be made to look and taste more like white wine – can indeed be passed off as such to the ignorant or sufficiently intoxicated. 'Royal cider', produced in the 17th and 18th centuries, was a potent liquor comprising the spirit distilled from one hogshead of cider added to a second hogshead. Brandy (in Normandy 'Calvados') can be distilled from cider or perry. After two centuries during which the excise authorities in Britain prevented its production, Bertram Bulmer obtained permission to distil it at the Cider Museum in Hereford and began to do so in 1984 under the brand name 'King Offa' (the local King of Mercia in Saxon times). Cider vinegar is also made: in 1891 Bulmers were charging 5s for a dozen wine-bottles of it.

These drinks were known in some form in antiquity. Palladius (4th century A.D.) indicates that the Romans preferred perry to cider, and gives instructions for making it. We catch glimpses of them, as products of ascetic monks, in the Dark and Middle Ages. St Guénolé of Brittany (414–504) chastised himself by living on a diet of water and perry. St Radegunda (died 587) is reported to have drunk only perry after her retirement to a monastery. In the 8th century St Ségolène in Lent drank only perry apart from water. But in the 9th we find the Abbot of Ferrier proudly inviting fellow-monks to taste his perry. Cider-makers were among the employees of Charlemagne, cider being at that time probably the crudely extracted and watered juice of wild, unselected fruit. Nevertheless in the northern part of Gaul (later France) the national drink was ale (Latin *cervisium*, French *cervoise*), until in Normandy and Brittany cider challenged it in the 13th century and overtook it in the 14th, continuing to grow in popularity, with intensive planting of orchards, in the next two centuries. There is some reason to believe that the impetus for improved production of cider came into western Christendom from the Basque country, and northern Spain still exports considerable quantities of it to Spanish America.

In England the crab apple at least was indigenous, and no doubt there were plenty of apple trees even before the coming of the Normans. 'Aplewin' was highly esteemed by the Anglo-Saxons. The Romans introduced the vine also, and 38 vineyards are mentioned in Domesday. The drinking of imported wine was stimulated by the union, under Henry II, of England with the whole of western France, though cider also came in from Normandy, mainly into Kent and Sussex (large quantities were arriving at Winchelsea about 1270). The latter must now have been strong enough to remain unspoilt in the cask for some time and stable enough to survive sea transport. The earliest firm reference to cider in England comes in 1205,[2] when Robert de Evermue is found paying petty sergeantry for his lordship in Norfolk to the Exchequer with 200 pearmain apples and 4 hogsheads of 'wine' made from pearmains. (The word 'wine' was misleadingly used of any fermented fruit juice.) The death of King John in 1216 was, according to Matthew Paris, due to a surfeit of peaches and new cider. There are several references to cider in that century, concerning various counties as far north as Yorkshire. Hitherto the Celtic ale had been the island's national drink, but there is a story of the monks of Canterbury preferring cider to Kentish ale. We find many instances of tithe being paid in cider, especially in Sussex, from the fourteenth century onwards; and in that century William of Shoreham had to forbid its use for the baptism of infants.

It is probable, however, that in the Middle Ages cider was chiefly a drink for yokels; perhaps for soldiers too, for we hear of supplies being obtained in 1497 for the followers of the rebel Perkin Warbeck. But it would seem that the West Midlands, which were to become the great area for cider, took to it comparatively late. It is noteworthy that the inventories of Worcester Abbey as late as about 1533 contain no mention of cider (nor, for that matter, of wine, though vines were once much cultivated in that area; perhaps climatic changes may have been ousting the vine.)

Great impetus was given to orcharding in England by one Harris, fruiterer to King Henry VIII, who, as the diarist John Evelyn tells us, planted with fruit the fields and environs of about 30 towns in Kent alone. This may well have set an example to landowners in other counties, including those of the West Midlands. At any rate John Gerard wrote in 1597: 'I have seen in the pastures and hedgerows about the grounds of a worshipful gentleman dwelling two miles from Hereford called Mr Roger Bodnome so many trees of all sorts that the servants drink for the most part no other drink than that which is made of apples. The quantity is such, that by the report of the gentleman himself the parson has for tithe many hogsheads of cider.'[3] (One can only hope he was able to sell off some of it.) But the greatest pioneer among a number of landowners now interested was the first Viscount Scudamore, particularly at Holme Lacy on the River Wye a few miles south-east of Hereford, during the years of his retirement there, 1628–37. We shall hear more of him in the next chapter.

The first known writing on the subject of cider was a work apparently composed in the 1570s by a Frenchman, Julien Le Paulmier ('Julianus Palmerius'), a physician who, despite anxious periods due to his conversion to Protestantism, prospered through curing King Charles IX and his brother, and became Baron de Grentemesnil before his death in 1588. While visiting Normandy he was impressed with the physique of its cider-drinking population and became a propagandist for the beverage, regarding it as a sovereign remedy. He knew of no historical record of it, but was aware that it had been drunk in Biscaye, south of the Bay, as well as Normandy from time immemorial, and observed references to it in the oldest leases of property in Cotentin in the Cherbourg peninsula. The work in question, Volume 2 of his *Treatise on Wine and Cider*, is known to us in texts both French and Latin dated soon after his death.[4]

In England books on the subject began to appear in the seventeenth century. The interruption by wars of trade with the Continent gave cider a chance to take the place of wine on gentlemen's tables, now that men like Lord Scudamore were improving its quality by experiment and skill. Francis Bacon found it a 'wonderful and refreshing drink'. Ralph Austen, in his book of 1653, suggested (to Cromwell, unsuccessfully) that there should be a law compelling men to plant cider apple trees (instead of stealing the fruit by night). 'This liquor passes in many gentlemen's houses, and others, instead of wine' (it was incidentally cheaper); 'so much the better if it be burnt, with some sugar, spices, rosemary etc.' 'It can be coloured with the juice of mulberries, raspberries or the great-bearing cherries, making it like claret-wine.' Cider made of the best fruits was less windy: windiness occurred only at first, to those unaccustomed. This was a wine-like drink, undiluted, not to be confused with the 'small' or 'common' cider of the farm labourers which co-existed with it.

Cider, made seasonally in October–Christmas (when other farm work was conveniently slack), could be stored from year to year.

This required larger cellars, with doors big enough to admit a hogshead. Since these had to be above the water-table, we find, from the seventeenth century onwards, 'ciderhouses' above ground being added to old houses, or incorporated in new ones. Sometimes a complete building was purpose-made for cider production.

John Beale (1656) remembered that 'when the late King (Charles I) of blessed memory came to Hereford in his distress, and such of the gentry of Worcestershire as were brought thither as prisoners, both King, nobility and gentry did prefer cider before the best wines those parts afforded.' He says elsewhere that 'very few of our cottagers, yea, very few of our wealthiest yeomen, drink anything else in the family save on very special festivals'; and he speaks of the credit of cider as being recently so much advanced in the opinion of 'our best gentry'. ('Our' here probably means 'of the West Midlands': he was a Herefordshire man.) Discriminatory epithets for cider were now bandied about: 'brisk', 'smart', 'fierce', 'masculine', 'full-bodied', 'sprightly', 'oily', 'winy', 'nappy', 'nitty', 'luscious', 'feminine', 'tame', 'dull'. Beale avows: 'I did once prefer the Gennet-Moyle cider, but had only the Ladies on my side, as gentler for their sugary palates and for one or two sober draughts; but I saw cause to relent, and to confess the Red-streak to warm and whet the stomach either for meat or more drink.' The topographer Richard Gough alleges (1780) that within a few years of the publication of Beale's book his native county gained some £100,000 by the fame of its orchards.

Another powerful impetus was given to cider-drinking following the foundation of the Royal Society at the Restoration. One of the first things it did was to commission John Evelyn to compile his famous book on trees, *Sylva* (1664). This had a large appendix entitled 'Pomona', covering fruit-trees in relation to cider, admittedly a digest of the work of others, notably Beale. He hopes that King Charles II will set an example 'by planting some acres of the best cider-fruit at every of his royal mansions, till the preference of cider, wholesome and more natural drinks, do quite vanquish hops and banish all other drugs of that nature.'⁵Evelyn realised that without security there was no incentive for tenant farmers to plant trees. He proposed that Lords of the Manor should set an example and also favour tenants who planted, indeed oblige new ones by covenant to plant a certain proportion of their holding. An Act of Parliament should compel owners to plant two or three trees per acre. As it was, 'the nation drinks its very breadcorn'. He was also in favour of enclosures, 'whatever the clamour': orchards could be planted 'on very poor arable land, and even in strong gleab, gravel and clay, and that pretty high, on the sides and declivities of hills.'

Sir Isaac Newton was interesting himself in 1676 in the planting of trees for cider-making.[6] Opinion at Cambridge was that although the tree of the famous Redstreak grew well enough there, the cider made of it was harsh and churlish and would not keep above a year, as contrasted with three years in other parts of the country. This was generally imputed to the soil, but Newton was inclined to impute it to failure to blend it with other varieties. In a letter to Oldenburg in November of that year he asks not only for scions or grafts, but for information as to what sort of fruit is used for blending with it in the cider countries, in what proportions and by what method. The persons from whom he hoped to obtain grafts were Austen at Oxford and Beale at Yeovil, whom we have already met.

Cromwell's Navigation Act of 1651 was designed to destroy Dutch trade with English ports, and the Dutch ships were the chief means by which the wines of the Rhine and Moselle and much of those from France entered the country. Foreign wars continued to interrupt wine imports. 'Our design', said Evelyn, 'of relieving the want of wine by a *succedaneum* of cider (as lately improved) is a kind of modern invention.' He tells a story to illustrate its improvements. About 30 years ago a well-known Herefordshire man, Captain Sylas Taylor, had challenged a visiting London vintner that he would produce a cider which should excel the best French and Spanish wine. The wager being deposited, he brought in a good Redstreak. In three rounds with different judges (in one a triad aged respectively 10, 30 and 60) the vintner lost. John Worlidge, in his *Vinetum Britannicum*, a landmark in cider literature (1676), reckoned that erroneous methods had previously impaired the reputation of cider, a drink which was 'more suitable to our English bodies than any of those corrupt and adulterated wines that are daily consumed.' Taylor had defended cider against the accusation that it caused 'windiness', and decried boiling or spicing it as an imagined remedy for this imagined fault; and Beale had agreed.

We here encounter another factor in favour of cider, its reputed medicinal virtues.[7] True, Sir Thomas Elyot (1541) found that people in cider-drinking districts looked pale, and 'had the skin of their visage rivelled', even in youth; and in 1542 Andrew Boorde said that 'cyder is cold of operation and is full of ventosity, wherefore it doth engender evil humours.' This fitted in with the rediscovered medicine of the classical Greek authority Galen, but fashionable views soon changed. The physician Le Paulmier asserted that good (as distinct from coarse) cider and perry were valuable for all arthritic complaints, gouts, catarrhs and fluxions. Francis Bacon observed that cider and perry were notable beverages in sea voyages; and in his *New Atlantis* (1626), that ideal scientific society, travellers were greeted with cider. This discovery was highly important. Though news of it spread somewhat haphazardly, it pointed the way to the elimination of that most deadly scourge of seamen on long voyages, scurvy. Evelyn was informed that cider was 'specifically sovereign against the scorbut'. About 1740 Edward Ives, surgeon on HMS *Yarmouth*, prescribed a quart of cider a day per patient, and lost none of the ship's complement of 500. James Lind of HMS *Salisbury* in 1797 tried a controlled experiment. He gave two patients fresh oranges and lemons, two a quart of cider a day, and the rest the other remedies then prescribed. By the end of the voyage the first two were cured, the cider drinkers had improved, the rest were no better. (Since 1920 we have known that what scurvy needs is vitamin C. Only a strong cider such as was made in the eighteenth century, especially in South Devon, would have had the necessary amount.)

Evelyn also believed that 'all strong and pleasant cider excites and cleanses the stomach, strengthens digestion and frees the kidneys and bladder from breeding the gravel stone.' Worlidge echoes these views. As for longevity, we hear of one landlord who refused to grant life-tenancies to cider-drinkers.

The first attempt to test such claims scientifically was made by Dr Denis Dumont (1830–86), Professor at the Hospital of Caen in Normandy. His work was summarised by Dr H.E. Durham of Bulmers in 1929. There were statistics to show that stone in the bladder, a common complaint in wine-drinking Burgundy, was almost unknown in cider-drinking Lower Normandy. As for gout, if indeed cider-drinkers suffered less from it than wine-drinkers, this might be because (contrary to what used to be supposed) cider differs in being free from tartaric acid and its salts. And as for kidney trouble, cider, and perry still more, does promote urinary secretion, and so might help to eliminate unwanted substances. Durham concluded that the whole subject deserved further study.

Worlidge continued the campaign against people who still thought cider 'a dull drink'. Incompetence in past ages both in orcharding and in manufacture was responsible for this opinion. But lately there had been great improvements, and cider was likely to be still more widely drunk. Now sent in large quantities to London (by sea to Southwark wharves) and several other cities, it fetched a high price and was valued above French wines, which suffered both from travel and from adulteration. This kind of cider was indeed a wine, a 'short drink', not a 'long drink'. Cider was more wholesome than malt liquor, and it might in time become cheaper too, since an acre of apples yielded more than two or three acres of barley, let alone the annual expense of tillage. When corn was dear, cider was cheaper for rustics than ale. As to diffusion of new knowledge, Evelyn's digest issued 12 years before was nearly sufficient. Worlidge's chief reasons for writing were to record the results of some experiments with trees and soils; to publicise un-familiar means of purifying and preserving cider; and to introduce his own invention of a grinding machine which greatly reduced labour and costs, called the Ingenio after a Cuban sugar grinder. To those who might object that cider led to inebriety his answer was that 'that vice is not so regnant in this realm as it hath been in former ages'. If so, perhaps the Puritans had had some effect.

The increased popularity of cider had, however, one drawback: it attracted the attention of the Exchequer. In 1643 the Long Parliament introduced, among a number of duties designed to help pay for the Civil War, an excise duty of 2s per hogshead of cider, levied on the retailer (one of 1s levied on private householders was repealed in 1653). This was not removed at the Restoration; indeed it was increased to 2s 6d for English and 10s a tun for imported cider.

The advantage given to cider over imported wine by Marlborough's wars further increased its popularity. This, together with an unprecedented vogue for Virgil's poem of rural life, the *Georgics*, emboldened John Philips to produce his *Cyder*, a poem in two books totalling 1,465 lines, published in 1708. In treatment it is an imitation of Virgil, in verse and style, of Milton. The medium of *Paradise Lost* gives it a certain air of pomposity. Like the *Georgics*, it varies practical precepts with ornamental digressions, on matters ranging from how glass is blown to the 'earthquake' (actually a landslide) on 17 February 1575 at Marcle Hill in Herefordshire.

A few lines will serve as a sample (he has been speaking of the ordinary 'Musk' apple);

> Yet let her to the Redstreak yield, that once
> Was of the sylvan kind, uncivilised,
> Of no regard, till Scudamore's skilful hand
> Improv'd her, and by courtly discipline
> Taught her the savage nature to forget
> Hence styl'd the Scudamorian plant....

The poem had a considerable success. It was translated 41 years later into Tuscan Italian. James Thomson, in his day perhaps the foremost poet of Europe in repute, hailed him as

> Philips, Pomona's bard, the second thou
> Who nobly durst, in rhyme-unfettered verse,
> With British freedom sing the British song

(that is, second to Milton in blank verse). We may be more inclined to agree with Dr Johnson. While praising the poem for being 'at once a book of entertainment and of science', he disapproved of Milton's grand style being applied to so mundane a subject, and concluded 'He seems not born to greatness and elevation'. There was an element of propaganda and of patriotism, not to say chauvinism, local and national, in this cider literature. It resounds in Philips' finale.

> Where'er the British spread
> Triumphant banners or their fame has reached
> Diffusive, to the utmost bounds of this
> Wide universe, Silurian [8] cider borne
> Shall please all tastes, and triumph o'er the vine.

In 1726 we still find cider praised, by Defoe, as 'so very good, so fine and so cheap'. He notes that great quantities of it were sent to London, even by lane carriage, though so very remote. Indeed the Duke of Chandos in 1720 sent his Genovese picture-dealer a dozen of Herefordshire Redstreak cider. But it is undeniable that before the middle of the eighteenth century cider did go out of fashion with the wealthier classes, when the wars were intermitted and wine was obtainable from the Continent again; and one factor was precisely the difficulty of 'lane carriage'. There was a further setback when, in 1763, Lord Bute's Government, to pay retrospectively for the Seven Years' War, imposed an additional and higher duty of 4s on a hogshead of cider, this time levied on the makers, to match the duty on beer. The outcry was nationwide, and not only outcry: the bells of Ledbury were rung with muffled peals of mourning for a whole day, and village church porches were draped with black crepe. The imposition was particularly unpopular because for the first time Government supervisors were given the right to enter private property in search of dutiable goods. (It was in opposing it that the elder Pitt popularised the dictum 'An Englishman's home is his castle'.) Plaques and painted cider mugs reinforced the protest. An extant caricature, 'The Roasted Exciseman or Jack Boot's exit', celebrates its withdrawal and the concomitant fall of Bute's Government. Private makers were exempted, though higher duties were imposed on retailers.

But there were other reasons for the decline of common cider. As population grew, agriculture was increasingly called upon to supply the more essential articles of food, corn and cattle. Corn was less fallible than orchard crops, and the area available for its production was almost unlimited. Also barley was plentiful, and beer became the drink of the big cities, encouraged by a Government concerned to divert drinkers from the ravages of gin. Again, apple trees took long to mature, and the price obtainable for fruit, juice or cider varied widely with the size of the crop. So orchards either degenerated through neglect or were grubbed up; and as less care was taken to produce cider of quality, what reached the cities gave it a bad name. Farmers forgot the good practices of their forebears.

Of course common cider continued to be drunk by farm labourers. 'Ciderkin' or 'Purr' was made for them by the addition of water to the apple-cake as it was passed a second time through the mill. It was fermented without any addition of yeast, and the process was carried through to completion, so that little or no sugar remained. Labouring people told Evelyn that they worked much better on weak cider than on the best beer. In haytime and harvest it was allowed to them in almost unlimited quantities, as a harmless and invigorating drink. At times when polluted water caused cholera and typhoid it was, because of its acidity, a comparatively safe drink. In the eighteenth century it became customary to pay about a fifth of their wages in 'truck' consisting of 'Zeyder' or 'Scrumpy', 3–4 pints a day in normal seasons, 6–8 or even more during haymaking and harvesting. A labourer's performance was rated by the amount he drank: a two-gallon man was reckoned to be worth the extra quantity he consumed.[9]

Down to the end of the nineteenth century at least, in central and northern Herefordshire if not elsewhere, at a ceremony called 'Burning the Bush' on New Year's Eve, chanting of the words 'Auld Zeyder' (the final syllable a low growl) accompanied drinking of that liquor. *The Times* for 18 January 1982 carried a photograph of a 'Wassailing Queen' being carried shoulder high through apple orchards at Norton Fitzwarren in Somerset so that she could attach toast soaked in mulled cider to the trees with the object of attracting good spirits (in the shape of robins). Earlier in the evening 400 cider-makers had banged sticks and fired shotguns, originally done to frighten evil spirits away from this annual wassail ceremony.[10]

Surplus production led to the rise of middlemen, called 'cidermen'. These resided principally at Ledbury and Upton, but they had buyers for them in Hereford, Gloucester and Worcester besides sending buyers out into the West Midlands. Bristol dealers also processed their own cider and perry at Hereford, and London dealers at Upton. Most was bought as cider straight from the press: growers did not want to pay the costs of conveying apples, nor to lose the liquor consumed in the home. Some liquor was also exported in bottle from Bristol to the East and West Indies and other foreign parts. This could only be done when it had acquired some considerable age, otherwise the bottles were liable to burst. Middlemen were accused of watering cider down, making about five hogsheads out of three, and of doctoring it for sweetness and colour in accordance with what they believed to be public taste. Until the coming of railways made transport much easier and increased competition farmers were at the mercy of dealers who met annually at the Hereford Fair about October 20 to fix the price of common cider for that and the adjoining counties, without consulting the growers and producers. In the 1780s, the latter on average got less than 20s a hogshead for juice.[11] To set against that was the cost of picking, carrying, grinding and pressing, totalling about 5s. If they had to use a public mill, they might be charged about 1s a hogshead. That left a profit of only 14s a hogshead, or half of that if they had to rent house and orchard.

Interest in quality cider and its wider distribution resurfaces in William Marshall's *The Rural Economy of Gloucestershire*, published in 1789. Volume II, pages 239–401, forms a separate section on 'The Management of Orchards and Fruit Liquors in Herefordshire'. Marshall says that this is a subject much misunderstood, and claims (strangely, when one thinks of Austen, Beale, Evelyn and Worlidge more than a century before) that the art has never been duly investigated. This shows, at least, how much had been forgotten. Such farmers as did make good cider for sale were reluctant to share their knowledge. But now the possibilities of marketing had been much improved by the 'present facility for land carriage' (and Macadam was soon to revolutionise this further), and by canals that were being dug, notably one linking the Severn and the Thames.

Marshall has much to say about prices. Towards the end of the eighteenth century quality cider again became remunerative. One farmer in Ross sold in one year 50 hogsheads of Bareland perry at 10 guineas a hogshead, or two shillings a gallon. Higher prices were paid for superior ciders. A Mr Bellamy, from near Ross, was offered 60 guineas for a hogshead of Hagloe Crab cider, or exchange, bottle for bottle (without freight, duty or carriage), of the best wine or spirits.[12]

As to common ciders, most farmers had only enough fruit to supply their own enormous drink-houses; but some cottagers on enclosed land made up to 10 hogsheads in a plentiful year, nearly all for sale. It was estimated that the four West Midland counties produced 15,000 hogsheads a year for sale to dealers and as much again for their own consumption. Distribution was not extended beyond farmers to local inns and cider-houses. A fillip was also given in 1830 by the abolition, by the Duke of Wellington's new Government, of the original tax paid by the retailer, along with that on beer.

There were however inherent drawbacks in the cider trade. Damage to crops by drip and shade from orchard trees was annual and certain, whereas a general glut or 'hit' of fruit was most uncertain—rarely more frequent than every third year. And when there was a glut, the price of apples could fall so low as hardly to repay the labour, carriage and attention. But much could be done by the clearing away of inferior trees and the better spacing of more suitable young trees in their place.

Hard on Marshall's heels came T. Andrew Knight, the father of modern scientific pomology, with his *Treatise on the Culture of the Apple and Pear and the Manufacture of Cider and Perry* (1797). Knight was a Fellow of the Royal Society and President of the

Royal Horticultural Society, a great friend of Sir Joseph Banks and Sir Humphry Davy. He was the younger brother of Richard Payne Knight, the well-known Hellenist and poet, M.P. for Leominster (1780–84) and for Ludlow (1784–1806). When Banks asked Payne Knight who could provide him with certain rural statistics, the latter suggested his brother. This was a turning point. Andrew began his researches into fruit trees, and became a world authority on the subject. He showed, for instance, that 'blights' of fruit trees were caused, not by lightning or by some latent noxious quality in the air, but by aphids and other insects.

The revival of quality cider hoped for by Marshall proved to be of limited extent. In the Napoleonic Wars, though the importation of French wines was interrupted, the price of corn and meat rose dramatically, and many farmers grubbed up their orchards for arable or pasture. By the time that peace returned and this boom subsided the loss could not be made good by planting slow-growing fruit trees. Meanwhile the trees that remained had been neglected, not to mention the malpractices of the middlemen. The degeneration began about 1830.

Ill-repute was also caused by contamination. A painful complaint known as 'Devonshire colic' had been attributed by William Musgrave early in the eighteenth century to rough and acid cider. Then in 1767 George Baker, observing that this was peculiar to Devon among cider counties, traced it to lead poisoning due to the custom there of sealing the joints between the stones of the mill with lead, or lining the bases of the wooden presses with sheet lead. It emerged that some farmers also used sugar of lead to sweeten cider. The cider of Devon appears to have been much stronger than the diluted common cider of Herefordshire, though not than the wine-like liquor favoured by the gentry. At all events, Baker's revelation provoked a resounding row in Devon; and after a series of scandals the gentry in general were put off drinking cider for several generations. Knight warned against the use of lead in soldering cider-mills, and so did Bull (1886), in capital letters. H.E. Durham of Bulmers (1929) recommended that, wherever possible, wood, rubber or glass enamel should be used instead of metal in cider-making machinery.

Another source of contamination was ignorance of the importance of absolute cleanliness at every stage. According to Cooke (1898), out of 20–30 hogsheads the contents of only 2–3 might be good, some of the rest indifferent, most frankly bad. Only the bad tended to reach the public, so again cider was discredited. Imported cider from Germany or America was preferred; and cider apples were being exported to France from Somerset in the nineteenth century.

So far we have not distinguished between the fortunes of cider and perry. Small perry ('piriwhit') is mentioned by Langland in *Piers Plowman*. Pear trees were no doubt introduced into Britain by the Romans, but there is no mention of them until Saxon times. They are twice as long-lived as apple trees, sometimes surviving for 200 years, so that they occur in medieval maps as serving for boundary marks of manors and parishes. There are pear trees at Much Marcle which were planted in the reign of Queen Anne. 'He who plants pears plants for his heirs' was an adage. They are also larger than apple trees (Worlidge tells of one near Ross which could only be encompassed by the outstretched arms of three men); so they are less readily grubbed up. Unlike apple trees, he says, they will prosper in 'strong, hungry, gravelly land, yea in tough, binding and hungry clay'. One of them will bear almost its weight of 'sprightful, winy liquor, sometimes 2–4 hogsheads in a year'.[13] They are also splendidly ornamental, with their profusion of white blossom in spring and rosy fruit in autumn. Perry is a speciality of Herefordshire and the neighbouring counties.

The arms of the City of Worcester incorporate 'three pears sable', added by direction of Queen Elizabeth I when she visited the city in 1575. But Gloucestershire, in the areas of soils derived from Old Red Sandstone, is best for pears. Daniel Collwall, in Evelyn's 'Pomona', says that Taynton, five miles from Gloucester, abounds in red squash pears which make the best perry in those parts. Perry has, however, been generally less highly esteemed than cider both in France and England (though not in Germany). Beale defended them in one respect: 'Pears make a drink fit for our hindes, and is generally refused by our gentry as breeding wind in the stomach; yet this drink (till the heat of summer has caught it) is most pleasing to the female palate, having a relish of weak wine mixed with sugar.' He also conceded that the neighbourhood of Bosbury in Herefordshire yielded a perry which had many of the qualities of cider. Philips assumes the inferiority of perry:

What though the pear-tree rival not the worth
Of Ariconian products?....[14]

Nevertheless Taynton Squash has been highly valued; and Evelyn entertained some friends to perry made from Turgovian pears which had travelled 800 miles from Central Europe.

From Andrew Knight to Durham perry has had doughty champions. Knight discovered the virtue of the Holmer pear (from a tree found growing in a hedge on Charles Cook's farm, 'The Moor', Holmer). It was illustrated by him with four others in his *Pomona Herefordiensis* (1811), a landmark in the history of perry as containing the first published illustrations of such pears, in hand-coloured engravings by William Hooker. Good perry pears, says Knight, are always bad for eating (Bareland pears are rejected even by pigs); so they have also the marginal virtue of not attracting thieves. Perry, he maintained, should be made from a single variety of fruit, whereas for cider different varieties should be blended. It is however possible to blend even apple with pear juice with great success. So Durham says (1944); and he adds that perry is a necessary ingredient of a satisfactory cider cup; its vinegar is better than cider vinegar in salads; and it is important for the distilling of industrial alcohol.

Revival of interest in cider after the 19th century slump in England seems to have been stimulated by events in France, in whose north-western departments it has always been far greater than anywhere in England. The vines of the wine-growing areas there were languishing, smitten with the disease phylloxera. In 1864 the French Government summoned a congress for the study of cider fruits, to meet at Rouen. The results of its labours were published in 1875 under the title of *Le Cidre*. Production rose from an annual average of 210,000,000 gallons for 1866-76 to 517,000,000 for the hit year 1883. By 1884 the Central Horticultural Society of the Lower Seine had analysed nearly 400 varieties of cider apples and perry pears and classified them both for overall merit and for various qualities, and a great exhibition of them was then held, also at Rouen.

In England the effects of the repeal of the Corn Laws in 1846 and the establishment of free trade had finally worked through to cause the agricultural depression that began in 1875. Every district had now to concentrate on producing the things for which it was especially suited, in the best possible form. Orcharding was presented to farmers as a modest opportunity for offsetting some of the damage. Farmers also collaborated with itinerant cider-makers such as are described by Thomas Hardy in Chapter 25 of *The Woodlanders*, who managed to make a fair profit in a prolific year (at least one of them survived World War I in Herefordshire). Meanwhile one J. Trowbridge, who reckoned that few of his fellow Americans had ever tasted a perfect cider, was composing a *Cider-makers' Handbook*, which appeared at New York in 1890.

The strength of cider made in past times is hard to assess, owing to uncertainty about the validity of methods of analysis. At the Rouen Exhibition of 1884 the French chemists gave about 1067–1080 as the specific gravity of their best varieties, so that the strongest contained some 12% of alcohol (similar to the strength of red wine), with about 3% of the sugar left unfermented for residual sweetness.[15] The British experts Bull and Hogg (in a poor season for apples) gave their highest figures at 1073 for Forest Styre and 1068 for Foxwhelp. But these are still very high by modern standards, representing a short drink rather than a long drink. Their average however for 47 varieties was 1044.5, or less than 6% of alcohol, which would be normal enough today.

Prices in a historical context mean nothing without constant reference to modern values, and these now change almost from year to year; but it may be worthwhile, for comparative purposes between different brands at one time, to give some prices for 1885 as reported by Dr Bull. (The weekly wage of a navvy at that time was 3s 6d.)

Best quality cider sold in cask: 1–2 shillings a gallon.
Same quality fresh bottled: 8–12 shillings a dozen.
Second quality (somewhat watered): 6–10 pence a gallon.
Common farmhouse cider: 20 shillings a hogshead (100 gallons).
Perry: 4–18 pence according to quality.

Special brands matured in bottle:

At public auction in 1880 Mr Mason's Foxwhelp sold freely at 30 shillings a dozen, Taynton Squash perry at 28 shillings a dozen (champagne bottle size).

Such was the general situation in about 1886, the year before H.P. Bulmer began the enterprise shortly to be described. We turn now to Herefordshire in particular.

[1] The famous Redstreak cider apple is know in Normandy as 'La Basquette'.

[2] We read however in *Henry of Huntingdon* (1154) that when a great feast had been prepared at Hereford in the reign of Edward the Confessor an enemy broke in and slaughtered all the host's attendants, stuffing their heads and limbs into receptacles for wine, mead and...cider *(sicera)*. (He carelessly tells the story as implicating Tostig, son of Earl Godwin, instead of the Welsh prince Caradoc, who made such a raid in 1065.)

[3] John Philips the poet of cider could still admonish his reader in 1708:

> Nor let thy avarice tempt thee to withhold
> The priest's appointed share.

[4] Translations of both versions, in typescript, have been made by Mr R. Harold Bulmer, who observed that the French, though dated 1589, may follow an earlier version, since it has some passages lacking in the Latin one, dated 1588. He suggests that the French version may have been intended for landowners, the Latin for physicians.

[5] As to relative prices, the Holme Lacy accounts for 1662 show that of cider to be £1.14.0. a hogshead, of beer £1.4.0. But prices very considerably from year to year with the apple crop.

[6] *Memoirs of Sir Isaac Newton*, by Sir David Brewster (1855), Vol. I, pp.128–31.

[7] There is an admirable chapter on early linkage of 'Cyder and Medicine' in R.K. French's *The History and Virtues of Cyder* (Hale, 1982).

[8] The Silures were an ancient people of the Welsh border country.

[9] The Truck Act of 1887, promoted by temperance campaigners, forbade the practice, but by collusion it often continued. Fred Bulmer was told by a labourer that his pay was so much money a day 'and a quart of belly-vengeance'. In November 1925 a Herefordshire farmer was successfully summoned for deducting an allowance for cider from the minimum agricultural wage payable to an employee.

[10] There is an interesting article on 'Cider and Folklore' by W.E. Minchinton in *Folk Life* XIII (1975), 66–79.

[11] The term 'hogshead' causes much confusion because it was not standardised. For purposes of excise duty it was 63 wine gallons; but in Herefordshire usage it varied from 100 to 115 gallons, 110 being normal, whereas in Devon, for instance, it was always 50, the duty being adjusted accordingly. There is a historical note on this in R.K.French, *op cit*, p.184, n.40.

[12]Special cider-glasses similar to wine-glasses were made in the second half of the 18th century, with air-twisted or opaque white twisted stems. They were engraved with apple trees or branches, or with landscapes. Some, of 1763, were topically inscribed 'No Excise'. There are some good specimens in the Cider Museum at Hereford. Rustics drank their 'Purr' from two-handled pottery mugs.

[13] Worlidge (1676), pp.266–70, gives a catalogue of English pears.

[14] Kentchester, near Credenhill, was in Philips' time believed to be the Roman Ariconium, which is now known to have been at Bollitree Castle, near Ross.

[15] Edward Ball doubts whether 12% of alcohol can be obtained from apple juice; 9% would seem a more likely maximum.

CHAPTER TWO

HEREFORDSHIRE AND CIDER

In the famous chained library of Hereford Cathedral there reposes appropriately a noble specimen of the 'Cider Bible'. This is a copy, written about 1420, of the translation known as 'Wycliffe's Bible', which is believed to have been largely made by Nicholas of Hereford, Chancellor of the Cathedral from 1391. At Luke 1.15 the angel announces to Zacharias before the birth of John the Baptist, according to 'King James's Bible' of 1611, he 'shall drink neither wine nor strong drink' (in the Greek, *sikera*); but the bible at Hereford translates *sikera* as 'cider'.

Herefordshire however is not mentioned in the context of cider in three comprehensive surveys of the land, William Harrison's *Description of England* (1577), William Camden's *Britannia* (1586) and Michael Drayton's *Polyolbion* (1622); but by the middle of the seventeenth century its supremacy among the cider counties had already been established, so that Evelyn could write: 'By the noble example of my Lord Scudamore and of some other public-spirited people of those parts all Herefordshire has become, in a manner, but one entire orchard.' Having inherited Holme Lacy from his grandfather in 1623 and Cradock (Caradoc) from his great-uncles in 1631, Scudamore set himself to the improvement of cider fruit. We have seen how Philips praised him for developing a pure wilding, 'Scudamore's Crab', into the famous Redstreak. While Ambassador to France in 1634–38 he is said to have taken cuttings from Normandy orchards. At the Royalist festival in 1639 he kept open house at Holme Lacy from December 23 to January 11, but it is noteworthy that only 12 hogsheads of cider were drunk to 54 of beer. (It may be as well to acknowledge, here at the outset, that even in the cider counties, let alone elsewhere, the consumption of cider has never amounted to more than a small fraction of that of ale and beer.) Captain Sylas Taylor, his Herefordshire contemporary, in an appendix to Evelyn's 'Pomona', concedes that the Redstreak 'bears the bell'. In itself it was barely edible, but the juice pressed out was immediately pleasant in taste, clear in three months, and fit for drinking in six. At six years it was 'very pleasant but dangerously strong, sparkling yellow in colour, of good full body,

26

oily and tasting like peaches.'

Viscount Scudamore, originally Sir John, was son of Sir James, from whom Spenser named the gentle knight Sir Scudamour in Books III and IV of the *Faerie Queene*. A protegé of Buckingham and the future Archbishop Laud, ennobled in 1628, he kept a low profile in the Civil War and survived. On Laud's advice he restored to the parishes in 1632 all the tithes unlawfully appropriated by his predecessors. His work in the restoration of Abbey Dore church was almost the first such work undertaken since the dissolution of the monasteries in the previous century. He was M.P. for Hereford in 1627–28, High Sheriff in 1631, and from 1660 High Steward of the Lordships and Manors of the Dean and Chapter, whose interests he greatly promoted.

John Beale, D.D., author of *Herefordshire Orchards: a Pattern for all England* (1656) and one of the earliest Fellows of the Royal Society, was an alumnus and Fellow of King's College, Cambridge (later to be very much the Bulmer college). He lived at Hereford until 1660 and wrote his book there. Having tried Somerset, Kent and Essex cider for several years and Herefordshire for forty, he agreed with the general verdict that the Herefordshire was best. 'As no culture of grafts will exalt the French wines to compare with those of Greece, the Canaries and Montefiasco, so neither will the cider of Bromyard or Ledbury equal that of Holme Lacy or King's Capell in the same small county of Hereford.' According to Evelyn, one area in Herefordshire 20 miles in compass yielded 50,000 hogsheads of cider a year. This points to a considerable degree of external trade. Worlidge knew of a Herefordshire tenant who bought his farm with the profit of one year's retailing of cider. In the seventeenth century Hellens, Much Marcle, the future home of Radcliffe Cooke, was surrounded by at least 100 acres of orchard, and four avenues of pears were planted there in the reign of Queen Anne. About 5, 000 casks, each with 100 gallons of cider, were shipped annually down the Wye. John Kyrle, the philanthropic and hospitable 'Man of Ross' celebrated by Pope in his third *Moral Essay*, entertaining 12 neighbours every market day, never provided foreign wines, but beers, Redstreak and Styre cider, and particularly Taynton Squash perry. G. Gibson, who translated and edited Camden's *Britannia* in 1695, remarked on the growth of cider-making in Herefordshire since Camden's day: large quantities were now exported to London and other parts of England. John Philips' *Cyder* addressed

Ye Ariconian Knights and fairest Dames.

He lived himself in his mother's house at Hereford, and on his early death at the age of 32 was buried in the Cathedral there. A Latin eulogy of him, 49 lines long, is inscribed in Westminster Abbey, and there is a brass memorial to him in the S.E. corner of the North Transept of Hereford Cathedral. 'Herefordshire' was still in 1743 a name under which ciders from other counties thought it worthwhile to masquerade. In John Dyer's georgic poem *The Fleece* (1757) the county appears as an idyllic refuge from the newly industrialised Midlands.

When interest in cider revived after the long eighteenth-century slump, Charles Dunster produced in 1791 an annotated edition of Philips' *Cyder*. Its final note gives a full account of how the liquor was made in Herefordshire in his own time. William Marshall, in his work already mentioned, reaffirmed that Herefordshire had always borne the name of the first cider county. T. Andrew Knight, whom we have also met already, was a Herefordshire man who lived at Wormsley Grange, and later at Downton Castle on the border with Shropshire. He was a founder member of the Herefordshire Agricultural Society, one of whose activities was offering prizes for new varieties of cider apple; and he edited for it in 1811 *Pomona Herefordiensis*, with the novelty of coloured engravings, which was only superseded 70 years later, by *The Herefordshire Pomona*.

The belief that cider promotes health and longevity was nowhere stronger than in Herefordshire. There was the famous story of the 'Hereford Morris', danced at the Hereford Races in 1609 by 'a nest of Nestors'—12 men whose years totalled 1,200. Martin Johnson, Vicar of Dilwyn from 1651 to 1698, wrote besides a verse *Encomium of Cider*, a treatise concerning the longevity of the cider-drinkers of Herefordshire. 'The cottagers', he wrote, 'as well as the wealthy, for the most part drink little other liquors in their families but restorative cider. The ordinary course among their servants is to breakfast and sup with toast and cider through the whole of Lent, and the same diet continues in the neighbourhood on fasting days all the year round, which lightens their appetite and creates in them durable strength to labour.' The vicar gives a list of long-lived locals; and indeed the returns of the Registrar

General for 1885 still showed that county among the first for longevity. Radcliffe Cooke (1898) produces evidence that 'gravel' or 'stone' is unusually rare in cider-drinking districts, also gout (of which he claims to have rid himself by drinking cider and perry instead of whisky). Paris physicians at that time were prescribing cider for gout, a complaint significantly claimed to be unknown in Normandy. Both some eminent French physicians and *The Lancet*, like Evelyn's authorities more than two centuries earlier, were recommending it for improving digestion. In Herefordshire such ailments as diarrhoea were notably rare among the working classes. It remained for advertisers in this century to coin the slogan, 'An apple a day keeps the doctor away'.

In 1851, the year of the Great Exhibition, was founded the Woolhope Naturalists' Field Club (still active), named after a district of remarkable geological interest between Hereford and Ledbury. It proved exceptional among such clubs for its interest in cultivated fruits, and began in 1867 its 'Fungus Forays', designed to improve their quality. A special Pomona Committee was set up to organize the distribution among members of choice grafts supplied by the Royal Horticultural Society from its gardens at Chiswick, and also exhibitions of apples and pears. Its work over the years 1876–85 produced *The Herefordshire Pomona*, a monumental and splendidly illustrated two-volume work,[1] of which the originator and general Editor was Dr Henry G. Bull of Hereford and the Technical Editor was Robert Hogg, LL.D, of London, Secretary of the Royal Horticultural Society. Science was thus married to local experience. At Hogg's instigation the Society organised a great National Apple Congress on October 4–18 1883 at its Chiswick Gardens.[2] Bull, Hogg and a Mr Piper of Ledbury were the Herefordshire delegates to the Rouen Exhibition of 1884. The delegation was awarded a Gold Medal for its table fruits, a Bronze for its vintage fruit, a Silver Gilt for cider made from mixed fruit, and a Silver for cider made from a single variety of apple; also a personal Gold to Dr Hogg for his great services to pomology.

One result of this visit was that, since 16 of the so-called 'Norman' apples of England were found to be unknown in Normandy, these were, officially at least, renamed 'Hereford' apples, while eight of the best genuinely Norman apples were selected for introduction into Herefordshire.

It was reckoned that there were in Herefordshire some 30,000 acres of orchard of fruit suitable only for making cider or perry. One of the best places for orchards in the county was the village of Credenhill, five miles north-south-west of the city, the site of an Iron Age settlement dating from about 400 B.C. The cornstone marl surrounding the hill was analysed by G.H. With in 1877 and found to contain 26% of carbonate of lime, and to this the peculiar fertility was largely attributed. Oldfield Perry from Credenhill glebe in a good season fetched the high price of a guinea per dozen bottles. Now from 1861–1910 the Rector of Credenhill, where the poet Thomas Traherne was once incumbent, was a notable expert on cider and a great friend of Dr Bull, the Rev Charles Henry Bulmer.[3] To him was due what Dr Bull called 'the very able and exhaustive paper' on 'The Orchard and its Products Cider and Perry' in Volume I of *The Herefordshire Pomona*. Much the largest (pp.113–60), it was subsequently reproduced as the main section of Bull's compendium of that work, *The Apple and Pear as Vintage Fruits* (pp.1–86), published posthumously in 1886. Bulmer recommended (as Marshall had done before the lamentable period of neglect), that in order to exploit the surpluses of fruit that occurred, especially in 'hit' years, when the liquor fetched a very low price and all the home barrels were liable to be filled, cider and perry factories should be established with facilities for largescale storage of juice from one season to the next. That was in 1886. Next year his younger son, Percy, drawing on the glebe orchard at Credenhill, started one of these in Herefordshire which was to become the biggest cider business in the world. Had Henry not lost a leg as a young man in a shooting accident, he would have gone into the Army, and presumably Bulmers' cider would never have come into existence. 'God moves in a mysterious way....'

[1] It appeared originally in nine parts. Some of the originals of the fine hand-painted illustrations, mostly by Miss Bull and Miss Ellis, were bought for Bulmers by Edward Ball at the sale of Dr Bull's home, Harley House, in 1958, for just over £50—about 2s apiece. Some of these now hang framed in the firm's offices and some in the Cider Museum.

[2] Its centenary was celebrated on Nov 1–3, 1983. For an account of it see Joan Morgan, 'A Historic Centenary', in *The Garden* for October 1983, 383–88.

[3] Known as Henry. He was grandson of Edward Bulmer, who came from Bristol in 1802 to take over a wine business in Widemarsh Street in Hereford and

became Mayor in 1822. Edward and his son Charles made sparkling bottled cider from selected varieties of cider apple grown on their farm at Holmer. The wine business, then known by the name of his grandsons John and William, passed out of the family's possession only in 1920, after the death of the bachelor William on 1 November 1918. It survived until recently as 'The Pippin Vaults'.

CHAPTER THREE

ESTABLISHING THE FIRM (1887–1894)[1]

Henry Percival Bulmer, born on 28 February 1867, suffered so badly in childhood from asthma that he was not expected to grow up. His formal education was interrupted; but he was on the books of Hereford Cathedral School from the age of 13 to 19. At 17 he suddenly grew out of the asthma and became strong, a blessing commemorated by his parents with a window on the south side of the chancel of Credenhill church. By then however the disruption had been such that he had not acquired the necessary scholastic skills for him to follow his brother Fred (Edward Frederick, born on 26 May 1865 and educated as a boarder at Shrewsbury School) to King's College, Cambridge.[2] It was also unlikely that anyone would give him an acceptable job because of his lack of professional qualifications: he would have to be somehow self-employed. His parson father had been, as we saw, advocating the establishment of cider factories, and his mother (née Mary Cockrem)[3] sagely observed that anyone going into business had better choose something to do with eating or drinking, since these things do not go out of fashion. Further encouragement came from the famous expert Robert Hogg, a frequent visitor at the rectory, remembered later by the sons as a 'dear old man with an immense beard', to whose *Journal of Horticulture* their father often contributed, over the signature 'Herefordshire Incumbent'. As long as he lived Hogg was to provide them with a free advertisement on his front page.

So in 1887, at the age of 20, Percy began making perry and cider from the fruit of the Credenhill Glebe Orchard, using the old-fashioned stone mill of a neighbouring farm belonging to Mr Richard Whiting of Magna Castra (on the site of the reputed Ariconium). The mill was driven by the family pony Tommy, who also drew the cart, another loan, which carried the first two casks achieved, of perry, back to the Rectory for storage in the cellar. Fred was able to give his brother a hand towards the end of his Long Vacation from Cambridge; and in the late autumn of that year Percy left Credenhill to set up in Hereford.

His first premises there were a warehouse in Maylord Street, next to the old *Hereford Times* office. There he managed that autumn to make 40 casks, some 4,000 gallons, of cider, which realised £157. Unfortunately the landlord, besides (as Fred Bulmer alleged) drinking like a fish, was not above taking advantage of the young and trusting. Percy gave him notice of quitting, but he did so orally. The landlord held out for his pound of flesh, a second year of rent, because he had not had notice in writing; so that when, in August 1888, a move was made to the present site in Ryelands Street, there was the crippling burden of paying for what was not being used.

Ryelands Street was named after the home of the owner, a Mr Lane of Leominster. What the Bulmers acquired from him was an acre of a field of 10 1/2 acres on the east side of it. The land had not sold well round there; there were as yet no houses to the east of it, and only a few to the west. Hereford Town ended where the Breinton Road diverged from the road to Broomy Hill. But the former was then only a lane 12-14 feet wide, and corn still grew where St Nicholas' Rectory now stands. On 16 July 1888 the boys' father bought for £350 this acre of land, situated at the northern end of the future works where the office and gates were to stand, and later the Museum of Cider. The original premises consisted of a one-storey brick building with a tiled roof and a cellar underneath, put up by a local builder called Lloyd under the supervision of an architect, Edwards, on a contract of £700-800. It was paid for by a gift of £1,760 from the father, who raised the money by a loan on his life assurance. (The risk of their mother and their sister Bella being left in poverty if he died early must have been an additional spur to the sons' endeavour.) The balance did not run to a steam engine or hydraulic presses: the brothers turned the wheel of a mill by hand, and screwed the presses down with poles—splendid exercise for expanding the chest. At first no draught cider was sold. The fermentation took place in 100-gallon casks, and the cider was fed by gravity and filtered through dropping bags, rather like those which housewives formerly used for filtering jellies, into bottles in the cellar below. Nor did funds run to paving round the outside of the building, and by November the mud was terrible. This did, however, stand them in good stead on one occasion in 1894. A gentleman had come down from Somerset House to satisfy himself that the owners of the works so flatteringly depicted in their brochure had not sufficient income to be liable for income tax. After looking from the picture to the reality he said: 'I think this is drawn with the eye of prophecy'.

'No doubt it is, ' replied Fred; 'We are hopeful people here and we have need to be.' He then set out on a tour of inspection; but when mud closed round the top of his patent leather boots he retreated to his cab and, like the Dr Foster who went to Gloucester, never came back again.

The staff consisted of an old man called Thomas Kennett, (known in the family as 'Tummas'), who lived in a cheap cottage in Lawns Terrace, nearly opposite the works. When not working, he sat outside his cottage door. At sunset his wife prepared a pewter pot of tea and left it on the hob before they 'got on the sticks'. At 4.30am, whatever the season, he rose and boiled it. Tummas was a great character, illiterate but gifted with a remarkable turn of phrase, often 'blue'. Among the early investments in the firm was £100 from Thomas Kennett.

Fred took part again in his Long Vacation from Cambridge (June–September) in 1888. It was still his intention to go in for teaching of some sort, and Oscar Browning, the King's don whose penchant for royalty of all kinds is still legendary, procured him the offer of a post as tutor to the sons of the King of Siam—a tribute at least to the impression he had made. But he was very much attached to his young brother, and by June 1889, when he went down with a second class Honours Degree in Classics and a Half Blue for Athletics, he had decided instead to join him in forming H.P. Bulmer & Co. They proved an ideally complementary partnership, and were so close that an agreement they made at the outset to keep no account of credit and debit between themselves never gave rise to any friction—one of Fred's proudest boasts as he looked back.

In the cider-making season they began work on weekdays before 6.00am. Their lunch was bread and cheese. In the evening a little boy called Perkins came down by the last Midland Railway train from Credenhill (half-price return ticket 4d) into a station east of the works site, where its sidings now are, bringing a pewter pot with supper prepared by their mother. At about 10.00 pm they threw themselves down in their working clothes on the floor of the shack and fell asleep. If they had been up all night or started in the small hours, Tummas would bring them a cup of tea, occasionally accompanied, as a special favour, by a plate of chitterlings (pigs' entrails) chopped and fried. In those days they generally worked on Saturdays until 6.00 pm, then walked the five miles home to save the railway fare.

Fred owed to his college, and to his own personality, the acquisition at Cambridge of something that was to prove more valuable than any degree, devoted and trusting friends who lent him at a small rate of interest a large proportion of the money that was essential for supplying equipment. Arthur Berry (Senior Wrangler and later Vice-Provost of King's) lent him £1,000 he had inherited from an aunt. Of the two friends (both senior to him) who were to be closest to him throughout his life, Nathaniel Wedd and 'Jammie' Withers (later Sir John and a leading London solicitor), the former sent him in instalments all his savings, about £500, and the latter for some years did most of the firm's legal business for nothing. Such of this work as Withers did not undertake was done, also for nothing, by another King's friend, a local solicitor call A.D. Steel, Third Wrangler in Berry's year. Other private loans, mainly from relatives, totalling some £5,400 are recorded. The largest, of £1,800, came from a Trinity College, Cambridge friend, A.M. Daniel (later Sir Augustus, Director of the National Gallery.)

At this time much depended for the brothers on the cider-apple crop. In 1889 it was enormous, but so was the rainfall, which prevented the formation of any blossoms, so that in 1890 the crop was a complete failure. The struggling firm could barely obtain a ton of fruit from the whole of Herefordshire. It was only by calling on Somerset farmers and paying an unheard-of price that they were able to carry on for that year. They got about 100 tons altogether, with the addition of a few local pears. But Daniel's providential loan enabled them to try what proved to be a most profitable experiment. They got Wilsons of Frome to make them four huge, round, vertical oak vats holding 50,000 gallons apiece, (subsequently named and labelled 'Geoffrey', 'Howard', 'Esmond' and 'Bertram'[4] and still to be seen at the works). In these they were able to store a reserve of cider in a year when apples were very plentiful and cheap, and sell it next year, when the crop failed almost completely, to a large firm at a handsome profit, which put an end to their serious financial troubles. But the loans from friends would not have sufficed without a mortgage of £1,700 which was given them on the freehold, and if the bank manager, who had known the family for fifty years, had not sanctioned a loan of £3,000 without security.

The firm's earliest price list contains press cuttings and testimonials dated 1889. Particulars are given of awards won at the Paris

Exhibition of November 1888—a Gold Medal for 'Champagne Perry'[5] and a silver Gilt for 'Sparkling Cider', both the highest in their class. It is hardly credible that beginners should have achieved such standards without the guiding hand of the father; and indeed the *Hereford Times* for 1 December 1888 credits the awards to 'Mr Bulmer of Credenhill'. The circular asserts that 'our manager [i.e. Percy], by careful study of the works of Monsieur Pasteur[6] and constant experiment and research, had discovered that by an intelligent management of the fermentation process cider and perry could be made in a way that exceeded his most sanguine expectations.' It looked forward to a time when Hereford would be to cider what Rheims was to champagne. The trade press was enthusiastic. Thanks to Bulmers England had acquitted herself with high distinction at Paris. It was pointed out that a dozen bottles of Sparkling Cider (then priced at 10s) could be bought at the cost of one of Champagne Wine.

In the spring of 1889 Percy had started out on a tour of North Wales to see what he could do as a commercial traveller, but he returned discouraged and disgusted.[7] Thus it came about that it was Fred who, as soon as he had taken his degree that June, went, in the traveller's uniform of top hat and frock coat, to Windsor Great Park, where his brother had taken some cases of bottled cider and perry to compete for prizes at the Royal Agricultural Show. (He was there, he alleges, cut dead by three passers-by who had been at college with him for the past three years, one of them a future Bishop of Worcester. Such was the snobbery in those days about engaging in trade.) He did well enough to earn a pat on the back from his brother, a telegram saying 'Well done, good and faithful touter'. What is more their liquor won the second prize in every class, 'a very good average of excellence', as *The Times* commented. This experience at the outset proved crucial, for it revealed that Fred had a flair for salesmanship (whether he liked it or not), so that Percy was relieved of a task for which he had no bent and was left free to develop what proved to be his own remarkable flair, for manufacture and factory organisation. One day Fred called on a man in Leeds called Brindley. He was seated at the end of a large empty room. Fred handed him his trade card which, without looking up, he tore in two and flung on the floor, making a fierce gesture for him to get out. When Fred stood his ground and waited, Brindley looked up and said, 'Who the hell do you think you're staring at?' 'The rudest bugger I ever saw, ' said Fred. 'Ah!', said the Yorkshireman, 'That's how I like to be spoken to: come inside.' He gave him a good order, and they became firm friends.

Fred travelled indefatigably in search of sales. He visited every town from the Isle of Wight as far north as Dundee. Many of the people he approached had never heard of cider. Some said they would stock it, but only if there was a demand for it. When this method seemed insufficient, the brothers turned, since press advertisements and posters were beyond their means, to composing booklets to be sent out to addresses obtained from directories,[8] often sitting up half the night to do the addressing. By these methods they acquired private customers, eventually 20,000 of them. In their second circular, in 1891, they announced that they had decided to dispense with agents and sell directly to customers. This would cut out the middleman's profit and keep prices down. In July 1892 we first hear of wholesale trade. They had secured a contract from Brownings & Co., catering contractors to the Great Western Railway, to sell only their cider for five years, and to hang their show-cards for a rent of 100 guineas a year. They now negotiated a much more exciting one on the same lines with Spiers and Pond, the many-branched caterers, at a rent of 500 guineas a year. The show-cards would cost £300. Friends also used to help by demanding Bulmers' cider specifically in pubs, hotels, restaurants, dining cars, even liners. Wedd, on his way to Jamaica in 1901, is exhorted to do this: Elder Dempster's ships did not as yet stock it.

A ledger entry shows that in 1890 they sold cider to the Hudson Bay Company. By 1893 they were sending it to South Africa, India and Australia, as well as all over the British Isles. In July 1894 a Mr Moore, Secretary to the Tasmanian Council of Agriculture, wrote to say that they had a large surplus of apples which might be suitable for cider-making and suggesting that Bulmers might extend their business to Tasmania (but were they cider apples?). There should also, he added, be a good market for cider in the hot climate of Australia, 'in preference to the horrible beers and ales brewed from sugar and chemicals'. But any anticipation that exports would come to play as important a part in Bulmers' business as might be expected took a long time to fulfil.

One day about 1891, when the brothers were about to sit down on a cider case for their frugal lunch, in came their uncle-by-marriage Fred Bodenham, Fred's godfather, a forceful character who was also their family solicitor. While sharing their meal he inquired about their circumstances and prospects, and they told him with natural truthfulness that they could not survive unless they could obtain for expansion some adjacent land that was for sale. Bodenham, after wishing them good luck, went straight to the vendor's agent and signed a contract to buy for £3,000 the remaining 9 1/2 acres of Mr Lane's field. When, some weeks later, Fred Bulmer offered him £800 for two acres he refused, adding 'I have got you now and I mean to bleed you'. By rare good fortune, however, the solicitor and the owner having died on the same night and a legal complication having arisen from the solicitor's being found to have become insolvent meanwhile, someone had to be found to take over that contract. In May 1892 another, very different, uncle-by-marriage, William Ball, Percy's future father-in-law, took it over and had the property conveyed to his two nephews and mortgaged to himself, indicating that they might pay him off as and when they could. Then followed the happy conjunction of a boom in building with cheap money. In about two years they sold off three acres of frontage for building for the price of the whole 9 1/2 acres, so that they had acquired the remaining 6 1/2 acres as a gift.[9] Meanwhile in 1893 the area occupied by the works was extended from one acre to nearly nine.

A great advantage of the site so obtained was that there lay all over it, 2–3 feet below the surface, a bed of sand and gravel going down to water about 14 feet below. This enabled cellars to be excavated at little or no cost; for the Town Council arranged that the contractor for its new reservoir nearby should excavate the new cellars for them for no payment other than the resultant sand and gravel.

There were no specialised firms, such as now exist for most industries, to fit out neophyte cider-makers with machinery.[10] The Bulmers had to improvise and experiment. In the autumn of 1890 they installed a mill and press introduced from France, after a design exhibited at the 1888 Paris Exhibition. The mill was constantly being broken by stones. The press was of wine-press type, a large cylinder with vertical strips on the sides, into which a mallet descended when worked with a lever and ratchet by manpower. Next year they hired a second-hand Clayton and Shuttleworth steam engine of great antiquity, of the type used for driving threshing-machines. In 1892 they installed hydraulic pumps and an accumulator, and a second and third press. One of the pumps was to work at 2 1/2 tons per square inch, and the other, at one ton, to raise the accumulator. The hydraulic ram of the first press was only six inches in diameter. At such pressures the pump should have been supplied with oil instead of water. As it was, the leathers were constantly being cut through, and leaking, and had almost daily, and sometimes several times a day, to be renewed—a really trying job in frosty weather. The third press, bought from a candle factory, was of cast iron, to work at a pressure of 300 tons, and weighed in all about 17 tons. If you tried to press apple pulp in it in small crates, the pulp flew out between the bars like slag from white-hot billets under a steam hammer.

They were badly in need of engineering skill and ingenuity to help them over these teething troubles; and here again a friendly contact proved invaluable. Fred had been at school with one Harold Baldwin, through whose brother Arthur he met a man whom he found to be 'an engineering genius', Robert Worth. As a result Worth applied to the Hereford Corporation for the job of putting in new pumps at the Water Works. He was appointed, and his pumps (still in good working order) established what was reputed to be a world record for efficiency. Whenever he came to Hereford he stayed at Credenhill Rectory, becoming 'Uncle Robert'. Fred described him in 1897 as 'dry as dust, but kindly and simple-minded', and very deaf. But he added: 'He looks like the dissenting minister of a hedge-row chapel, but when he talks to you, you find that appearances are deceptive above all things.' Worth was so transparently honest that the brothers never asked him in advance the price of any machine he was to devise, such as one that enabled a crushing mill to pass stones from among the apples (hitherto inability to remove them had been a nightmare).

By the end of 1893, however, it had been borne in on the brothers that if they could not learn more about the real science of cider-making they could not survive. They had already in 1891 appointed Mr J. Parry Laws, F.I.C., F.C.S., of London as Microscopical Expert and Consulting Analyst. He reported to them at that time: 'I don't think much of the foreign cider yeast; on the other hand the champagne yeast is a very fine one.' Percy as a boy, helped by his mother, had taught himself French in the intervals between his asthma. He now decided to go to Rheims and

Epernay in Champagne to see what he could find out. The young men did not know a soul on the continent: their only connection was a firm at Epernay called Taillard from which they had ordered a corking machine through the post. So in 1894 Percy set out to visit them. He was most kindly received. M. Taillard introduced him to the firm of Desmonet, which made champagne in a small way at Epernay, and they in turn invited him to stay and showed him how they made it.[11] What was more, they passed him on to a M. Thomas, head of the Municipal Wine Laboratory at Rheims. There in the next few months Percy learned how to make the most important estimations in the production of good cider. And still better, he brought home from there all the best French literature on the subject, which became their 'Cider Bible'. So it was that the firm began making cider by the champagne process, marketed from 1906 as 'Pomagne'. Percy's visits to France and subsequently Germany were the foundation of the firm's ultimate supremacy.

The brothers were now living in a rented house called St. Ethelbert's, the solid building still standing in Ryelands Street opposite the old factory gates.[12] They tried taking in an apprentice to live with them: for a few months from 1893 one Richard Dawes, a parson's son, introduced by friends, was there. But he proved choosy about his work and dissatisfied with his pay and prospects, though he had no qualifications, and made others a vehicle for his complaints; and his departure was good riddance. They themselves meanwhile were still getting up to work at 6.00am.

But a great change came in August 1894, indeed a great shock to Fred, who took a long time to get over it: Percy got married, to their cousin Mildred Ball, daughter of the uncle-by-marriage who had been so helpful to them over the purchase of the Ryelands Street site, a ship-owner of Torquay. A letter to Fred from his great friend Nat Wedd, dated 11 October, gives a glimpse of the odd situation: 'I don't quite understand the position at St Ethelbert's. Have you left the house? I hope not. Of course it can't be the same between you and Percy now that he is married: that is inevitable, and nothing can alter it. But the difference can be made less if you give way in all non-essentials, even to the extent of washing during cider-making.' In fact the situation was impossible, and soon after that Fred moved into lodgings at 40 Ryelands Street, the home of one of his employees, Charlie Pearson. In all this there was no element of personal antipathy to Mildred, as he admitted to himself in the turmoil of his spirit; and the marriage proved an extremely happy one. In those early days Mildred had to be prepared for St. Ethelbert's to be a sort of hotel for business visitors to the works.

On 27 October the *Hereford Times* reported a meeting that had taken place at the Holborn Restaurant in London with the object of forming a National Association of English Cider Makers. In the chair was C.W. Radcliffe Cooke, Conservative M.P. for Hereford from 1893 to 1900, who became known in Parliament as 'The Member for Cider'. There were 26 people there. Fred Bulmer read a paper on the proposed Association as it would affect (a) cider-makers, (b) the public taste and health, and (c) agriculturalists and the land interest. As to (a) he took a firm line that, in a competitive industry, 'we cannot be expected to pool the knowledge we have individually acquired by hard experience for purely philanthropic and patriotic purposes'. They could however doubtless organise mutual assistance in such matters as defining and suppressing adulteration; railway rates; conditions as to imports of foreign cider fortified with duty-free spirits; and any other matters on which their interests might be threatened by legislation. They must support the cause of English cider made from English apples, guaranteed as such. He doubted whether farmers would be able to make cider of the required quality, or to market it readily if they did. Dry cider was what the medical profession would no doubt recommend; but the Americans had conditioned the public taste to prefer sweet cider, and this would be largely demanded. Any sweetness should be natural, not the product of saccharin.[13] Cider might also be made which alcoholically met the requirements of the Temperance Society. A proposal that an Association on these lines should be established was put by the chairman and carried unanimously; and a Consultative Committee was set up to arrange the details.

The fact that the policy thus endorsed was formulated and proposed by Fred Bulmer, aged 29, indicates the position his firm held in this comparatively new profession. A commendation of them in a letter written in February 1894 by one Charles F. Oldham of Grierson, Oldham & Co. to Messrs Lane of Kidderminster may be quoted, for although it is the testimony of a self-proclaimed friend it must at least have been plausible, otherwise he would not have ventured it:

'We have pleasure in introducing to you Mr E.F. Bulmer,

41

partner in the firm of H.P. Bulmer & Co. of Hereford, the celebrated cider makers, and we think it would be to your advantage to make arrangements with them, as they are no doubt the best makers of Cider and Perry in the Kingdom.'

So far sales had been as follows (in £. s. d.)

1888	157	1892	1405
1889	1265	1893	1003
1890	2475	1894	7558
1891	3387		

The jump in the last year is attributable to the accession of the large vats bought from A.M. Daniel's loan.

The year 1894 seems a good date for closing this chapter on the establishing of the firm, being marked internally by Percy's marriage and his crucial visit to France, and externally by Fred's prominent role in the founding of the National Association.

---

[1]This chapter is largely based on a 30-page booklet by E. F. Bulmer, *Early Days of Cider Making*, privately published in 1937 to mark the Golden Jubilee of the firm and reproduced in facsimile in 1980, with notes, by his second son, Harold. Harold Bulmer has also supplemented the account considerably in typescript, from press cuttings, letters, the firm's early circulars, etc.

[2]Asthma attacked Fred also, causing him to intermit one year from his Cambridge examination course; but it never troubled him further.

[3]She was the daughter of the founder of the *Torquay Directory* newspaper. She was an excellent wife, who kept her husband's sermons up to the mark, played the church organ, helped him to farm the glebe land, and nursed parishioners when they were ill. She was also an excellent mother, who had her sons' school-friends to stay in the holidays, for long periods if they had nowhere else to go.

[4]The three eldest sons of Percy and the eldest son of Fred.

[5]'Champagne' was used here in a sense traditional both in France and England to describe sparkling bottled liquor which had undergone a secondary fermentation in bottles with wired corks but had not been 'disgorged' (second corking) like champagne. This is not an anticipation of the making of cider by the same process as champagne, which was inaugurated a few years later by Percy Bulmer (see editorial note on p.82).

[6]Cider fermentation was first scientifically investigated in 1888.

[7]In later days he replied to a lady who asked if he had a job for her son: 'Dear Madam, With reference to your letter, I regret that the only vacancy we have

is for a commercial traveller. This however requires rare and special gifts, and a man may well thank his God if he does not possess them.' (Travellers at that time were expected to imbibe liberally with their customers.)

[8]A sidelight on this operation is thrown by a letter from a Mrs J. Randall to Fred Bulmer of 2 February 1894. She and her husband had acquired a copy of *Slater's Directory of Manchester and Suburbs*. He had lived there, and could pick out about 5,000 principal merchants. Nationwide advertisements in local papers for retired postmen who could supply relevant addresses also proved quite productive.

[9]History repeated itself in 1976 when 10 acres of Red Barn Farm were sold for £140,000. The whole farm of 66 acres had been bought by Bulmers in 1959 for £34,000.

[10]For the processes used in manufacturing cider see Chapter Eight.

[11]Some years later a young Frenchman, arriving unannounced when Percy was away, called on Fred and told him that he had been left the business by his stepfather, M. Desmonet; but that owing to certain provisions of French law he would stand to lose a considerable sum if he could not find £200 in the next 12 days. Fred, seizing the risky opportunity of repaying something of that great debt of gratitude, lent him the money, which was punctiliously refunded.

[12]It was bought by the firm, with 1 rood, 3 perches, of land in 1920 for £1,500, and subsequently enlarged.

[13]Circumstances were to make some of these requirements eventually unrealistic; but the regulations for the National Mark approved in 1931 (see below) were still stringent. In 1896 Fred Bulmer was sending Radcliffe Cooke evidence that the use of saccharin was frowned on by most European countries, but with no mention of France. The Geneva Conference of 1908–09 on the adulteration of food recognized as normal the addition to cider of tannin, tartaric acid and alkali bisulphites, sweetening, pasteurisation, clarification, colouring with caramel, treatment with citric acid. In England legal restrictions continued to be minimal.

CHAPTER FOUR

PERCY BULMER (1867–1919)

It is not easy, at this distance in time, to form a clear impression of Percy Bulmer. He died more than sixty years ago, at the age of 52. None of his sons survives, and his daughters-in-law never knew him. He was clearly very different in temperament from his elder brother, devoted though they were to each other, and their divergent experience in youth accentuated the difference. They had the same dislike of humbug and chicanery, and though Percy's sense of humour was less ebullient, his niece, Lady Hull, remembers his home as one of perpetual gaiety and laughter, of parties and dances. He himself was quiet, modest and retiring, but not distant; indeed he was kind and thoughtful for others, wide in sympathy and generous without ostentation, active also for the benefit of St. Nicholas's parish. His favourite recreation, not unpredictably, was fishing. He also sang and played the piano. (He and Fred sang Handel and music-hall songs together, sometimes accompanied by Ivor Atkins, the future organist of Worcester Cathedral; and he was a friend of that other Worcester musician, Elgar, whom he teased with a request to compose a 'Cider Symphony'.) He even wrote a play, which remained unpublished. The accident of his being unable, for reasons of health, to go to boarding school and university like his brother precluded him from the chance of making a wide and varied circle of friends, so that even if he had been a letter-writer his letters might not have been very revealing.

Yet it is clear that while he lived his contribution to the prosperous growth of the business was at least equal to the complementary contribution of his brother. The latter wrote of him years afterwards, that he developed the most remarkable judgement in the manufacture and organisation of a factory: 'I have never in my long life met anyone with such a natural gift of judgement. It almost amounted to second sight. If there were six possible ways of doing a thing and the evidence was deficient in all six, the way in which he invariably chose the right course was something uncanny. It was more due to his good judgement than to anything else that we pulled through in the end.' This may not be impartial evidence but it is nevertheless impressive.

It is clear also that he possessed other capacities. He was good at teaching himself. He learned enough bacteriology to profit from the latest researches of Pasteur into fermentation. As we saw, he learned French, which stood him in good stead when he came to visit Champagne. He had learned some German also, from a German governess at Credenhill, and in 1904 went to Germany to the Apollinaris factory, to study their methods of bottling, which subsequently led to the marketing of Bull Brand cider in 1909. Next he went to East Prussia, to learn how sugar beet was processed, something wholly unknown in England at that time. Other fruitful ideas he brought back from this memorable visit were that of floating apples to the mills and washing them on the way, and one for a machine to dry apple pomace based on the type which was used for drying spent sugar-beet chips. More will be said of these improvements later. In 1903 he bought the first mechanical vehicle owned by the firm, a Minerva Motorcycle for the use of a salesman. Obviously Percy was not only enterprising, alert, and receptive of new ideas, which to a large extent accounted for the go-ahead policies and success of the firm: he also had a personality which made people of other countries as well as his own willing to welcome him and initiate him into their mysteries.

After his marriage in 1894, Percy and Mildred (or 'Trot') continued to live at St. Ethelbert's. But in 1901, helped by a handsome dowry from her father, they built a comfortable but not ostentatious house called 'Longmeadow' on the western outskirts of the city, near the Breinton Road and the water tower, with a fine view to the south. This step was to have great importance for the family, for their relations came to occupy a number of sites beginning there and running along the ridge on the left of the Upper Breinton Road, most of them having a superb view for miles, south and west over the Wye Valley to the distant line of the Black Mountains in Wales. To get the complete picture we must anticipate.

Mrs Percy, first remembered by her niece, Lady Hull, as driving a pony and trap, survived until 1968. She became in fact one of the first motorists in the county, and drove her car, to the general trepidation, till she was over ninety. After her death her second son, Howard, continued to live at Longmeadow. In 1910 the brothers built 'Highcroft', above the Breinton Road near the water tower, to receive their parents on their retirement from the rectory at Credenhill. This passed in 1925 to their elder sister Isabel ('Bella'), and then to the widow of Percy's third son

Esmond, now Mrs Grace James. In 1905 Fred built 'Adam's Hill', a cheerful, well-windowed house with the Black Mountains view. Next door was 'Springfield', occupied by Mrs Fred's sister Nell and her husband, Major Ziegler. Before the Second World War Fred's eldest son, Bertram, built 'Little Breinton', a house with an equally fine view some way further along the Upper Breinton Road, designed by Hugh Hughes of Cambridge; and Percy's third son Edward built 'Pilliner's Hill', next to 'Springfield', where his widow, Mrs Margaret Rye, lived until 1981. Some time after that War Fred's second son, Harold, an architect, designed for himself below 'Adam's Hill' on the Hereford side, 'Broad Oak'(now called 'Warham Oak'). He also designed for Mrs Ziegler in her widow-hood 'Fairfield', on the ridge to the south of 'Adam's Hill', by the Lower Breinton Road, now occupied by Percy's nephew Edward ('Teddie') Ball, who joined the science side of the firm in 1927 and later was Technical Director until 1965. On the other side of the road there already stood 'Warham Ash', built in 1939 in the latest style for A.M. Hudson-Davies (later Sir Alan), Works Manager for Bulmers from 1933 to 1941, by the well-known architect Maxwell Fry. What a colony! The proximity of the homes of the two families helped to maintain the amicable cohesion of the firm.

For the most part it is impossible to disentangle the business operations of the two brothers. It is no surprise to find them in 1899 buying, for £24, a tandem bicycle for getting about the country. Glimpses of Percy's separate activities in Fred's voluminous correspondence give some idea of their range. *1898*: he is thinking of going to Rheims for a few days to take lessons in the laboratories of a good professor in analysing cider for certain constituents. *1899*: he is in France with George Marshall, prowling for apple trees. *1900*: he is going to Cardiff to see a big oak vat they are thinking of buying, holding 7,000 gallons. *1901*: he has gone to The Whettons (their orchards) to sack the people there for idleness. *1908*: he wants to start a farmers' co-operative in the district, and has invited C.R. Fay, the Cambridge economist, to come down and explain to him why co-operation should not work here as it does in Denmark. Next, orders have come in so heavily that he has to go and work in the packing room. In 1912 he had the satisfaction of being joined in the business by his eldest son, Geoffrey, born in 1895. He devoted himself particularly to the welfare of his employees. The hurly-burly of politics he left to

Fred; but in the First World War he was Chairman of the Hereford Advisory Committee on recruiting, supporting Kitchener's call for 30,000 recruits a week for six months and urging that the Herefordshire target should be ten a day.

In the summer of 1916, however, he came under the threat of serious illness, wrongly diagnosed next March as colic. The mistake was realised after a few months, and in March 1918 he went to Liverpool to have radium treatment for cancer. Sadly the brothers now felt obliged to turn their partnership into a private company. Percy had already had more than his share of trouble. His only daughter, Cecily, had died in 1906 at the age of two. Geoffrey had been through the terrible summer campaign on the Western Front in 1916 and in August had become the only surviving officer in his company (a bullet fired at him at point blank range hit the revolver in his belt). He was awarded the M.C. in February 1917. Transferring then to the Royal Flying Corps, he had further hair-raising experiences, and qualified as a pilot. But he was nervy for all his courage, and the horrors he had witnessed preyed on his gentle mind. In February 1918, on his way to the funeral of his grandfather Charles Henry Bulmer, he took his own life in a hotel in London. Howard (born in 1897) survived the war. He was transferred in the summer of 1918 from Palestine to France and then wounded in the leg, which necessitated nine months in hospital, at the end of which time the war was over. He joined the firm in March 1919, later to become Managing Director on the selling side, and Chairman from 1941 to 1965. This at least was a comfort to Percy in his last year. He died in December 1919. Howard survived till 1985.

Though Percy died at what should have been the prime of life, he was at least spared further blows that were in store. Esmond (born in 1900) was able to go up to King's College, Cambridge, as soon as the War was over, and he took an Honours Degree in Natural Sciences before joining the firm in 1921. There he worked in the scientific department under Dr H.E. Durham (of whom more anon). And he did well: in 1924 we find Durham, at the end of an article on perry in the *Journal of the Royal Horticultural Society* 49, acknowledging: 'Esmond Bulmer has been most helpful both in the orchard and the laboratory—in fact the major share of the analysis (in Appendixes that follow) is due to his work.' A rowing man, energetic and exceptionally strong and courageous, he was a lively, humorous and attractive personality, a great success as Works

Manager, admired and loved by the employees. It was a terrible blow when, in 1932, less than three months after his marriage to Grace Pethybridge, he died, quite unnecessarily it would seem, after an operation for appendicitis.

There remained Edward, born in 1907, another rowing man, a quietly impressive character who had graduated three years before at the same College, where he was probably taught by Keynes among others, with upper second class Honours in Economics. In the firm he was principally concerned with marketing and advertising. He was killed in an accidental explosion on a Midlands airfield in the Second World War, in June 1944, three months before Percy's nephew, Fred's youngest son Oscar Theodore ('Becket' or 'Beck') was killed in action in Belgium. Fortunately Edward had been married, in 1933, to Margaret Roberts, and he was survived by three sons, two of whom are Percy's continuing legacy to the firm, James Esmond, the present chairman, and David.

A year after Percy's death Fred and Mildred gave to the City Council in his memory a playing field for the children who lived in the neighbourhood of the works, primarily those of St Nicholas' parish and those attending the Scudamore Schools or any other school to be built thereafter in the parish. In 1938 Fred paid for a brick pavilion and shelter to be erected in the Tower Road corner of the field, and presented it to the City Council, again in memory of his brother.

CHAPTER FIVE

FRED BULMER (1865–1941)

Fred Bulmer was almost the opposite in temperament and in education to the younger brother for whose sake he had sacrificed the chance of a professional career more obviously suited to his bent. He was extroverted and ebullient, bursting with vitality and often satirical humour, impulsive and pugnacious for what he knew to be right, and demonstratively affectionate. He thoroughly enjoyed his schooldays at Hereford Cathedral School and at Shrewsbury, where he excelled in running and won an Exhibition in classics to King's College, Cambridge. That college was quite small in numbers—there were 30 others in his year—and it was easy there to form friendships with men in other years also, and indeed with some of the Fellows.

By far the most intimate of his friendships was to be with Nathaniel Wedd, two years his senior, who became a classical don at the college, a man unknown to history save for the intriguing avowal of the writer E.M. Forster: 'To him, more than anyone else, I owe such enlightenment as has befallen me.' Of Wedd, Lowes Dickinson, a King's don again two years his senior, once famous as a humanist and writer on historical, political and moral subjects, said: 'He is, I think, the ablest man I have known.' Nat Wedd, it will be remembered, was one of the first to invest money in the cider enterprise (Fred resisted his wish to receive 4% instead of 5% interest); and when he became, from 1908 to 1918, the victim of the rare, and in his case tardily diagnosed, Graves' Disease, for which he tried every kind of nostrum involving residence in all sorts of places, Fred was only too pleased to be able to repay him a hundredfold by bearing most of the extra cost, though the college helped by continuing his emoluments. With Wedd he kept up a lifelong correspondence, which has fortunately survived and in which there occur incidental references to the business that have been invaluable for this book.

Shrewsbury friends with whom he kept up included the author and journalist Sir William Beach Thomas, Nature Correspondent to *The Observer*, and Arthur and Harold Baldwin, cousins of Stanley, the future Prime Minister, who was also to become a friend of his in due course. (The Baldwins' Wilden Works[1] were to be the industrial model for the Bulmers'.) The chief friends he made at Cambridge were nearly all people who were to make their mark. In King's, besides Wedd, Lowes Dickinson and J.J. Withers, there were Roger Fry, the famous art critic, C.R. Ashbee, an architect and town planner whose reputation is still growing and who, like Roger Fry, founded an important craftsmen's guild, Robin Furness, who served Egypt as Deputy Director of Radio and Professor of English at Cairo, Arthur Hill, later Director of Kew Gardens and Robbie Ross, the faithful friend of Oscar Wilde. He made friends in Trinity College also, the philosophers McTaggart and Bertrand Russell, the politician Charles and the poet Bob (R.C.) Trevelyan (brothers of the historian G.M.) and the brothers Crompton and Theodore Llewelyn-Davies; and at Caius there was H.A. Roberts, the admirable founder-to-be of the Cambridge University Appointments Board.

These were all great readers, some of whom he joined for vacation reading parties, in the Lake District or some such place, in several years after they had graduated. Literature was to play a great part in Fred's inner life, and he had a remarkable verbal memory. He had been brought up on the Bible and Dickens. At school he was introduced to Homer, and all his life he kept a Greek text of the *Odyssey* at his bedside. (He had, as his son Harold has remarked, some of the salient characteristics of Odysseus, resourcefulness, perseverance and occasional wiliness.) He re-read Shakespeare all through his life, and among novelists he especially enjoyed Jane Austen, Trollope and Hardy. History too, especially on its personal side, was a constant interest, as in Pepys' diary, Gibbon's *Decline and Fall of the Roman Empire*, Boswell's *Johnson* and Cobbett's *Rural Rides*. He tells Wedd in 1898 that he has been reading with enthusiasm Froude's *Life and Letters of Erasmus*: 'I wanted to get some birdseye view of the period.' Speaking at a press dinner in 1926 he said: 'I was brought up on Aristophanes and Shakespeare (with especial attention to Falstaff), Smollett, Fielding and the family Bible. These early influences contended for the mastery; and thus it is that, while I am not unconscious that I am my brother's keeper, I can also see that he is a damned funny fellow.' (He meant – need it be said?—his brother in general, not Percy.)

The friends mentioned above were on the 'arts' side academically; but others were scientists (indeed Roger Fry himself got a First in Natural Sciences). There were the mathematical Fellows H.W. Richmond and Arthur Berry. There was H.E. Durham, who will recur in this book; and at Trinity Reg Langdon-Down, from whose father Down's Syndrome ('Mongolism') takes its name. These ensured that he did not under-value science, as some other classically educated people were liable to do (though he was a fanatical advocate of classical education). The *ethos* of his circle as a whole was free-thinking and anticlerical, yet more moral and socially conscionable (more truly Christian indeed, they liked to claim) than most of the 'bien pensant', respectable people whom they enjoyed shocking. Also they really did love one another; nor did Fred ever lose his love and respect for his parson father or for his fiercely Protestant mother.

Younger friends accrued from later generations, notably Hugh Meredith, the economist friend of E.M. Forster, and the classical prophet J.T. Sheppard, who was to be Provost of King's for 21 years. Revisiting the College four years after he left it he wrote to Roger Fry: 'My work is horribly uncongenial; but somehow nothing seems to matter except that one has been to King's.' At his father's rectory, and later at his own home when now he could afford it, he loved to have his friends to stay. A few weeks after the First World War broke out Lowes Dickinson was staying at Adam's Hill, miserable but anxious to see if any good could be extracted from catastrophe. All one morning he paced the lawn, then spent the afternoon writing. He was drafting a pamphlet he was to publish under the title 'A League of Nations', and this may have been the origin of the term.[2] It influenced the thinking of what came to be called 'The Bryce Group'; and Lord Bryce went over to America and converted President Wilson to the idea. The result is part of history.

For nine years Fred was, as he said, dependent on his old Cambridge friends for all the real interest in life. 'Business,' he wrote, 'is so brutal and so absorbing that I often wonder that it has not killed my inner life.' He had been saved, he concluded, by the affection he had for some few people. On changing his lodgings he had to part with sacks full of their letters. But then, in the summer of 1899, he got married. His wife came from a very different world. He had fallen in love with her when they met by chance at the alpine Theodule Hut near Zermatt on 24 July 1897. Sophie Rittner's parents were German immigrants settled for nearly 30 years at Liverpool, well-to-do importers of ivory and mother-of-pearl. They objected strongly to Fred as a suitor, as being of inadequate social status and unable to keep her in the state to which she was accustomed. For a long time he was allowed to write to her only once a month. But gallantly, though not without occasional misgivings (those shabby clothes!) she stuck to him and they were married. To mark the occasion a dinner party was given on the rectory lawn at Credenhill to which all the 150 villagers were invited, and (as at the previous marriage of Percy and Mildred) a silver plated tray to which nearly all of them had somehow managed to contribute was presented. The employees of the firm gave the pair a glass and silver claret jug and cigar stand.

Fortunately Sophie preserved all the letters they exchanged during their courtship, and a few others. Fred was most anxious that she should accept his friends, and generously she did so, Nat Wedd in particular. Only one proved too much even for her tolerance. On 7 March 1901 Fred wrote to Nat: 'What dust and ashes everything else seems compared with the love of friends.' We are relieved to find him adding a few days later that 'marriage does not make one love one's friends less, but rather more, if possible, because it raises one's standards of affection.' Sophie's character was a rare compound of sweetness and sturdy good sense which transcended the narrowness of her upbringing. Her father told her she was 'too masculine', which he explained as 'too decided'. She was indignant at the way men treated women, and Fred, an enthusiast for Ruskin and for Hardy's *Tess of the D'Urbervilles*, agreed with her, even going so far as to admit (if quite safely): 'I don't see why you should change your name because you are married: to be quite fair I should be Mr Rittner and you Mrs Bulmer'. He shared her contempt for men who preferred that the women they married should be sexually ignorant. 'How I do pity girls, ' he wrote: 'driven through this world, like horses, with reins and blinkers'. He protested that the customary fare of music and painting was not a sufficient education for women if these were to the exclusion of reading, which educated the *mind* as well as the sensibility; and he undertook to send to Wedd an annual subscription towards a Research Fellowship at Newnham, the fledgling college for women at Cambridge. (All this, remember, was as early as 1898–99.)

Sophie kept her end up well. 'Would you kindly tell me why men find it necessary to swear?' . . . 'As long as you don't swear at me I don't mind; but I should like to know why you do it at all.' She had been to school from the age of 16 at Kronberg, near Frankfurt, and she kept up with her many German relations, with only the painful but unavoidable interruptions of the two wars.

Fred came to be accepted by them, and this German connection was not without advantage to him: he imbibed some German ideas about insurance, education and baby clinics which were later tried out at Hereford. On one important matter only did they have to agree to differ: Sophie was religious, in an unobtrusive way (a fact which had given Fred scruples about marrying her which Wedd tactfully enabled him to overcome). To the end of her life she quietly went off to church when she felt inclined, but without putting any pressure on her children after childhood to accompany her.

Theirs proved a most happy marriage. At first they rented a small house called 'Bellevue', on the Hay Road, half way between Hereford and Credenhill—'brick, old, unpretentious, with a green verandah, cabbage garden, orchard and two pigstyes'. Two years later they moved nearer to Hereford, to the somewhat roomier 'Fayre Oaks Cottage', still to be seen on the south side of the Brecon Road, about 300 yards beyond White Cross. Finally, in 1905, they built and occupied Adam's Hill, which was subsequently enlarged to accommodate their six children (Dorothy, b.1900; Bertram, b.1902; Harold, b.1909; the twins Joan and Nancy, b.1910; and 'Becket', b.1913). They too, like Percy and Mildred, had more than their share of private sorrow; for in 1923 Dorothy developed a very severe disease of the brain and died three years later, and Richard, born in December 1905, died after three months. Fred, having lost two much loved nephews, was spared by his death in 1941 the distress of losing another, and finally his son Becket, a young man of rare vitality, intelligence and humour, in the War. Sophie lived on serenely to the age of 94, dying in the same year as her sister-in-law Mildred, 1968.

It will have become apparent that nothing could be fundamentally less like the stereotype of a successful businessman than Fred. 'Businessmen generally pay for their wealth with their souls,' he wrote. But that phrase 'my work is horribly uncongenial' requires amplification. To begin with, it was written in a brief, fleeting moment when he was back at King's with some of his closest friends. At that time (1893) his life was exacting, comfortless and often depressing. In autumn he was often up at 5.30am[3] One October day in 1897 he cycled 70 miles in 12 hours with only two ounces of food, buying apples. He was too tired to read in his evenings, so tired, he alleged, that he sometimes tossed hot coals from the boiler from hand to hand to keep himself awake. 'It is bloody hard work with Percy away. It is nearly three weeks since I was outside this building, except on Sundays.' He began to have sciatic trouble, which plagued him on and off through life. A leading Liverpool consultant only prescribed the impossible: 'rest and warmth and a change at Aix'. But the trouble went deeper. What he hated was the side of the business that chiefly fell to him, sales promotion, not manufacturing. In November 1898 he wrote to his fiancée: 'We are still very busy, but I always enjoy the work at this time of the year, as it is what I call decent work, organising men or making analyses to decide what sorts of apples must be mixed together . . . . The work I hate is selling. I can never do it without a sense of indignity. I detest touting, writing puffs and advertisements, and all those self-assertive methods without which it is impossible nowadays to conduct business. In any properly organised state of society such offensive proceedings would be unnecessary, as strictly speaking they are non-productive, neither do they conduce to anyone's happiness.' A few months later he is writing: 'Lord Tollemache's butler has just been in here, trying to get a tip in return for an order. However the brute got no tip from me, and we got no order! It is these things that make business so offensive.' Again (three years later): 'What jars on me so much in business is, that I don't like the feeling of persuading someone else to remove their custom from another and give it to me.' Significantly perhaps, he had been reading in the train a book by Lowes Dickinson, probably his latest, *The Meaning of Good*. Yet he could not help enjoying success in his trade: 'On my way from the station at Bath to Barts' [H.A. Roberts'] house I sold a grocer £20 of cider, so that paid my expenses.' And again: 'I opened a very good account with a large brewery company. They gave me an opening order for £130 of bottling cider. But it takes a long time to catch those people, for the bosses as a rule only stay in the office for an hour or so in the morning to see letters, and then have done for the day, and so have you.' He gives guidelines to Wedd, who has been put on to drafting a trade circular for him: 'Only enough for one page. We must be careful not to say anything against brewers and wine merchants now, as so many of them deal with us largely . . . . Wine of the country' might be one line, but not at the expense of other countries' wine.'

We should beware, indeed, of projecting into the twentieth century the mood created in him by nostalgia for Cambridge, distaste for the sordid side of business, the frustrations of his courtship and the depression of sheer fatigue which belong to the first ten years of his career, the nineteenth century years. It stays in the mind because most of his letters that survive are from those years. With the growing success of the venture, the relief afforded by the recruitment of two willing commercial travellers, his happy marriage, the acquisition of a comfortable, idyllically situated home and the arrival of children, he became much more buoyant and much more proud of the business, both for the good repute of its pleasing products and as a community of well-employed and contented people created out of nothing. This is the man that is remembered by the survivors of those who knew him.

He also valued the opportunity which his position and increasing wealth gave him of spreading happiness and doing good. As a young schoolboy, when walking up Aylestone Hill for his daily lunch with his older cousin Fanny Bulmer, he sometimes joined the Rev John Venn, son of the co-founder of the Clapham Sect. From him he learned how they had successfully improved the living conditions of the poor. This planted in him a lifelong care about housing, education and public service, which was nurtured at Shrewsbury by A.H. Gilkes and at King's by Oscar Browning. He was appalled by the unemployment and consequent poverty in Hereford, especially among ex-soldiers of the Boer War, and at having to turn down 40 starved-looking applicants for a job in one day (he gave preference for jobs to fathers of families).

He was willing to take up the cudgels for individual cases. Thus in May 1899 he found that the second gardener of a landowner reputedly worth two millions, earning 13s a week with a cottage and tiny garden, was being charged 15s a visit for five visits (including no medicine) by a Hereford doctor to his sick wife, and 5s 6d by a solicitor for writing a letter. Fred proposed to see the doctor and solicitor, but expected to have to pay most of the debt himself—not however without writing to the local paper to advocate the setting up of a Medical Aid Society, something (he said) which the local doctors dreaded. Three months later he was writing to the Great Western Railway's agent for the West of England to ask him whether he was aware that one of his employees had been sacked 'for old age' in his 60th year, after 20 years of excellent service, without a cent. If he would not do anything for the man, Fred proposed to close his account with the G.W.R. and tell him the reason. He loathed any abuse of privilege. In 1908 the Lord Lieutenant's car killed an old man at Credenhill. Fred wrote to the papers about it. When the Coroner's jury brought in a verdict of Accidental Death, he sent a report of the inquest to the Home Secretary. The Public Prosecutor sent a man down to investigate, and following his report the chauffeur was committed to the Assizes on a charge of manslaughter. It is symptomatic of the haphazard nature of the epistolary records that we do not know the outcome of these cases.

Writing from the firm's new orchard farm at Broxwood in 1899 Fred said: 'We have about 15 yokels working here. They are thoroughly nice men. Their conversation is most amusing, and it is like reading Thomas Hardy to listen to it. They know the history of every field in the parish, and sometimes in several parishes. It is really pathetic to hear them discuss the merits of bacon and other sorts of food, and which go furthest with children. I am very fond of this sort of life, and these persons. They are so simple, homely and sympathetic to the troubles of life, and so patient under the injustice of their poverty.' Welcoming two parties of Welsh miners on a visit in 1927 (both Tory!), he noticed as he shook hands that about half of them showed signs of severe injuries. One of his own workmen was a drunkard who had to be sent to prison for neglecting his children to death's door. 'A lot of people like this are a queer family to have on your hands', he commented to Sophie. But he added: 'Some few are brutes, but most of them are wonderfully kind—much more so than we who call ourselves the upper class.' To him they were a family.

Alcoholism was indeed something he came across everywhere. Warm weather, so good for trade, could result in some employees coming drunk to work. 'Our cooper, John, has been awfully on the booze, which is very awkward as he is our only cooper . . . But one never knows who drinks. Trot's nice nurse has turned out boozy, and got drunk as an owl.' Had he a conscience about being a maker of alcoholic liquor? It did not seem so. He used to say that he liked to think that he had provided millions of people with a good drink. He was in favour of moderation, not of abstinence or prohibition, misnamed 'temperance'. He was amused that (in 1893) 'the Temperance people' should be prosecuting the barkeeper of the House of Commons. But he did see that there were two sides to the question. Lady Henry Somers of Eastnor Castle was addressing temperance meetings in the streets of Hereford in 1899. 'She may be mistaken in some ways, but she is courageous and anxious to help the poor.' She subscribed indeed

56

to his scheme for rehousing them. We have seen that in 1894 he proposed, as one of the objectives of the new National Association of English Cider Makers, that some cider should be made which alcoholically met the requirements of the Temperance Society. In 1928 the firm, about to launch a new non-alcoholic cider, offered a prize of £5 round the works for a name for it (existing names in use elsewhere were Cydrax, Pomol, Pomril and various compounds of *Pom-*). The word should be easy to shout round a bar, and preferably of two syllables. (Three might be acceptable, however; indeed they got as far as asking their patent agents to find out if Wedd's suggestion, 'Philomel', had been anticipated.) The ultimate choice was 'Cidona'.

You may have noticed some phrases Fred let fall—'the injustice of their poverty'—'in any properly organized state of society'. In his early years of struggle Fred was a keen radical. He hated the squirarchy. 'There is no better sport in life than to be heckled by squires and parasites before a big yokel meeting.' In 1898 we find him giving a lecture to an audience of working men on John Ruskin's *Unto this Last*, of which he said, 'It answers to silence . . . the greedy and idle rich'. Due to give another to the Brotherhood Club of Non-conformist workers founded by the Rev Basil Martin (father of Kingsley Martin), who lived in Ryelands Street, on 'Ruskin as a Social Reformer' and having 'no time, no books, no knowledge', he had recourse to Lowes Dickinson for help. He also asked Dickinson to get him the Webbs' *Industrial Democracy* from the Cambridge University Library, armed with which he gave an eloquent lecture to the Hereford Literary and Debating Society on 'State Socialism'. He was very keen on the nationalisation of the railways, and envisaged that of the coal mine, and even of the drink trade! He was in touch with socialist circles in London, and interested in the new Independent Labour Party. But he found his ideal society when cycling on his honeymoon in remote parts of Brittany where the people had never seen an Englishman before: 'The Brittany peasants are most delightful people, and when we curse the French should be especially exempted from our maledictions . . . . In Brittany everyone seems happy and industrious and contented, and no one is rich or overworked. There are no squires and the result is all the peasants are frank, unsuspicious and full of fellowship. I want to behead all landlords all the more.' His criticisms were not reserved for local magnates either. On 9 July 1908 the King and Queen (Edward and

Alexandra) passed by train through Hereford; but 'though they stopped at the station, the miserable pair would not check the train just outside, where 5,000 children were assembled to have a look at them but never had a glimpse. It is enough to make one a republican.' (One wonders whether the Royals had been warned of their presence. Or were they expected to pull the communication cord?)

In 1895 Fred had given up, for the present, the idea of active politics because his radicalism distressed his parents, his sister and even his brother. (Percy was conservative by temperament: 'You think that many things can be improved by Government action: I don't.') Thereafter he resisted frequent attempts to get him to stand for Parliament, for the radical wing of the Liberal Party. By 1898, however, he was Treasurer of the Liberal Association for both city and county. He was very friendly with Robert Hudson, Secretary of the Liberal Federation, and gave a luncheon talk at the National Liberal Club in London on the South Herefordshire constituency. Instigated by Wedd (one of the early Fabians), he contributed to *The Independent Review* an article on the plight of farm workers, four months before the Liberal landslide in the election of December 1905. Summarised in the London press, it caused more than a ripple nationally. Seven years later he returned to the charge with his friend the economist Hugh Meredith. Realising that circumstances made it improbable that farm labourers could ever organize a trade union, they proposed the establishment of an Agricultural Wages Board consisting half of employers and half of representatives of the National Trades Union Executive.

He had little respect for most of the politicians he met. Sending Wedd an account of the Tory speeches and doings in Hereford, he commented: 'They give us as good an insight into snobbery and jobbery as the best of novels.' Nor did he by any means approve of all Liberals: 'The two rejected Harmsworths are bringing out a Liberal Review'—another filthy jingo wolf in sheep's clothing.' From 1893 he was involved in the choosing of Liberal candidates both for the city and for South Herefordshire. One prospective candidate he described as 'thoroughly worldly, with an equally rich, pushing wife who ran the show and pretended to be hugely for the working classes.' The man thought the Boer War was just.[4] 'My Gawd, what a Party!' Another a few years later, 'the biggest and most shameless bugger of them all'. On one occasion he called a meeting for the purpose of sacking an M.P. for allegedly continuing to neglect South Herefordshire. The Labour Party was still in its infancy; but in January 1907 à propos his becoming a magistrate, the *Hereford Times* described him as 'a radical with strong sympathies for the Labour Party'. He was never drawn into it however.

His own political interests were in housing, education, health, law and order, and women's rights. What he did about these, and about local politics in general, will be dealt with later, in the context of Hereford and of employees; but it may here be briefly recorded that he was on the County Council from 1898 to 1904 and from 1907 to 1913, and an Alderman from 1913 to 1919; and on the City Council from 1905 to 1911 (Mayor in 1908–09) and from 1925 to 1931 (Mayor in 1925–26).

When he was courting Sophie, Fred asked her to explain to her parents why his views were so radical: 'They do not realise that I have lived like a working man and worked *much* harder'; and just before his marriage he said: 'For the past twelve years I have always systematically endeavoured to seek my riches in the fewness of my wants.' But as the hard work bore fruit the workman turned into a capitalist. In 1916, to allay Mrs Wedd's scruples about accepting money for her ailing husband, he told her that, despite wartime restrictions, he had paid income tax on some £8, 000 in two years. In 1929, after a wonderful summer, he took comfort in the thought that he could see no chance of having to deny any of the Bulmers anything necessary for their moral or spiritual welfare. But it was, as he told his son Harold three years later, consciousness of how lucky they were that urged him to do all he could to make the lot of the less fortunate more endurable.

How did this change in his fortunes affect his own life and political outlook? Certainly he enjoyed having his friends to stay, occasional holidays abroad, and good food and drink, but ostentatious living he despised. When he saw examples of it he would murmur with a sly twinkle the words of the Litany: 'In all time of our wealth . . . Good Lord deliver us'. But he became disenchanted with left wing politics. In a moment of exasperation in May 1915 he wrote: 'Organised Labour has been so concerned for years with its own class interests that is has forgotten that the nation exists, and thinks only of its own booze.' But the old radical naturally felt a need to justify his position. On 22 October 1931, stung by some local criticisms, he summoned his workforce of 438 and gave them an address on 'This business and the political situation', printing this *Apologia pro sua vita* for subsequent private circulation. He began by telling them how he and his brother had built up the business until now it paid out £50, 000 a year in wages: 'and I, who used to wear clogs and a shirt without any collar and to sleep on the floor, became what many call in present day language "a bloody capitalist" . . . . There has to be capital, but the capitalist must be judged by the use he makes of it and the amount which he spends on himself. By that test I am content to be judged by any tribunal. We have not drawn out of the business since we have been here an average of more than 2 1/2% of the capital we have put into it, and my personal expenses do not even now exceed the cost of the stamps on your cards. I venture to submit to you, that my services have brought greater benefits to the people of these works than all the stamps they have affixed to their cards'.

So much for 'This business'. There is nothing here of the social-istic radicalism of 30 years before; instead, a defence of enlightened capitalism.[5] But what about 'the political situation'? That was the other occasion of the speech. In an effort to maintain the value of the pound, which he had recently taken off the gold standard, Ramsay Macdonald, the Prime Minister, had broken with what proved to be the majority of his Labour Party, and was going to the country for support for his National Government, in alliance with the Conservative Stanley Baldwin and the Liberal Herbert Samuel; and Fred ended with an appeal to his employees to sup-port it. (Next week it was returned to power with an enormous majority, and continued, under the name at least, of 'coalition' to govern the country for the next 14 years.)

When Fred was elected Mayor in 1925 his friend Alderman Steel quoted his father as having said: 'You know, Fred thinks he's a radical, but there's no more thoroughgoing conservative than he is.' In any case, there's nothing unusual in a man's becoming less radical as he gets older; and no one who knew Fred could doubt that he considered the issue at stake in that election to be vital, though one cannot help wondering whether his friendship with Stanley Baldwin may have fortified his decision.[6] His whole record of work for the community and the whole way he ran his business (which will be dealt with in subsequent chapters) are evidence enough that there was no diminution in his social concern.

On the day of his wedding in 1899 a *Hereford Times* contributor prophesied a brilliant future for this young and talented townsman:

'He possesses the attributes which go to make up a successful leader of men. First, he has great knowledge of history and a true insight into the lives of men, and a strong sympathy with all shapes and forms of it . . . the power of expressing his own thoughts clearly, thoughtfully and intelligently . . . unbounded faith in the people.' When he died on 2 September 1941, less than a year after his beloved Nat Wedd, at the age 76, the same paper described him as among the most notable men of Herefordshire of the present century: 'A man of unique capabilities and outstanding intellect, he carved for himself a niche in the history of the county, and particularly in that of the city, surpassing in importance even the position that he occupied as the joint creator with his brother, H.P. Bulmer, of the biggest cider manufacturing business in the world.'

[1] Described in K. Middlemass' *Life of Stanley Baldwin*, pp.22–7.

[2] For 20 years Fred's wife Sophie was to work tirelessly for the League of Nations Union, and after the War for the United Nations Association. She also advocated 'family planning' at a time when this was an unconventional thing to do.

[3] Even after his marriage, six years later, it was the same story in November: 'I get up daily at 5.15, make cider till 6.00 or 7.00pm, feed at 7.45, get bloody sleepy and useless at 8.30, and by 9.00pm asleep on the sofa'.

[4] Like many Liberals, Fred was against the Boer War: 'The Press seem more horrible than ever,' he wrote on 2 October 1899; 'they want the land, and they mean to have it' ('the land' was the Transvaal).

[5] On 10 August 1929 he had written, about plans for the Hereford City Electrical Works: 'The lion in the path is the socialist Government, which will probably raise objection to the transfer of our concern to a capitalist body.'

[6] Baldwin, then Lord President of the Council, visited Bulmers' works on 2 January 1933.

CHAPTER SIX

BULMERS AND HEREFORD: (to 1919)[1]

The plan to start the works in the Ryelands had an inauspicious hurdle to clear. There was an acrimonious row, ventilated in the *Hereford Times*. On 14 August 1888 a deputation from 83 owners and occupiers of property in the vicinity objected before the Roads and Sewers Committee of the City Council that the value of their property would be likely to be diminished by nuisance from rotting apples. The committee ruled that the manufacture of cider was not an offensive trade within the meaning of the Public Health Act 1875 and that the plans conformed with the by-laws. But in view of the importance of the matter and the positions of the objectors they referred it to the Council, hoping that they might get the Rev C.H. Bulmer, purchaser of the property, to come to some arrangement satisfactory to the memorialists. On 25 August three representatives of these told the Council that, having approached Mr Bulmer, they had received a discourteous refusal. He for his part, in a letter to the Mayor, took exception to their addressing him as 'Rector of Credenhill and Cider Merchant', insinuating that he confused his religious calling with one purely secular. Thereupon they cited an advertisement he had issued in 1885: 'Sparkling perry, quarts, taken prizes wherever exhibited, equals finest champagne, which it excels in keeping; 30s the dozen hamper. Also same price, extraordinarily luscious, pure and highly flavoured cider.' However, he protested also that he had no connection with the proposed business, to be carried on by his son on land he had purchased for him. The Council accepted that, unless and until a nuisance could be proved, it had no right to interfere. Fortunately so. But one can see that the memorialists had a point: land bought in the vicinity by the Hereford Freehold Land Society six years before at a ratable value of £60 was now rated at nearly £2,000. One wonders what an environmental planning committee of today would have decided.

It will be remembered that Radcliffe Cooke, Conservative M.P. for the Borough, and Fred Bulmer were respectively President and Secretary of the National Association of English Cider Makers, founded in 1894. During one of his campaign meetings before the parliamentary election of 1895 Cooke read out a letter from Bulmer thanking him for what he had done for cider and assuring him that, although he was doing the most he could to turn him out, that would not prevent him from joining him in future to promote the interests of the cider industry; and indeed they did continue to collaborate. But at a Liberal campaign meeting Fred was less urbane: 'I would as soon think of looking for toleration of political opinions in a cathedral close as for a decent Land Act [to help farm labourers] from a Conservative Government. The electors of Hereford were misled by the many people telling them lies at the last elections, and in consequence they have been smitten with a member like Mr Radcliffe Cooke. But we mean to get rid of that disease.' The victorious Cooke smugly advised the young man to keep out of politics; but Fred felt much too passionately about social justice as he saw it. Nevertheless the collaboration continued, and in the autumn of 1897 Cooke accepted 'a not inconsiderable testimonial' from the cider-makers of the district (a bicycle).

Next summer, in the course of which he published a small work entitled *A Book about Cider and Perry*, Cooke announced in the *Hereford Times* and in a circular somewhat derogatory about the present state of the industry and describing himself as 'The Leading Authority on Cider', that he was setting up as a cider-maker. There was an explosion. An open letter to him from H.P. Bulmer and Co. and five other Herefordshire cider-makers appeared in the *Hereford Times* for July 16th 1898. It was drafted by Fred, as anyone could tell, and begins: 'In the words of Dr. Johnson, let us advise you to "clear your mind of cant".' The gist of it was that Cooke was simply out to make money; that he had appealed to the electors of Hereford to return him to Parliament as a *disinterested* advocate of the cider industry, and that when he accepted that recent testimonial from the cider-makers he must have been already preparing to compete with them. An extract will convey the tone:

'In your circular you arrogate to yourself the title of "The Leading Authority on Cider". Let us consider how you have established your claims. By virtue of your office as a Member of Parliament, and your reiterated professions of disinterestedness, you obtained the confidence of the cider-makers of this county, and the same professions enabled you to secure in the columns of *The Times*, and the press generally, a publicity in connection with cider and its manufacture which thousands of pounds spent in fair and legitimate advertising would have failed to procure.

Armed with credentials of a public character, you obtained the entrée, and frequently inspected the works and manufactories of cider-makers, whom you systematically cross-examined in great detail both as to the theory and practical methods of their several businesses. You yourself have justified your intrusions on the score that unless you were well posted up on the subject you could not to the greatest advantage give effect to your benevolent intentions. But pray what ground have you for the statement that you *are* "the Leading Authority on Cider Making"? What apprenticeship have you served to justify this title? No doubt you have obtained the necessarily superficial training which can be got by using the brains of others who have had to pay heavily in cash and labour for their experience; and this too while professing to act in the public interest.'

This letter did not go unnoticed by the national press. The *Westminster Gazette* described it as 'one of the most diverting documents we have seen for a long time'. Whatever the rights and wrongs, someone at least thought Cooke an authority, for he was commissioned to write the article on cider for the 11th edition of the *Encyclopedia Britannica* (1910; Vol 6, pp.362–4). It is pleasant to record that when, having resigned his parliamentary seat in 1900, he left his Herefordshire home of 'Hellens' at Marcle in 1909, Fred as Mayor wrote a letter on 23 January to the *Hereford Times* supporting public recognition for Cooke's services and saying that 'his political opponents had in him a courteous and kindly antagonist'. The Bulmer brothers subscribed ten guineas each to a purse of £175 which Fred presented to him at a public meeting on July 28 together with a testimonial.

To Fred Bulmer life in Credenhill village seemed to have changed very little since the Middle Ages. Writing to his fiancée he said: 'The county is one of the most lovely in England, and from my home we have an extensive view of some 40 miles, stretching from the Black Mountains in Wales to the Malvern Hills.' But closer acquaintance with the county town when he went to work there produced a much less idyllic impression: 'a slum cathedral town', he called it. The juxtaposition of words was pointed; for he was further appalled to find that some of the worst slums belonged to three ecclesiastical bodies in the city, who raised the rents whenever the employers raised wages. When, some years later, he reported these facts to the City Council as Chairman of its Housing committee his comments were widely headlined in the Midlands press: 'Clergy Grind the Faces of the Poor?' Realising that there was a desperate need for new accommodation, sanitary but simple and at low rent, to rescue the slum-dwellers, he began to organise a limited company, semi-philanthropic, to raise money for building such cottages. The authorised capital of Hereford Dwellings Ltd. was registered as £10,000, to be raised by £1 shares at a fixed interest of 4%, income tax being deductable at 1s in the pound. Again Fred appealed to his old friends, and again they responded – Wedd, Berry etc., and Gibbins, 'a Quaker turned agnostic by King's and in practice a good Christian'. The difficulty proved to be not raising the money, but finding the land. No one seemed willing to sell. When he approached the Rev Dr Innes, Custos of the College of Vicars, he received the reply: 'Mr Bulmer, the housing of the poor is not a matter that would in the slightest commend itself to the College of Vicars.' However, he managed to collect a board of directors consisting of 'all the most able men in the town', and finally, after several years of hard work and some setbacks, the first block of 12 cottages in Moor Street was opened at the end of 1901, and flats in Bewell Street and Bath Street followed. Applications for tenancies were overwhelming.[2]

It should be said at once, to the credit of the Church, that one of his staunchest supporters had been Bishop John Percival, sometime Headmaster of Rugby, who was appointed to Hereford in 1895. He subscribed to the scheme and gave it his blessing. The two became great friends. Fred often sought his advice; and when in 1904 the Liberal Bishop was accused of meddling in politics because he criticised the morality of Joseph Chamberlain's protectionist measures, Fred routed the organisers of a round robin of protest by recalling that no one had protested when Bishop Atlay had allowed his Palace to be used as headquarters for the Tory Primrose League in Herefordshire. In later years the Bulmers were to be particularly friendly with Dean Waterfield and his family, and with the scholarly canons Rashdall, Bannister and Streeter. It was not anticlericalism as such (not only Fred's father, but three of his uncles were parsons), but justifiable moral indignation that had evoked those earlier strictures on local ecclesiastical authorities.

Now deeply interested in improved housing, and having inspected over 100 more slum houses, Fred went on to more ambitious schemes. On missing a train at Watford, which meant a wait of forty minutes, he had picked up at the bookstall a book by a Mr Nettlefold entitled *Garden City*. Letchworth Garden City had been a pioneer in 1903 and Hampstead Garden Suburb in 1905: why he asked himself, should Hereford not have its Garden City? Inspired by this thought, Fred in 1908 convened a meeting at the Town Hall to be addressed by Mr Nettlefold; and Hereford Co-operative Housing Ltd was launched, with promises to take shares amounting to £5,000. In 1909 the Garden City was inaugurated, on rising ground, the former Penn Grove Estate, beyond the railway station. It comprised modest semi-detached houses with small back and front gardens, the first 'working class' houses in Hereford to be set back from the road frontage. It was a success, and still remains as a pleasant residential area, with names such as 'Geoffrey Avenue', and 'Esmond Avenue' besides 'Bulmer Avenue' to recall its connection with Percy's family also. Some of the 120 houses have four bedrooms, but most have three.

In 1910 an appeal for £500 was launched to build a social centre there, but the outbreak of war caused the plan to be shelved. In 1935 however, when the fund stood at over £700, Fred laid the foundation stone, which recorded his name as founder of the Garden City, of 'a social institute for indoor and outdoor recreation'. It was to be the finest club house in Hereford.[3] Four years later Fred rolled the first wood at the new bowling green, next to the hard tennis court, which he had presented along with a challenge cup.

As Chairman of Hereford Co-operative Housing Ltd. Fred explained to a meeting of the Trades and Labour Council on 22 September 1917 how the building of the Garden City had been organised. The City Council was responsible for planning the site, determining the number of houses to the acre and laying out roads. (These last proved quite inexpensive, as stone and brick rubble was available from the demolition of some of the worst slums in the City, in Bewell Street.) A committee was formed to enable future tenants, if willing to buy shares, to have a say in the size and design of the houses. The Garden City was registered as a Friendly Society and paid the co-operative an annual sum in interest and sinking fund so that ultimately it would be freehold. A sum of £9,252 was borrowed from the Government at 3 1/2%, to be repaid in 30 years. The balance of £2,000–3,000 was raised by the sale of ordinary shares. The co-operative appealed to public-spirited people to buy loan stock at 4% without sinking fund. Tenants could become shareholders by paying a small weekly subscription with their rent. Meanwhile, before 1919, hardly any municipal housing was built in Hereford. By the Second World War all the available land in the Garden City had been built on, and the loans nearly all repaid.

Another cause on which Fred was particularly keen was that of medical care. At the beginning of the century he became County Treasurer of the National Association for the Prevention of Tuberculosis, a disease rampant in those days. He continually pressed the Council to provide more sanatorium accommodation for it. When the Insurance Act of 1911 came in, the beginning of a national health service, he was appointed by the County Council to be chairman of a committee to negotiate with the doctors the administration of the new 'panel patient scheme'. Herefordshire doctors were predictably the last in England (bracketed with the Isle of Ely) to come in. The official in charge of the Bill summoned Fred to come and see him in London on Christmas Eve before returning to Hereford the same evening to meet the doctors. He arrived at St Peter's Church House on a freezing night at about 8.00pm, and they kept him waiting for two hours until, by a narrow majority, they agreed to hear him under protest. He told them that the Minister had doctors with their bags packed ready to come down and administer the scheme if they were not prepared to do so. It took ten minutes then for him to secure the 50–60 signatures sufficient to form a panel. Years afterwards, addressing the Annual County Dinner of the Medical Association, he claimed that as chairman of the National Health Committee he had received many proofs of the doctors' confidence. 'How so?', interjected the somewhat inebriated chairman, giving him his chance to reply: 'They told me what they thought about each other.' He was a master of the complicated details of the Act, and always got the most out of it for the insured individual, being especially helpful to sufferers from tuberculosis.

A further service he performed for the community was by helping the National Telephone Company, in the autumn of 1898, to find enough subscribers for them to set up a telephone exchange in Hereford.

Education was another of his great interests. On the County

Education Committee he secured the co-option of women. He played a prominent part in the founding in 1904 of the College of Education (then known as Hereford Training College), in 1912 of the High School for Boys, and in 1915 of the High School for Girls, of whose governors he was for many years chairman. He also helped to organize technical and agricultural education in the county. His papers show that he was conversant with modern educational ideas in the U.S.A., Germany, Denmark and even Japan.

The immorality and corruption of Hereford politics was another thing that came as a shock to Fred. Here again the Bishop was to agree with him, saying that Hereford was 'hopeless', the whole atmosphere so bad that political work was almost useless. In 1894 Fred stood for the City Council as a Liberal candidate. Besides the replacement of slums by new council houses at low rents, the platform included a demand for a minimum wage of at least 18s a week instead of 16s for municipal employees, and for meetings of the Council to be transferred to the evening so that employed people with regular hours of work could be participant members. A letter in the *Hereford Times* of 13 October 1894 from a 'Progressive Liberal', in which Fred was praised, advocated Trade Union wages in all municipal contracts; ensuring that shops conform to the Shop Assistants' Hours Bill, which prohibited work for more than 74 hours a week (some young people in Hereford were working in hotels and refreshment rooms for 90–100 hours); and providing a central hall for trading and friendly societies. Fred was defeated. Four years later, however, he was elected unopposed to the Above Eign ward of the County Council, at whose meetings he and two like-minded friends sat together and harried the die-hards, earning the name of 'The Three Musketeers'. He hoped to be able to help on its Agriculture and Technical Education Committees, but in March 1904 he lost his seat. Bitterly he reflected on his misfortune in living in such an obscurantist and reactionary place: 'Agriculture hates Education and Radicals'.

County Councils were a novelty, established in 1889. At the outset one-third were co-opted as aldermen. They included men Fred greatly admired, such as Colonel Prescott Decie. Looking back in 1939, he wished that councils would make more use of their power of co-option. Unfortunately there had been able members who thought their only duty was to limit public expenditure to the minimum. Proposals for improvements were often postponed and then, when the First World War brought a change of heart, finally implemented at immensely greater cost.

Shortly after Fred lost his County Council seat in 1904 (he regained it in 1907) the Earl of Chesterfield recommended his name to the Lord Chancellor for a seat on the City Bench as a Justice of the Peace. Nothing happened, and eventually inquiries elicited the explanation that he had been 'worse reported on than any man in the Kingdom'. But others proved to have had a similar experience, and there was such disquiet that a Royal Commission was appointed under Lord James of Hereford to inquire into the affairs of the Borough and how its Justices were appointed. Fred was summoned as a witness, and in answer to a question from Arthur Henderson, the Labour representative, expressed himself as willing to name names to substantiate his allegations; but the Chairman intervened to forbid him to reply, saying, 'Aren't you forgetting, Henderson, that this witness has to live in Hereford?' The evidence of corrupt practices and malicious reporting was overwhelming, and shortly afterwards Fred was appointed not only to the City (1906) and County (1909) Benches but to the Lord Chancellor's Advisory Committee for both (1911). In this last capacity he succeeded, against much local opposition, in obtaining the appointment of new men from a wider social spectrum, and after 1918 he secured the appointment of women.

At the end of 1905 the political atmosphere underwent a considerable change. The Liberals had a landslide victory in the parliamentary election. At the same time Fred was elected to the Hereford City Council (he held his seat until 1911), and in November 1908 he was elected Mayor for the ensuing year. One senses that from 1906, in politics as in attitude to business, his early violence and feelings of frustration had been somewhat softened by marriage and the mellowing effects of the years. In February 1907 he had the satisfaction of seeing one of his passionate campaigns end in his favour, when his motion that a minimum wage of 18s a week should be paid to all able-bodied Corporation workers was passed.

The birth of his son Harold during his mayoralty was marked by the presentation to him by the City and County Councillors, Officials and Magistrates of a two-handled silver loving-cup surmounted by a silver 'cradle', the first time in ten years that there had been a birth to a Mayor in office. In his speech of thanks he

was able to announce: 'Before the end of the year we ought to
see 200 persons living in better surroundings than they have been
accustomed to.' The Garden City was another breakthrough
in his battle against conditions of poverty. On 7 December 1909,
when his term was over, both he and his father were ceremonially
admitted as hereditary Freemen of the City.

But he did not relent towards the county magnates (one of
whom he called 'The Bloatocrat'). A letter to the *Hereford Times*
of 14 April 1906 signed 'Old Tory' had concluded: 'All honour
to Mr Bulmer for his sturdy advocacy of the just claims of the
underdog. Of course the upperdogs growled and yelped. In the
long run the Bulmer dog may be master of the kennel'. An interesting sidelight on his relations with the 'upperdogs' comes from
an unexpected quarter, from Vyvyan Holland, the son of Oscar
Wilde, who at the age of 24, with his father dead and his name
changed at the behest of his elders, spent six months in 1909–10
in a solicitor's office in Hereford. The solicitor did not introduce
him to anyone, even his own wife: his first friends there were the
Bulmers. Robbie Ross had written on his behalf, and Fred sought
him out. This is his recollection nearly 60 years later:

'Bulmer was extremely unpopular in the neighbourhood, for
three reasons. First because he was a Liberal and organised political
meetings at which he made converts to his own views, which was
a heinous crime in such a Conservative stronghold as Hereford.
Secondly, because he was a successful business man in an almost
exclusively agricultural community. But most of all because when
Fred had been Mayor of Hereford and therefore chief magistrate
in 1908, he had developed a habit of inflicting heavy fines and
even imprisonment on local worthies, some of them even being
magistrates themselves, for being drunk in charge of horses on
Market Day in Hereford . . . . This unpopularity had no effect at
all on the Bulmers, who were a very united family who did not
mix much with their neighbours.'[4]

Fred lost his seat on the City Council in 1911 and on the County
Council in 1913. He was appointed an alderman, but resigned
this position in 1919 because of Percy's illness. On that occasion
the *Hereford Times* characterised him in the following terms: 'He
is a destructive critic of no mean order, but even in his most
iconoclastic performance can always be reckoned upon to suggest
an alternative policy. He has the gift of imagination—a real asset
in the humdrum routine of administrative work—and the capacity

to inspire men with a new vision.' For six years after that he was running the business almost single-handed; but in 1925, with Howard and Esmond now run in, he was less encumbered. The City at that time was hard pressed to find a mayor, and at the combined invitation of the Liberals and Conservatives, encouraged also by Sophie, he agreed, as a preliminary, to stand for the Council. Elected on 6 November, he was made Mayor for the second time with acclamation a week later. An alderman said on this occasion: 'Mr Bulmer has made it quite plain that he must have a free hand', adding, 'He is a gentleman of a penetrating mind, a clear brain and a vocabulary that is never at a loss.' In responding Fred assured them, among other things, that they would not be let in for the expense of a present such as Harold's birth in his previous mayoralty had caused them: 'The days of Abraham and Sarah are over.'

The ensuing year was an unhappy one for him in his private life, for in it he lost both his mother and his eldest child, Dorothy. Publicly however it was one in which, as another alderman said in retrospect, 'it was almost impossible to enumerate his many activities.' They included generous hospitality to visitors for the celebration of the 1,250th anniversary of the see of Hereford. But his most lasting work was in financial reorganisation, by which the projects of spending committees should be co-ordinated, with priorities discussed and established every April, and in general economising.

Not that he thought the political scene in Hereford had improved much. In 1927 he reckoned that there were six criminals on the Council. Their leader, who (he alleged) had twice deserted from the Army during the War and had never got as far as France, walked in a robe in the procession to the War Memorial on Armistice Day. 'Hereford took this as a matter of course: it would', was his comment to Webb. No member could be found who was willing to succeed him. Fred himself was urged to stand again, but unhesitatingly refused.

His career in local politics came to an end in a strange way. It will be remembered that in October 1931 he nailed his colours to the mast of the Macdonald-Baldwin-Samuel National Government. A week after that speech he made to his employees urging them to do the same, there were local elections. Defending his seat for Leominster Ward as an Independent Liberal, while the party put up an official candidate, he split the Liberal vote and so lost his seat to the Labour candidate. He remained, however, a magistrate until 1938. For the year 1934 he was appointed High Sheriff for the county (as Viscount Scudamore had been three centuries before). The photograph of him in his court dress may seem rather incongruous to those who knew him and remember the stories of his radical past: one fancies one detects a trace of amusement as well as pride in his face.

[1] *The Book of Hereford*, by J. and M. Tonkin, (Barracuda Books Limited, 1975), has at the end a bibliography of the city and a list of principal dates concerning it.

[2] The Moor Street houses are still in use, but were eventually sold, partly to tenants, partly *en bloc*. The Bath Street flats were also partly sold to tenants, and the Bewell Street ones to British Canners Ltd. (Cadbury).

[3] Unfortunately it was destroyed some 30 years later by juvenile arson, and Council flats now stand on the site.

[4] *Time Remembered* (1966), 17–8. I have amended plurals to singulars, since Holland should not have included Percy. 'In the neighbourhood' should perhaps read 'in the county circles'. I am also sceptical about the 'imprisonment'. Another person in the neighbourhood who was kind to Holland was Edward Elgar.

CHAPTER SEVEN

FRUIT AND ORCHARDING: (to 1919)

Now back to cider-making. The history of varieties of apple is
complicated by the fact that they appear and die out, and that not
only has the same variety been given different names in different
parts of the country, but the same name has sometimes been used,
concurrently or successively, for different varieties. Knight (1797)
reckoned that no variety cultivated in his day had existed for more
than 200 years, and pointed out that apples known in his day did
not correspond with descriptions given of ones of the same name
by Parkinson in 1629. He estimated that Scudamore's famous
Redstreak and the highly reputed Gennet-Moyle were in the last
stages of decay, and the Foxwhelp and Styre hastening after them.
Bull, in *The Herefordshire Pomona*, gives a list of highly esteemed
stocks that had disappeared. Out of Duncumb's list of 18 cider
apples grown in his day (1805) Edward Ball reported in 1944 that
only half a dozen—Hagloe Crab, Foxwhelp, Dymock Red, Ten
Commandments, Redstreak and possibly Gennet-Moyle—still existed. But skilful grafting could rescue varieties. Thus the Pomona
Committee rescued the Foxwhelp and the Taynton Squash pear
with complete success by this process, though it was sometimes
hard to obtain good grafts. The Forest Styre and the Hagloe Crab
were not reprieved until 1883. A single tree found in Herefordshire
rescued the Gennet-Moyle, which has the rare capability of being
propagated by sticking a twig or branch into the soil, where the
roots readily form.

The Woolhope Club's Pomona Committee imported eight
Norman varieties and sent them to Cranston's Nurseries at King's
Acre, Hereford, which propagated from them and distributed
the results to the orchards of Herefordshire, along with Forest
Styre and Hagloe Crab. A Worcestershire nurseryman produced
and distributed 8,000 young specimens, in vigorous health, of
Foxwhelp, Skyrme's Kernel and Taynton Squash pear. In 1899
a committee of the Herefordshire Fruit Growers Association was
set up to designate vintage apples best suited to the county and
adjoining districts. A list of 21 were approved, of which five had
been recently introduced from Normandy. But when Percy Bulmer
went over to France in February of that year to buy nursery apple

trees, he found there was a dearth: only rubbish was likely to be put on the market.

Approved varieties of tree must be propagated by grafting, to avoid genetical disturbance. New varieties may be discovered by improvements such as artificial cross-pollination or radiation treatment, and by those methods some useful ones have been produced.

The chief elements in cider apples—sugar, tannin and malic acid —are in proportions different from those present in eating apples. The sugar produces the alcohol and the tannin adds 'body'. Cider apples actually require less acid than eating apples, because in the finished product there is less sugar left to counteract it. It is the bitter and astringent tannin that makes cider apples unpalatable for eating. What the balance should be is ultimately a subjective matter determined by connoisseur tasters in laboratories. Formerly different apples were blended; now it is different ciders. There are four recognized categories, distinguished according to relative proportion of acid and tannin. 'Sweet' is low in both, e.g. 'Sweet Coppin'. It is useful for blending with ciders from the more strongly flavoured fruits. 'Bittersweet', e.g. 'Ball's', gives English cider its characteristic flavour, being high in tannin and low in acid. Its tree flowers late, and its crop is therefore less liable to be spoilt by frost. 'Sharp' is predominantly acid, like cooking apples, which can be used to replace it, e.g. 'Crimson Sharp'. 'Bittersharp', e.g. 'Kingston Black', is fairly high in both acid and tannin, though with less varied tannin effects than those of Bittersweet; but cultivation of Sharp and Bittersharp is likely to be stepped up, to make good scarcity and diminish consequent expense. Eating apples can be used along with cider apples for making cider, but not to a proportion beyond 25%, according to Fred Bulmer.

When Bulmers began, they advertised locally simply for 'good cider apples', usually bittersweets, or sometimes with a bonus for certain varieties, such as Foxwhelp or Kingston Black, whose blending produced 'The Imperial Tokay of Herefordshire'. There was also a bonus for 'Upright French', if it was kept so as to be ripe in e.g. mid-December, so that the period of processing apples could be staggered. A limited amount of 'culls' (cooking apples) could also be used in the admixture. A list of reliable suppliers was gradually compiled. At first each kind of cider was made from one or two kinds of apple; but soon others were blended in, without however altering the name and general characteristics of each. A list gradually established itself, more or less as follows (prices per dozen are here given for early years of the century):

Cider

No.1	Redstreak and White Norman (medium sweet)	9s
No.2	Foxwhelp and Kingston Black (sweet or dry)	18s
No.3	Strawberry Norman (fruity)	10s
No.4	Cherry Pearmain (medium dry)	9s
No.4a	Cherry Norman (extra dry)	9s

Perry

No.5	Holmer (medium sweet)	9s
No.6	Longland and Moorcroft (dry)	9s
No.7	Still cider (extra dry)	7s
No.7a	Tankard cider (medium sweet)	7s
No.8	Still Perry (dry)	7s

As to prices paid for apples, in October 1913 cider-makers were offering 30s a ton; but South Herefordshire growers, not content with this, were banding together, and Bulmers raised their offer to 40s a ton.

In former times apple trees standing in hedgerows were a useful addition to farmers' assets. John Norden (1610) estimated that a surplus of their fruit could fetch about £10 a year. But orchards have also been cultivated from time immemorial, and ones specifically of cider apples for several centuries. Formerly all apple trees were 'standards', trees with a trunk more than 7 1/2 feet high and a canopy spread of about 25 feet. These when planted at 40 trees to the acre produce very little for the first 5 years, 3–4 tons an acre by 15 years, 6–7 by 25, and steadily less after 70. They look splendid, and have the advantage that their branches are out of reach of grazing farm animals; but they are difficult to harvest when heavy with fruit in autumn. There used to be a good deal of cultivation between apple trees in orchards, of wheat or rye or vegetables, but in recent times the rising cost of labour has made this unremunerative. Otherwise grass was let grow, for grazing animals, which had the additional advantages of providing natural manuring and a firm surface for harvesting machinery. Grass, and even arable crops, are still sometimes grown in orchards while the trees are young; but in recent times the smaller 'bush' trees have become more popular. These, with a trunk of up to 2 1/2 feet, grow to about 12 feet high, and have a fruiting spread of about

20 feet. Some 160–240 of them can be planted to the acre, as compared with 40–60 standards, and they come to full cropping in 8–10 years of about 10 tons an acre; but their life expectancy is shorter than that of standards, so the capital outlay is larger. A strip of soil between them is usually bare, spray having been used to kill grass and weeds that would have competed for moisture and nutrient with the trees.

The trees are cultivated in nurseries, by either grafting or budding tested varieties on to virus-free stock. Farmers used to replace individual trees in their orchards as they deteriorated, so that a confused variety of kinds of apple resulted. They are now encouraged, if their farms are large enough, to segregate and to specialise more, and to produce fruit that matures at different times of the year, so that the cider mills may be kept regularly busy with fresh fruit and the harvesting may be spread out more throughout the season.

The cider apple harvest starts at about the beginning of October, a slack time otherwise on the farm. Worlidge (1676) tells how apple harvesters used to go out into the field with a horn corked up at the narrow end and filled with cider. After it had been passed round for all to drink to a good harvest the cork was withdrawn and the horn blown as a signal to begin work. Harvesting goes on until late November or early December. The traditional method was to shake the apple tree's branches with a long hooked pole and then gather the fallen fruit into bags (which Bulmers provided free to their suppliers). Nowadays various kinds of mechanical harvester are continually being tried, including 'shakers' clamped to the trunk of the tree and vibrated. But mechanical harvesting, though rapid and labour-saving, does bruise the fruit more than hand-work, so that processing of the fruit has to take place with the minimum of delay.

The importance of satisfactory storage of apples was early recognised by good cidrists. Francis Bacon, on the ripening of fruits by proximity to one another, wrote: 'Our cyder makers have an excellent way of imitating the operation. For they care not to bruise or squeeze the apples till they have lain together in heaps and so ripened by mutual contact, that the great acidity of the liquid may be corrected.' Here is the gist of Austen's instructions (1653). Gather apples when seeds are brown or black (cut open a sample and see). Avoid bruising. Spread them thinly on mats or boards.

Keep them dry, with draughts from the north on dry days. (It is important that as much air as possible should circulate between the apples.) Pick out rotten ones and leaves. Cover the good ones with mats or straw in frosty weather. Beale (1670) recognized ripeness by fragrancy. He thought that cider apples, if unbruised, should be left a week or more before grinding. The harsher the wild fruit, the longer it must lie. Cadle (1863) said that apples should at first be spread in the loft about 12–18 inches deep, but that after a week or nine days the depth could be increased to 24–30 inches.

These measures were all very well for farmers, but the bigger production aims of factories presented more problems. In the early days of Bulmers the apples, as they arrived from the farms, were spread out in heaps on acres of fresh green turf, as shown in contemporary pictures, 'a reservoir of fruit for the mills to draw an uninterrupted supply'. Later it became recognised as important that the arrival of fruit should be so staggered, according to the time of ripening of each variety, as to limit the area needed for storage while keeping the mills nevertheless in full production. The soft and early varieties should not be left for more than a week or ten days before pressing. Most however will keep from when they are picked in November until around Christmas. The 'hard', late-ripening Redstreak often stood for six weeks before being processed in January.

A ton of apples yielded about 180 gallons of juice.

CHAPTER EIGHT

MANUFACTURE: (to 1919)

'A low thatched shed, a huge round trough, a ponderous rolling stone impelled by an aged horse, whose movements were ever and anon impelled by the human voice and shovel blows . . . '
'In the trough is a kind of porridge of green and ripe and rotten apples, sloppy with water from the nearest horse-pool. The veteran cider-maker shovels off the gruesome compound to the press hard by, and builds in hairy cloths his pyramid of pulp. With gravity and circumspection the rusty screws are turned, the heavy beam descends, the muddy stream flows out. Long rows of mouldy casks stand ready in the cider-house. Into these the pressed juice is poured, and mixes with the aged lees of many years.'

This is no doubt a wilful caricature, 'knocking copy', the drabbest composite picture that could be painted of cider-making on a Victorian farm. It occurs in a pamphlet on *The Revival of Cider* issued by Bulmers about 1908, and was intended to bring home to the public the transformation in the methods of manufacture that had been effected by the cider factories which had sprung up in the past 20 years, particularly their own. (It is only fair to say that respectable cider was apparently being made by a minority of more enlightened farmers.) The Bulmers' principles had been set out in their circular No 4 of 1893: no handling in the process of manufacture or possibility of contamination; no contents except the juice of the fruit—no water, no sugar, no chemical compounds added. An interview between a representative of the *Hereford Times* and 'the senior partner' (?Percy) published on 18 November 1893 gives an idea of the situation at that time and of the processes involved in cider-making.

Harvesting of apples having begun in September, the factory was very busy, with employees working on shifts. Some 1,000 tons of apples had been bought in the season, and the heaps covered nearly two acres of the yard turf. As men piled fruit into the two-wheeled, horse-drawn 'tip-carts', women stood by to pick out any rotten specimens. The apples, as required, were moved on a portable railway in light trucks, wound automatically up an incline to the first floor, and then tipped into the mills (revolving steel drums with toothed knives projecting about 1/16 of an inch), through which they were crushed at the rate of a ton in five minutes, the pulp being received in two receptacles alternately in the room beneath. While one receptacle was being filled with newly crushed pulp the other was being pressed by means of hydraulic power. About 15 hundredweight of pulp was pressed at a time, the operation lasting for 5–10 minutes, so that from 3,000 to 4,000 gallons of clear-run cider could be made in a day. The juice from the press streamed down into a reservoir beneath, and from there it was conveyed by pumps in due course to all parts of the building—the racking-vats, the fermenting-vats, the filtering department, and finally to the storing casks. The machinery throughout was driven by a 30 h.p. gas engine. The fermenting room was maintained at a temperature of 60–65 F. After about three weeks the cider was conveyed through glass-lined pipes into the filtering department. This was surmounted by a tower with a tank at the top which enabled the casks, stacked one, two or three high, to be filled by gravitation with equal rapidity in any part of the building, with no use of buckets and not a drop spilt. There were three centrifugal pumps, running at the rate of 3,000 revolutions a minute, to convey the cider from one part of the building to another in the process of manufacture. The cellars held 30,000 gallons, but this was not enough, and another was to be constructed in the coming year.

This account may be supplemented by one given by Fred Bulmer to his fiancée in a letter of January 1899:

'The brew consists of about 80 vats or cuveés', all of course identical. Each one of these lots has to be analysed many times over, and constantly examined to see if the proper fermentation is present. If not, healthy ferments must be added. The juice is quite thick at first; but if the fermentation is healthy and your analyses are adequate, it is possible, by using exactly the right quantity of gelatine (the stuff cooks use for blancmange and jellies) and isinglass, to clarify the juice completely. During the process it has to be racked' (i.e. drawn out of one cask, in which the sediment is left) several times and put into a clean one. But it is also of great importance to choose the right time for all these things.'

The improvements introduced by Percy Bulmer after his visits to Germany have already been mentioned. One of them was the method by which apples were propelled into the elevator by water pumped along earthenware channels which had pits ('stone-catchers') at intervals to intercept any pieces of stone or metal washed off in the process. A further advantage was that, whereas good apples float, rotten ones do not, so that these too were trapped. Another improvement was a machine, based on that used to slice sugar-beet for slicing apples prior to processing. (At first the 'pomace', the residue of the apple, had been simply buried on the site, which spoiled the ground for building. Later it was used to fuel the large boiler that provided steam for the equalising of temperature and for cleansing and sterilising casks and vats; or else it was carted out, at some expense, into the country and dumped under the hedge of some benevolent farmer, to be spread over the land when it eventually decayed.) Next a German dryer was introduced. Dried pomace could be profitably sold to manufacturers of cattle cake.[1] (Its use for the production of pectin was to come in later.)

The special characteristic of Champagne*** or Sparkling Cider made by the process that Percy learned on his visit to Champagne in 1894 was, that its manufacture carried on when that of wine normally ended. After undergoing the first fermentation and filtration, about the end of February, the different varieties of cider made from selected fruit had to be suitably blended, by expert connoisseurs, so that each should contain the desired balance of sugar, alcohol, tannin, acidity, etc., elements that vary greatly in apples from year to year. Specially selected yeast and sugar were added, to ensure a suitable second fermentation in the bottle. Some yeasts are capable of converting certain sugars—sucrose, glucose, fructose—to ethyl alcohol and also of producing carbon dioxide gas. As fermentation proceeds, the natural sweetness of the liquor diminishes in proportion to the alcoholic strength and, in theory, the liquor eventually reaches a state of absolute alcoholic dryness. Not only do yeast strains have an effect on the flavour of cider, but careful selection of yeast may be used to produce an especially high alcoholic level, or a particular aroma, or a more rapid fermentation. But this proved effective only if the juice was sterilised, just before yeasting, with sulphur dioxide ('sulphiting') to kill the majority of the natural 'wild' yeasts in it, and a sulphur-dioxide-tolerant yeast then added.

The next consideration was effervescence. This depended on the amount of carbonic acid gas which the cider already contained and the further amount it was likely to develop, which in turn depended on the amount of natural sugar present. Too much gas would shatter the bottles: too little would result in corks that refused to pop and liquor that refused to sparkle.

Bottling took place in March–May. The cider was rapidly drawn off into bottles, which were immediately corked and lowered in baskets through holes to the cool cellars. (Speed was essential for the liquor could change drastically otherwise in a single day). It now underwent its second fermentation, designed to produce in every bottle a pressure of about 70 lb to an inch. Stacked horizontally to form immense walls reinforced by wooden laths, the bottles underwent the pressure of fermentation for at least a year. During this time the carbonic acid and the liquid contents became intimately incorporated, so that when the bottles were opened at a low temperature the effervescence was nearly all retained.

The sediment resulting from fermentation was removed by a rather expensive process known as 'disgorging'. The bottles were laid on racks ('pupitres'), sloping cork downwards, and given a quarter turn by hand daily until all the sediment had settled in a layer on the cork. They were then inserted into a freezing tank of brine two inches deep so that the contents of the neck of the bottle were frozen solid and the sediment was imprisoned between the plug of ice and the cork. Finally the bottles were set upright again, the cork was drawn, and the plug of ice shot out carrying the sediment with it. They were then topped up with the small quantity of purified cider required, recorked, foiled, dressed and labelled.

A particularly strong variety, known as'Cider de Luxe', made of special apples and, if necessary, fortified with sugar before fermentation, had been marketed by Bulmers since 1906, from 1916 as 'Pomagne', in bottles decked out like those of champagne wine. Every bottle was matured for years. In due course the advertisements claimed that it was 'acknowledged by cider connoisseurs to be the world's best cider'.

Up to 1895 Bulmers sold cider and perry only in bottles. Then sale in casks began, and rapidly became the mainstay of the business. This 'still' or 'draught' cider cost about 15s for a ten gallon cask. Containing about 5% of alcohol, it could be diluted with water, if desired. 'Woodpecker' sparkling cider, fermented once (and after 1919 artificially carbonated), originated in 1896. It was sold in bulk to brewers and others (in 'pipes' of about 110 gallons or hogsheads of about 65) at 1s 3d—1s 9d a gallon, for them to bottle themselves under their own label. Many recipients bottled the cider so badly that Bulmers preferred that their own name should not appear on the label. It was not until 1926 that they began to bottle Woodpecker under their own label for the retail market. 'Bull Brand', a cider naturally fermented with yeast in tanks for second fermentation in a warm room was introduced in 1909 and sold in full-sized bottles, halves or quarters ('splits') at 5s 6d per dozen bottles. It was still obtainable in the 1930s.

How long will cider keep? Lord Scudamore had a repository at his Herefordshire seat in which, according to Worlidge, cider was preserved for many years; but most seventeenth century writers on the subject did not claim so much; Sir Paul Neal, indeed, reckoned that cider would keep for two years if boiled, otherwise for only one. Beale held that Bosbury perry could improve over two or three years. Bolder claims were made at the end of the eighteenth century, when cider began to be bottled. Marshall had heard of a gentleman near Ledbury who had cider in store of every fruitage for 20 years past. Knight (1797) said that in good draught cider a considerable portion of sweetness remained for three or four years, then gradually disappeared. It was best bottled at two years, after which it would keep for 20–30 years if the cork was good. That was the period still reckoned for Herefordshire cider in the mid-nineteenth century. Cooke (1898) thought it *could* keep for 50–100 years, but at 50 he found only three bottles out of twelve to be good: the rest had been ruined by bad corks.

In the Edwardian period Bulmers reckoned that draught cider would keep for 2–3 years in a ten-gallon cask, and proportionally longer in larger ones. As for sparkling cider, it would keep for twice as long as champagne wine in a cellar kept as cool as possible short of freezing, and the small trouble of laying it down would repay the connoisseur. They always kept the old vintages of Foxwhelp in store.

It should be made clear at this point that when the term 'champagne cider' is used in this record, as it must be for historical reasons, it means *cider* made by the same process as the sparkling wine of the Champagne district of France: there is no suggestion that it is other than cider. The term is no longer used. In particular, the term does not indicate any intention to deviate from the permanent injunction granted to the Champagne producers in 1975 which restrains the use of the expression 'Champagne' in connection with cider or perry.

[1] In 1925 Bulmers drew attention to the value of dried apple pomace as feed: lambs fed on it put on flesh remarkably; it kept ewes in good condition in bad weather; for cattle it could be mixed with roots, for store pigs, ground to a fine powder. It cost 70s a ton.

CHAPTER NINE

DEVELOPMENT OF THE BUSINESS: 1895–1919

Let us now resume the story of the firm, which we left at the end of 1894 and of Chapter Three well rooted and ready to grow. By September 1895 enough building sites had been sold off on the Ryelands estate to repay to William Ball the last of the money he had advanced for the purchase of the land, and some were still in hand.

Winter that year came early and with exceptional severity: by November 15 more than half of the water mains in Hereford were frozen, and ice on the Wye eventually reached a thickness of 15 inches. But the works were a hive of industry. 'We are hard at it,' wrote Fred in January, 'bottling cider, which is excellent, very different from last year.' They were expecting a shipload at Gloucester of 24,000 dozen new bottles. In November 1896 Fred was partially relieved of the work he hated by the appointment of a commercial traveller, who worked for half the year for commission and travel-expenses. Mr Edwards was just the sort of man they were looking for, entirely self-made, one of the nine children of a Shropshire gardener, 'a jolly, genial, human fellow'. He was an immediate success, especially at agricultural shows. His reputation for wit and for extracting orders was such that people would gather round his stall to watch. To someone who heckled, 'You don't expect me to believe that sort of thing, do you? I am not a fool,' he replied promptly, 'Sir, you surprise me.' At the Royal Agricultural Show at Manchester in 1897 he and Fred took orders worth over £1,000 in the four days, a considerable achievement at that time. Two additional agents, Mr Cope and Mr Gilbert, were appointed in 1901.

Sales of cider naturally depended on the vagaries of the English weather. Take the year 1898. On 3 June Fred wrote to Wedd: 'This is the bloodiest weather for summer I have ever known, and it simply plays the devil with trade. The statistics show that in the Midlands we had only 27 hours of sunshine last month, so no wonder our sales for the month have fallen by 25%.' But in mid-October there was a heat-wave, and sales soared; there was not enough skilled labour to cope; 37 women were handling bottles;

two new coopers had been engaged; a lot of ready-made new casks had been bought; nearly £300 a day was being taken instead of the normal £60. Next April the firm was doing better than it had ever done before. In June 1900 there was a heat-wave and the British public was 'simply raving for cider'; orders were coming in at the rate of £400-500 a day; there would have been no coping but for an extra 'typewriter' (i.e. typist). But a fortnight later we hear: 'The weather continues cold and stormy, and it is simply fatal to business.' A month later the heat has been terrific, and they may be sold out by the end of September. It seems that in selling cider, as in politics, 'a week is a long time'.

The vagaries of the English weather affected another vital factor, the supply of apples. The year 1898 was a bad one owing to drought: Fred had to cycle 500 miles in seven days, and even so he could not get enough apples at any price. Next April he wrote: 'If we could get a cheap year of fruit, we should be comparatively opulent. So far there is every indication of a very big crop, as the blossom is plentiful and the weather has been moist, which is very good for it; but the crop can never be considered safe till the end of June. We have had so many lean years that it ought to be our turn soon; and a good year would be worth £2,000 to us.' His hopes were fulfilled (but not before his bicycle had finally died on him): that October apples were plentiful and cheap. 'The farmers come in droves, and sit humbly in our outer office, for our convenience.' (He had no great tenderness for the farmers: in a bad year, he alleged, some were capable of repudiating any contract that was not in writing.) Even so, it was now pouring with rain (which came through the office roof, under repair, on to them), so that the abundant apples could not yet be picked.

The traditional cider-orchard was geared to producing farmhouse cider as a by-product to the pasture of sheep and cattle beneath the trees. The decline of individual stocks was slow enough to be unapparent, while any new planting or grafting would involve some years of unproductivity. In 1893 Bulmers were to the fore in insisting that, in return for higher prices, farmers should specialise in and segregate certain varieties of cider-apple, as Knight had recommended long ago. If all sorts were harvested together, the earlier ones soon decayed and infected the rest. Windfalls should not be included with consignments; nor should 'pot' fruit.[1] Meanwhile improvements in scientific analysis were making it daily more apparent that certain varieties of cider apple were more desirable for blending than others. There was a great deal of education and indoctrination to be done. Fred Bulmer proposed that the County Council should appoint a committee to interview growers at fruit shows and collate their experience. It should then issue a hand-book, to be paid for out of the rates, specifying which early, medium and late varieties respectively were desired. It should also contain a list of soundly established salesmen in each of the larger towns. The land in question, 30,000 acres of Herefordshire, could be made to yield an increased profit of £2-3 an acre, enough to pay the rates of the whole county. A private 'black list' was also compiled, of farmers from whom it was undesirable to buy.

Bulmers regularly put advertisements in the local paper such as 'Wanted: apples, all round' and selected fruits'. Bags sent to nearest stations. Foxwhelp wanted at once. Early pears wanted at once.' (Autumn 1899.) They bought between 2,000 and 3,000 tons of fruit in 1899. But it was becoming apparent that, as the business grew, there would sometimes not be enough fruit to meet demand, and that the quality of desired varieties would not always be adequate. So in November 1898 they bought, for £1,500, 'The Whettons', a farm at Broxwood, 15 miles N.W. of Hereford, with 68 acres of land to plant experimental orchards of their own. On the 11th Percy and Fred went there with an agreement for the tenant, one Lloyd, to sign. They were confronted with the sort of situation to which they were sensitive and vulnerable. Lloyd had been brooding since their previous visit. He had been there for 45 years, and the idea of leaving was hell for him. It took them and his wife an hour to persuade him to sign. Three weeks later they had to go again, as he was refusing to leave. This was doubly awkward, as by now there were 1,000 apple trees on the way which would die if not planted at once. Finally, five days later, Fred wrote to Sophie: 'I have just returned from the farm. I went to see the tenant and his wife. They are old, and poor, and pitiful, and their son, a great strong man of 35, has injured his spine from carrying a sack of barley, and will have to sit by the fire for the rest of his life. So I could not find it in my heart to turn them out, as they had no other farm to go to; so I just took two fields for the trees we have ready, and told them they could stay on till a year next February, which will leave them plenty of time.' In October 1899 there were 4,000 more trees due to be planted.

In a retrospective article published in 1944 on the cider orchards of Herefordshire in the past 60 years Edward Ball of Bulmers reported on the performance of four out of the eight varieties of Norman cider-apple tree selected by the Woolhope Club's Pomona Committee for introduction into Herefordshire and directly imported for testing in the orchards at 'The Whettons' planted between 1901 and 1907. In an appendix he names 40 varieties of French bittersweets that had been tested there. One very strong-growing prolific bittersweet, excellent for cider-making, proved to have no name. It was called 'Bulmer's Norman'.

The Bulmers were also much interested in the manuring of trees, a subject little understood. Percy told a meeting in 1900 that they planted 'standard' trees in the autumn with 14 lb. of 'shoddy' round each. Three years later he read to another meeting a translation of a French paper on a chemical manure composed of nitrogen, phosphoric acid, potash and lime. With this it was no longer necessary to assume that a tree which had borne a good crop would have to take it easy for a year or two. Bulmers offered the County Council facilities at The Whettons for experimenting in chemical manuring.

Inevitably there were odd setbacks. Harold Baldwin, Fred's schoolfriend, was set up with an assistant, Mumford, at The Whettons, where he superintended the planting of the first 60 acres. But Baldwin suffered from epilepsy. His increasingly frequent fits not only incapacitated him for work, but caused his assistant to become more and more like a body-servant until finally he felt he could not cope. Then the secretary of the firm, one Jackson, was found to have been embezzling. The amount was all recovered save £150, but he had to go, along with others, and could not be given a testimonial, which was distressing for his employers, especially as he had four children. A letter of 7 September 1900 from the firm to Mr Edwards explained that Jackson had misled them. The profit for 1899 had been only £250. Over the past three years Edwards had received about £350 in commission. A falling off in the year of £1,000 in show and trade sales meant that 'the trade' must be abandoned, as a source only of loss. Finally, at the climax of a cider-making boom, one of the big presses broke down. All this in one year, 1900.

We have seen that research both into the botany and the chemistry of cider-making had begun in the 1880s to be put on a more scientific basis. In 1903, largely at the instigation of Radcliffe

Cooke and Neville Grenville from Somerset, but with Bulmer support, the National Fruit and Cider Institute was set up at Long Ashton, near Bristol, with the backing of the Board of Agriculture and of interests in the West. It was built up by B.T.P. Barker, who was Director from 1904 to 1942, and by 1917 had 50 orchards. In 1912 it was taken under the wing of Bristol University.

We have seen also that Percy Bulmer in particular took an interest in scientific experimentation, and we hear of Fred too experimenting in their modest laboratory. In 1893 they were sending apples to their consultant in London, Mr. Parry Laws, for cultivation. In 1898 they obtained a certificate of 'searching chemical analysis' of their cider from Dr. Granville H. Sharpe, late Principal of the Liverpool College of Chemistry. They also employed a French bacteriologist, M. Bayer, who stayed with them at least twice round the turn of the century. In December 1904 they were seeking a man from Cambridge for their laboratory, 'not excluding a non-scientist capable of learning'. This last clause indicates how modest was the scope envisaged. In the event, however, they landed, quite unexpectedly, a very large fish.

Herbert E. Durham, grandson of William Ellis the inaugurator of secondary technical schools, was yet another of Fred's friends from college days at King's ('Durban' to him). After taking his F.R.C.P. at Guy's Hospital he took part in the Liverpool Yellow Fever Expedition to Brazil of 1900, the London Beri-Beri Expedition to Christmas Island in the Indian Ocean in 1901–03 and other expeditions. Returning in 1905 with his health impaired and at a loose end, he was one of Fred's first guests at Adam's Hill; and he readily accepted an invitation to become Director of Research for the firm. He was wisely given his head in the laboratory, with no obligation to confine himself to research directly relevant to cider. Durham took his Sc.D. in 1908, and continued to publish articles on bacteriology and zoology, and also horticulture. His name is perpetuated by the 'Durham Tube' he invented in 1897 for measuring fermentation, a standard item of bacteriological equipment. A keen gardener all his life, he introduced a number of plant varieties into England. It was unfortunate that an idea he had for avoiding garden digging by small dynamite explosions proved less feasible than some of his ideas. His photographic skill earned him the medal of the Royal Photographic Society in 1927; and of two albums of photographs of trees and fruit which he left, one is in the Lindley Library of the Royal Horticultural Society. He was also a talented draughtsman and wood-turner. To the Hereford City Library he presented a fine set of books and slides on apples and pears. He also served for many years on the Board of Management of Hereford General Hospital; and from 1907 he was an active member of the Woolhope Club, its President in 1924.

Bulmers owed a great part of their phenomenal success to Durham's flair and devotion. For instance, at the time when he joined the firm, despite recent advances since Pasteur, fermentation still presented problems. His department solved them in two years. He worked out methods of estimating the amount of tannin and sugar in any juice; and he chose one of the best yeasts to aid fermentation of cider in bottle, cask or vat, so that for the first time its control became possible. Again, when the business was in danger of being ruined by 'cider-sickness', from a form of yeast that causes very rapid fermentation and a most unpleasant flavour, he found an antidote.

Durham was immensely admired by his juniors in the laboratory, who knew him affectionately as 'The Doctor'; but it must be added that, for all his qualities, he was never an easy man. On those old expeditions he had quarrelled with his colleague F.T. Manson, and disagreed so violently with Hamilton Wright, a scientist of Kuala Lumpur, that he came home in a huff. He also felt that he did not receive his due either of credit or profit from 'Derris Powder', an insecticide he had brought back from the Far East. At Bulmers' he had to be kept out of the works as much as possible, since he upset people by his astringent criticisms. When Esmond died he was so upset that a well-qualified and agreeable young man imported from King's College, Cambridge, to take his place had no chance: he had to be sent back, with acute embarrassment, after 24 hours. It was a bitter tragedy for this lover of children and his wife that neither of their own two children survived infancy. When he retired in 1935 he insisted, against her inclinations, on their going to live in Cambridge, and it was not a success. When she died in 1950, five years after him, he was found to have made provision in his will for nearly £9,000 to establish a fund to promote work in the University on the life of man or other animals in health or disease, to be administered by King's College, but with the proviso that no woman should ever benefit from it. (After the passing of the Sex Discrimination Act, King's having also become one of the first Oxbridge colleges to admit women, the proviso was set aside by Order in Council).

With success the firm began to afford new buildings. A new cellar was constructed in 1896 with a building over it. In 1900 they put up an elevated vat house for a high blending vat which was expected to save about 30% of the money spent on wages for cider-making. In the first few years storage had been in 100-gallon casks. Next came the four vats already mentioned. In 1904 came eight holding 10,000 gallons each, followed in due course by a series holding 50,000–60,000 which are still in use. The large volume assured a uniformity of blend not easily attained otherwise. To wander among these round oaken giants is like wandering in a dark Californian red-wood forest. The catalogue for 1906 shows a new pressing house capable of dealing with 100 tons of fruit in 24 hours.

Marketing was, of course, a prime concern of the growing business. In September 1895 Bulmers proposed that the National Association of English Cider Makers should draw up an alphabetical list, to be available to any inquirer, of makers who had undertaken (1) that they would not do anything to promote the sale of American cider in Britain and (2) that they would not add any saccharin to their cider. The dual object was, to encourage English growers of cider apples, and to protect pure cider from adulteration. (The proposal was defeated by the casting vote of Radcliffe Cooke, with the explanation that he thought the matter would be more suitably dealt with by legislation.) Twelve years later Fred had still to report to Lord Carrington, who was receiving a deputation as President of the Board of Trade, that spurious ciders had greatly hindered the sale of the genuine article. In their advertising Bulmers regularly emphasised the purity of their product and also its medicinal properties. Their dry 'Cherry Norman' was especially recommended for sufferers from rheumatism and gout and also from diabetes.

Prestige stockists were mentioned in the firm's brochures, leaflets and price lists[2]—the Euston Hotel, for instance, the Criterion Restaurant, the Zoo, the Royal Aquarium and the establishments of Messrs Spiers and Ponds. Shipping lines were important—the Orient, the Union. Show cards and labels printed with the bottler's name were supplied to any stockist ordering more than 50 gallons, provided the liquor was not retailed at less than a stated price. Bulmers' Cider was 'Highly Recommended by the Old Nobility'! In June 1899 Percy and Edwards entertained a most aristocratic *clientele* at Windsor and sent back a lot of orders, mostly from the peerage. An attempt was made to popularise Cider Dances as the novelty of the Christmas Season of 1901. 'Good champagne is ruinous in price. Bulmer's cider is the solution.' Railway stations and restaurant cars were also important. In 1899 the firm was paying nearly £1,000 a year to the London and North Western, presumably for their patronage.

The railway companies were important in another way. They were by far the chief transporters of both apples and cider. It mattered a great deal what their freight charges were. In January 1895 Fred complained that he had been charged 5d. a gallon for the transport of cider, 'enough to destroy any industry'. He managed to get the Great Western to reduce their charges for transporting it between Hereford and certain named stations, and eventually with its help to persuade other railway companies to do the same. After two years his efforts, according to Radcliffe Cooke, had been largely successful. But ten years later, when the charge was 3d. a gallon, we find Cooke leading a deputation of cider-makers to the Board of Trade to seek its help in getting the railways to charge less for the transport of cider apples: they wanted them to be classed with potatoes, not with dessert fruit. The railways, however, would agree only to extending the number of stations to which there were concessionary rates. It was a great step forward for Bulmers when, in 1912, the Great Western decided to extend a private siding into their works.

In the *Journal of Horticulture* for 5 June 1913 an article on cider-making at Bulmers appeared. By then they had two acres of cellaring below ground, and buildings to a much larger extent above. They were the only firm in the world engaged in production of cider on a large scale by the champagne process. Of their vats ranging from 10,000 to 50,000 gallons in capacity, nine were of the latter size. Their total vat capacity was 1,000,000 gallons. Between 1895 and 1919 sales rose steadily from 8,715 to nearly 80,000 gallons and profits from £1,516 to over £9,000.

The steady progress revealed by these figures is reflected by other evidence. The long series of high awards at important shows culminates, perhaps, in the Grand Diploma of Merit (the highest possible award) at the International Exhibition at Buenos Aires in 1910. Next year the firm received the Royal Warrant as Purveyors of Cider to the new King, George V. Other large firms had meanwhile sprung up elsewhere. Gaymers in Norfolk began in 1891 (largely using the Ribston Pippin, a pot apple), and Whiteways in Devon soon after. Moore began in 1913, becoming the Taunton Cider Company in 1921. Factory production enhanced the reputation of cider by increasing its average quality, uniformity, stability and presentation. But in 1920 farmers still accounted for 76% of the output in the U.K., and the rise of quality cider must be seen against a background of the steady decline in total consumption of cider in the U.K. from an estimated (though perhaps exaggerated) 55 1/2 million gallons in 1890 to 21 million in 1920.

In August 1912 a 'Peace Delegation' of four had come over from Düsseldorf. A tea party was given for them, and they were shown over Bulmers' works. Two years later England and Germany were at War. One of the first people to suffer was Sophie Bulmer, as being German by origin. She was obliged to resign from the local Red Cross Committee. The Indian Army Major renting Springfield next door asked Fred to return a small piece of ground he had leased to him as 'he did not want it trampled on by Germans'. A family of Belgian refugees came and lived for nine months at Adam's Hill. Wounded soldiers were entertained there and at Longmeadow. Percy and Fred meanwhile became enthusiastic special recruiting officers.[3] Out of 46 eligible male employees at the works 45 volunteered for service in due course (the remaining one, medically low grade, was exempted when conscription came in). Geoffrey Bulmer joined the King's Shropshire Light Infantry, Howard the Cambridgeshires. Yet somehow the business managed to carry on unabated. Cider was considered to be good for the health and morale of the nation. When the Royal Household at Buckingham Palace abjured alcohol for the duration, an exception was made of cider and perry. There were some harmless economies; thus to save labour the decoration of bottles was discontinued for the duration. But plans for building offices opposite St. Ethelbert's in Ryelands Street were allowed to go ahead, and these were completed in 1915. The front office originally had a high counter surmounted by a grill. Here Percy and Fred took turns, having cycled down before breakfast, at opening the mail. Their shared office was a room with dark oak panelling, later the Board Room. In a small adjacent room sat Reginald Phillips, the Secretary. Here there was a grill at which the employees appeared once a week, shepherded by 'Father' Pearson, to receive their wages in a cup, which they returned after counting them. Nearly every Saturday Fred drove in his three-wheeler Morgan 'runabout' car over bumpy lanes to The Whettons to discuss management of the farm with their bailiff, Mr Baker.

The figures indicate that, even taking some monetary inflation into account, business held up remarkably well during the war, with 1917 as an extraordinary peak year. There was the usual compensatory boost from the fact that foreign wines were not imported in wartime; and some returning soldiers had acquired a taste for cider in Normandy. The supply of beer was also somewhat restricted, whereas at first cider was left alone. There were, of course, special difficulties. Sugar and fuel became expensive. Apples were scarce because farmers could not afford to have them picked, at least not for wages they were prepared to pay. They feared, with reason, that if they offered higher wages to seasonal workers, their regular workers would be unsettled. In 1916 it was uncertain whether the firm would be able to raise 1,000 tons of apples; but they were. In December 1915 Fred had written to the *Hereford Times* deploring the state of agriculture in Britain and advocating the exemption of registered farm labourers from military service. But wages were too low to attract anyone, and now he was advocating the employment of German prisoners on the land. In 1916 the U-boats were sinking shipping at a rate which would eventually reduce Britain to starvation. At the end of it Lloyd George took over, just in time, and both these measures were adopted. Fred Bulmer was put on a seven-man County Agricultural Committee. He was the first in the county to advocate that women should be employed on the land, supplied, as at his works, with suitable clothing and stout clogs. (To the objection, 'You can't teach us farmers anything' he replied, 'That remark is applicable in more than one way.')

A tax on cider and perry was introduced—4d a gallon on sales— as a war-time measure.[4] The most this raised was in the excellent crop-year 1917, £144,000. 'Money seems plentiful, ' wrote Fred; 'I suppose it will be, so long as the Government keeps the printing presses going, but it doesn't go far, at least in cider. We have had to put our prices up shamefully; but it only makes them order more than ever.' 'If it were not for the Excess Profits Tax, which consumes 85% of them, we should make our fortunes.'

In May 1918 the Food Production Department proposed to put

up a big plant at Hereford for concentrating the juice of cider apples. Fred anticipated that, unless there was a large crop of apples
(which from the scarcity of blossom seemed an impossibility), no
cider-making would be permitted anywhere, even on the farms; but
the plant did not materialise. The War Office Medical Department
also took over part of the works for producing serums, etc., for the
whole Army, under the supervision of Durham. But in the event
some cider was made.[5]

The end of the War in November brought immense relief, of
course, to Fred, but no euphoria. His father and Geoffrey had died
recently, and now Percy was dying. The Russian Revolution and
the breakdown of law and order and of health in Central Europe
were profoundly disturbing. He hated the cries for vengeance,
resented the exclusion of the Asquithian Liberals from the peace-
making process, and deplored the vindictiveness, as he saw it, of
the Peace of Versailles. More than most he realised, like Keynes,
that it was a Pyrrhic victory. But his hope was, that the national
spirit which had brought the country through the war might save
it from the perils of returning peace.

[1] Dessert or cooking fruit, 'culls'.
[2] A copy of one of these was sent to the firm by Mr R.A. Butler in 1934.
He found it in a copy of the *Strand Magazine* for 1899.
[3] At a meeting of the South Herefordshire Joint War Arms Committee on
1 December 1918 Fred was praised by the Chairman for securing co-operation
between the political parties. He made a speech on reasons for carrying on
despite war-weariness. He and Wedd were estranged temporarily from Lowes
Dickinson and permanently from Bertrand Russell by their whole-hearted support of the War. But he was acutely conscious of the sufferings of the troops,
especially through letters he received from a Private Cummings, to whom he
sent regular weekly parcels till Cummings was killed in action in 1917.
[4] It was abolished in 1923, but reintroduced in the 1976 Budget at 22p. a
gallon, estimated to bring in £10,000,000 of revenue.
[5] In 1918 the cider apple crop was disastrous. The Government fixed the
price at £20 a ton.

CHAPTER TEN

EMPLOYEES: (to 1939)

A letter dated 24 October 1899 from Fred to his fiancée was written while he was engaged in supervising the first nightshift of the casual workers engaged for the cider-making season, always the worst night, since they had to be taught or reminded how to do the job and they got very tired. Some had come drunk and were only just drying out. They were always liable to be clumsy and accident-prone. How much easier it would be if cider-making went on all the year round! People would get used to the work, and the bad workers would get weeded out.

The permanent workforce was a different matter. An efficient and loyal staff was gradually built up. It is clear that Fred, like his brother, got on exceptionally well with their employees. Indeed within living memory one had only to go round the works with him in the 1930s to see that, or while out on a walk with him to be asked to wait outside some terrace house while he looked in to talk to some workman or his wife who was ill. It was said that once, when the mates of a man who was suffering from syphilis were worried because he was unwilling to be seen going to the V.D. clinic, Fred had a talk with him and came up with an idea: 'I know: we'll go together. Then people won't know which of us it is!' He also allowed for eccentricity. 'Old Shin' the cooper was a splendid craftsman but prone to bouts of violence, when he would hurl tools at some apprentice or fellow-worker who happened to be near. Fred provided him with a little shed in the yard where he could work alone. He himself, indeed, could be arbitrary on occasion. There is a story that once on his rounds he came upon a boy assistant in the crate factory who was resting after a stint of shovelling sawdust and, assuming that he was just idling, told him to collect his cards and go. Thomas Barnes, the Works Manager, told the boy to lie low in the cellars for a few days. A week later Fred found him shovelling. 'Glad to see you working, ' he said; 'I dismissed a lad last week for not working.' The employee so providentially reprieved was Arthur Evans, who drove the firm's first lorry, a one-ton Morris, and eventually became the foreman of the cider mills, 'King Arthur'.[1]

Fred learned from experience. For instance, being worried about the monotony of much of the work, he mooted a scheme for moving the workers round, hoping that they would find interest in the variety and in getting a conspectus of the processes of manufacture to which they contributed; but in the event he found that most of them, especially the women, preferred to do something they had learned to do automatically, without having to think and perhaps with the chance of incidental chat.

In another letter to his fiancée, dated 23 November 1898, Fred wrote: 'I very nearly boiled over when your father said it was the duty of the Guardians of the Poor to pay their officials as little as they could get them for. No person or corporation could owe such a duty as that except to the Devil himself. We are going to start a superannuation fund for our workpeople, as we shall feel it less if it is started now rather than later on, when the men begin to get old. It will, I expect, cost nearly £100 a year, and we shall invest it in trustees, so that even if the business did go wrong, or we died and sharks bought it, there would be some provision for the oldest of the men. Do not mention this to your father: he would think it unbusinesslike; and moreover we don't like that sort of thing talked about, or it is apt to become advertisement, which is disgusting.' Such provision was far from normal at that time.

On 2 February 1918, in one of the darkest times of the war, Fred gave an address to the Hereford Trades Council in the context of the Whitley Report, which was designed to secure a permanent improvement in relations between employers and employed and to arrange for systematic reviews. Before the war, he said, powers of leadership had been diverted from constructive work to unprofitable strife. During it there had been much more co-operation. National Joint Standing Industrial Councils with representation of both sides should be set up. Trade unions rules suspended during the war should be revived. There should be District Councils for close co-operation, and Works Committees in particular works. The practical knowledge acquired by workpeople should be put to better use, and there should be better means of learning about conditions of work. The scheme should be carried out forthwith, before the onset of the vast amount of other post-war work that could be foreseen.

In 1920 a life insurance and pension scheme was instituted by Bulmers, an advance on what had been done in 1898 but modest, of course, in comparison with what has been done since. A sum of not less than £1,000 was set aside out of profits to provide for pensions or gratuities to men over 50 who had served the company well, to be invested in trustees. The policy of providing housing for workers was also continued: a site for 16–20 houses was acquired quite near the works, on the Broomy Hill Academy site and adjacent land, between Breinton Road and Tower Road. It was conveyed by the company to 'Hereford St Nicholas Co-operative Housing Ltd'.

There were, of course, bounties of various kinds for employees. One learns, for instance, from an entry in the Wages Book, that all clerks got a week's extra wages in honour of the coronation of King George V in 1911. Annual works outings took place. From 1927 Blackpool was the favoured destination. A special train left Hereford at 5.20 a.m., and returned next day at 4.30 a.m., the firm providing free tickets and light refreshments at Crewe. In 1935 there were 435 excursionists. A Sports Club was started, which eventually was to include cricket, football, hockey, netball, bowls, skittles, rifle-shooting, golf and fishing. In 1935 an excellent sports ground of nearly 21 acres was established off the Brecon Road on the outskirts of the city, with a pavilion said by the *Hereford Times* to be 'undoubtedly the best in the Herefordshire League'. Courts were made there for the Tennis Club, which already existed. A Sports Club Social was held every March. From 1928 the clerical staff had an annual Social Evening: in 1932 we hear that all the Bulmers had been able to be present except two. At a Works Social on 15 March 1939 about 350 people were present. It provided an opportunity for tasting the firm's new non-alcoholic apple drink, Cidona, due to go on the market that summer.

When he became Mayor again in 1925, one of the pieces of advice Fred Bulmer gave in a speech to the Council was: 'Mitigate class distinctions, which are at the root of our troubles. In America the social gulf between employers and employed is much less than in this country, which enables them to get in touch with each other more easily.' Five years later he told the Council: 'I look forward to the day when there is only one class in the land, and when any man can marry any other man's daughter.' But one of the difficulties was sheer numbers. In his own business these had risen now, as a result of success, to some 300. In the previous October he had written to Wedd: 'I am more than ever convinced that it is the size of businesses that is the root of the trouble, but how this can be got over I don't see. Certainly mass-production

1 The Revd C. Henry Bulmer 1883–1918, Rector of Credenhill, who grew apples and pears for cider and perry on his glebe.

2 H. Percival Bulmer 1867–1919, first Chairman.

3 E. Frederick Bulmer 1865–1941, second Chairman.

4 Credenhill Rectory, where the enterprise started, as built for the Revd
C. H. Bulmer in 1882.

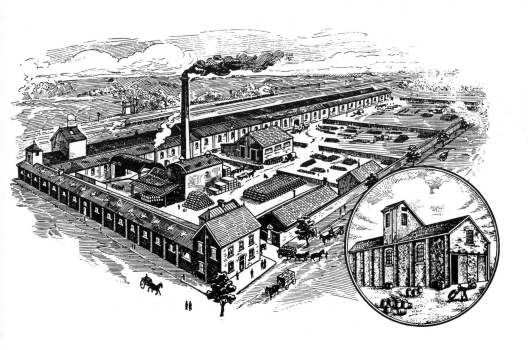

5 *Above*, the first building, Ryelands Street, 1891; below, general view of the works as seen with the eye of faith in publicity material of 1907 (and still used on the No. 7 label) and inset the reality.

6 Cider apple picking at the turn of the century, by courtesy of the Herefordshire County Record Office, Bustin Collection.

7 *Above left*, H. Howard Bulmer 1897–1985, third Chairman; *above right*, G. H. Bertram Bulmer 1902–   , fourth Chairman; *below left*, Peter J. Prior 1919–   , fifth Chairman; *below right*, J. Esmond Bulmer 1935–   , sixth Chairman.

8 The famous locomotive King George V lent to Bulmers by the National Railway Collection which hauled the Pullman coaches used for entertaining visitors.

9 Visit of H.R.H. The Duke of Edinburgh 12 November 1958.

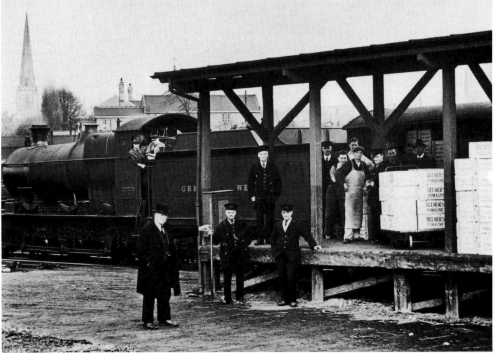

10 *Above*, packing Pomagne for export to the United States in 1934 on the repeal of prohibition; *below*, dispatch at the Barton sidings adjoining the works for shipment.

11 *Above*, unloading of apples on the ground at the Ryelands Street site in the early days; *below*, a standard cider apple orchard.

12 Two oak vats in the Ryelands Street Vat House (one with Fred
Bulmer's initials), each capable of holding 60,000 gallons.

13 Strongbow steel vat at the Moorfields mills, the largest container of alcoholic liquor in the world, with a capacity of 1,630,000 gallons.

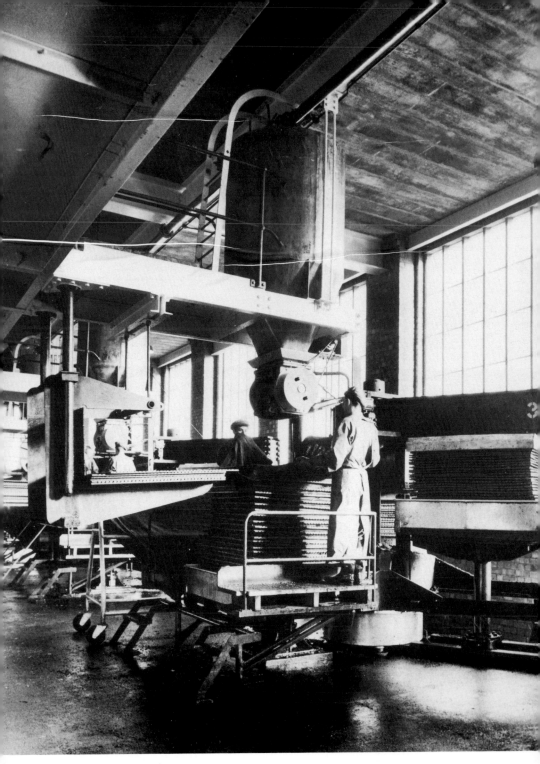

14 The Press house on the Moorfields site.

TRADE · MARK

15 *Above left*, first trade mark based on an Elizabethan engraving with the motto *A stirpe ad vinum; above right*, label for King's Acre cider, *below left*, label for Woodpecker cider; *below right*, wartime advertising (1942), when stoppers could not be obtained.

16 *Above left*, Dr Herbert Durham 1866–1945, First Scientist; *above right,* Edward Ball 1901–   , Chief Scientist, among seedling apple trees at Bulmers' King's Acre Nurseries; *below left*, Brian Nelson 1930–   , Group Managing Director since 1975; *below right*, Patrick Wilkinson 1907–1986, friend of the family and author of this book.

is no remedy. In a big business it is only the system which men feel they are up against, and if they don't like it, it does not seem unreasonable to change it. In a business like ours that would mean getting rid of us all, which I don't think they want.'

His defensive speech of 22 October 1931, already noted, was made to a workforce which now totalled 431. Stung by being referred to in public as a 'bloody capitalist', he said:

'It is a great benefit to workpeople to be associated with a well-conducted and prosperous business, because such a business has reserves of cash. But, you will say, what good have these done us? Well, a few years ago, owing to the hardness of the times, people could not afford to buy our sparkling ciders: they cost too much. It was necessary to change over to the cheaper and more popular flagons. We had to find £15,000 for bottles, cases, machinery and such like for the turnover, and the result has been a great increase in the number of people employed. But failing these reserves, numbers of you would have been in the street. Also, owing to the decrease in the number of apples grown in England and the increased demand for them owing to the growth in the cider trade, it has become necessary to buy more and more apples from France. But these apples will not keep: they have to be used in a very short time. This also require the expenditure of further reserves on the new Press House, amounting to another £15,000. In addition we have had to face savage competition from large competitors in other parts of England, who have been paying their workpeople an agricultural wage of 31s a week. How has it been done? It has been done by thought, by organisation, and has necessitated getting rid of incompetent workpeople, which has been for the benefit of those who were left.'

After his appeal to his audience to vote for the National Government he continued: 'There are a few more things I want to say. Since the war I have received numerous offers to buy this business at very big prices. These offers have no attractions for me. I have lived among you, and hope to die among you; and I am confident that I tell you the truth when I say that my nephews and son take the same view of the matter. You may rely upon it that as long as the workpeople will stand by the Bulmers, the Bulmers will stand by them.

'To those who have recently been unemployed, and may unfortunately again be unemployed before long, I would say: keep up your courage in better times to come, believing that it is better to receive a slightly reduced unemployment pay which will bring you a reasonable quantity of food than a larger pay which will buy you little or nothing.

'That is all, except this: you are entitled to ask yourselves whether you can trust me and whether I am disinterested. A man's motives are between him and his Maker. I cannot prove to you that I am disinterested. I can only appeal to my record, which has been known to some of you for nearly 45 years. Those who have not been here long, I would ask to do me the justice of taking my record from the people who have worked here for years with me, and not from the prophets of the street corners.'

In these days, when 'paternalistic' has quite widely become a term of abuse as applied to industrial concerns, such a speech would hardly be thinkable. It was, however, not only delivered but circulated in print, and if there was any resentment among the audience, it does not seem to have been apparent. On 2 September 1933 a dinner was given to celebrate the marriages in that year of Bertram and Edward Bulmer at which 400 employees were entertained. In his speech of welcome Fred recalled that for Percy's wedding in 1894 two horses had sufficed to draw the whole works staff to Credenhill (four survivors were among those he was addressing). For his own in 1899 the numbers had risen to 30, of whom seven were in his audience that evening. The secretary of the company, Reginald Phillips, spoke of the happy relations that existed between Bulmers and their employees. It is easy to say, 'Well, he would, wouldn't he?'. But the fact remains that there never was—never has been—serious unrest in the works; indeed, there has been a prevailing spirit of good will.

This was remarked on by Charles Pickard, who had entered the firm as a boy in 1900 (at a time when there were only 10 clerks, half of them girls come straight from school) in a speech he made at its Golden Jubilee celebrations on 18 December 1937. He attributed it to the accessibility of the principals. It was remarked on again by Arthur Evans, looking back in 1969 on his retirement after 48 years with the firm. He recalled Howard and Esmond the elder shovelling a record of 125 tons of apples into the canals at one shift. 'This was—and still is—the great thing about the family: they were always ready to get stuck into a job and to help out on the shop floor when necessary'. Besides such involvement, sick employees were always helped, and often sent to convalescent homes. During the war steps were taken to ensure that serving employees did not lose their homes. Many retired ones were enjoying pensions to which they had not contributed, widows also in some cases. Some very old pensioners were present on that day – Robert Bethell, Thomas Eversham, Tom Jones, Thomas Page; and Charlie ('Father') Pearson, aged 83, who had joined three years after the business began, the same man in whose house Fred had lodged when he moved out of St Ethelbert's after his brother's marriage.[2] A silver fruit bowl was presented by the employees to Mildred and a silver rose bowl to Fred, along with autograph books signed by employees all over the country, whose numbers had by then risen to more than 800. Pickard singled out three things as Fred's greatest contributions—the Garden City, the Sports Ground and the Pension Scheme; and Fred in reply attributed the success of the firm to Percy, Durham and the workforce.

Although it remained very much a family firm, it was possible for employees to gain promotion by merit. Thus Reginald Phillips, who started as an office boy at the age of 12 in 1893, became the company's first Secretary (he died a month after war broke out in 1939); and Thomas Barnes, who entered in 1894, rose from the bottom to be Works Manager. Recruitment from outside to higher posts continued to be by personal knowledge rather than advertisement. It cannot be said what effects casting the net wider would have had; but neither can it be denied that the business prospered. Of important figures from between the wars whom we shall meet again, Vernon Beach Thomas was son of Sir William, a school-friend of Fred's, well known as a writer on nature; Harold Robinson had been in the Army with Howard in the Middle East; Stanley Lewis was another old army friend of Howard's, and Adam Cochrane was a second cousin of Howard's. Alan Hudson-Davies came from the old stable, King's College at Cambridge, and he introduced Richard McBride. In this friendly atmosphere decisions could be taken without time-wasting discussions and formalities. One who eventually became Works Manager, Richard Ankerson, was originally recruited in the following way. Bertram asked him to come for interview to Platform 1 at Paddington Station, but was delayed so that as he arrived his train was already moving. He jumped in, and Ankerson ran along the platform answering questions. As the train drew away Bertram shouted: 'You'll do: start on Monday at 50s a week.'

An adjunct to the workforce still consisted, inevitably, of seasonal casual labourers. Thus in October more than 100 aged

21–45 were needed for 6–10 weeks. For a 48-hour week the pay was 1s 1¹/2 an hour for day work, 1s 2d for night work, during which a full meal was available for 3d. There were also possible bonuses. Some of the labourers came from South Wales, but some came from Ireland. These had to be carefully pre-selected, as it cost quite a lot to transport them.

At the beginning of 1938 Fred retired from active participation in the business, though he remained Chairman of the company until March 1941, five months before his death. He marked the occasion by establishing a Welfare Trust consisting of 10,000 old £1 shares in Bulmers. It was to provide, in the first place, family allowances for every permanent employee of the firm who had more than two children and was in need of help. Until further notice the grant was to be 5s a week for every child in excess of one who was under 16, still at school, and not in an earning capacity. This was well in advance of the Welfare State: indeed at that time probably not more than a dozen firms in the country provided such allowances. Provision was also made for non-contributory sickness benefit and for holidays with pay.

[1] He was noted for his malapropisms, such as 'intimate' for 'interim'. These were so often bandied about the works that some newcomers imagined they were correct technical terms.

[2] One of the big vats was named 'Pearson'. On his death a few weeks after the Jubilee Fred told the *Hereford Times*, 'My brother and I always regarded him as a friend rather than a workman. We never had a misword.'

CHAPTER ELEVEN

BETWEEN THE WARS

In talking of employees we have, for convenience, trespassed on our next period, 1919–1939.

The articles of association of the private company of H.P. Bulmer & Co., signed on 27 June 1918, had as subscribers Percival, Frederick, Mildred and Sophie Bulmer, H.E. Durham, J.J. Withers the London solicitor, and J.H. Todd of Findlater, Mackie, Todd, from 1912 the firm's London agent and sole export agent. Reginald Phillips was appointed company Secretary. The initial capital was £70,000 in £1 shares. The first directors (who were also Governing Directors) were Percy and Fred. Their remuneration was to be £1,000 a year, and a further £1,000 in any year in which profits exceeded 8%. Each of them was allotted 27,000 £1 shares in satisfaction of the purchase price. But the whole arrangement was made with Percy's deteriorating health in view, and 18 months later he died.

By then the war had ended, and now in 1920 Fred found himself in sole charge as Chairman and Managing Director, Howard, now a director, being still a beginner, Esmond at King's and Bertram still at school. His style continued to be highly personal: he opened all the firm's mail himself before breakfast, and twice a day went round all the departments. Durham was a great standby, but mainly on the scientific and orcharding sides. If Fred had to go away, Thomas Barnes, the Works Manager, and Reginald Phillips were left in charge. By 1925 Fred was receiving a salary of £3,000.

Meanwhile wartime limitations continued. Emergency taxation – Excess Profits Duty (reduced from 80% to 40% in 1919, but raised again to 60% in 1920) and a new Corporation Tax of 1s in the pound—would have been more easily stomached but for the sight of palpable waste at the new Government factory at Hereford. However, a deputation in April 1923 to Stanley Baldwin, then Chancellor of the Exchequer, led to the abolition of the duty on cider (at the cost to the Excise of £100,000 a year). The full benefit of this was passed on to customers.[1] Dividends on ordinary shares were 10% in 1919, and after sagging were back at that figure in 1923.

In 1920, as we have seen in Chapter Nine, 76%, about 16,000,000 gallons, of all cider made in England was still being produced by farmers; but now the era of cider factories was setting in. The National Association of English Cider Makers formed in 1894 had apparently not lasted long; but a new National Association of Cider Makers, with 46 members and Fred Bulmer as its first Chairman, was founded in 1920 (and still functions). Some of the larger firms have already been mentioned. In addition, Redvers Coates, a Bristol graduate, set up in 1925 at Nailsea, near Long Ashton. Brewers were already handling cider in the 1920s, some establishing factories of their own in the West of England with the intention of binding their tied houses to sell only their cider, thus further squeezing out the farmers, who reacted bitterly. Bulmers made agreements with brewers for the sale of their cider at the latters' public houses. Despite reported increases in the consumption of cider, this was so small compared with that of beer that most brewers were content to make what they could out of it instead of treating it as a potential rival to beer.[2] By 1933 some had drawn up a select list of cider-makers from whom their tied houses were allowed to buy supplies. By 1937 the farmers were making about 6,000,000 gallons, 32% of English cider, the factories, 13,000,000.

The period following the war was one of rapid expansion for Bulmers. At the end of 1919 they had 200 employees. Though after that date unemployment was fast increasing in Herefordshire, in the summer of 1921 none of them had been discharged (the only threat to employment that was feared was shortage of power). During the General Strike of the summer of 1926 all the employees, now numbering 300, continued to work full-time, though if it had gone on for another week short-time working would have had to be introduced for lack of rail transport (road transport was not yet found suitable even for distances no further than Hereford to London).

One symptom of expansion was the increase in the size and number of storage vessels, though small storage vats were still to be needed. In August 1923 Fred was in France with Durham and Esmond to find out about new rectangular ferro-concrete vats lined with glass tiles which were replacing oak casks in the French wine and cider trade. Everywhere they were praised, and Fred wrote, 'It looks to me as if the days of the picturesque oak vats are over.' In 1924 Bulmers acquired two ferro-concrete ones of 40,000 and two of 50,000 gallons; but the standard size proved to be of 100,000 gallons, as compared with 60,000 for the biggest oak ones; and 22 of these were erected between 1929 and 1935.[3] Being glass-lined they were easier to clean than the wooden ones, and they required no maintenance to compare with cooperage;[4] and because of their shape they could be installed in two tiers, which saved space.

Another important innovation in the cider-making was car-bonisation, a process developed in the 19th century by the mineral-water industry. By 1913 Bulmers had been advertising cider suitable for bottlers to carbonate, and after the War they began to carbonate it themselves. The liquor was filtered and sweetened, and compressed carbon dioxide was forced into it during bottling. This enabled it to be sold much more cheaply, and therefore widely, than when it was fermented in bottle. In 1926 Bulmers began to sell Woodpecker cider in quart flagons provided with internal screw stoppers with rubber rings, which were much more convenient than corks or even than metal caps. This again boosted trade.

Though the period between the wars saw a decline in the overall consumption of cider in Britain, this was mainly due to a decline in consumption by agricultural labourers. Fewer men were working on the land, and increasingly mechanised methods made those who did less thirsty. But the rise of the factories led to standardisation and improved quality, and so to the reinstatement of cider, which had been begun by Bulmers' Pomagne Cider, in higher social circles. In the autumn of 1923 the national press carried articles alleging that cider cup was becoming a favourite drink in a number of London clubs and hotels. On 7 June 1924 the *Daily Mirror* asserted: 'Everyone is talking about cider now that the King has introduced cider cup on state occasions' (it had been served at two evening courts and a state ball). The *Evening News* reported that Devon brewers were setting up as cider-makers, and that some Devon public houses were selling ten hogsheads of cider to every gallon of beer.[5]

For the great Wembley Exhibition of 1924 Bulmers decided not to have a stall of their own: it would have cost £2,000–£3,000, and they would have had to give away, not sell, what they exhibited. Instead they made an agreement with Messrs Lyons, for a quarter of that sum, to stock their cider and quote it on all their wine lists. But at the Brewers' Exhibition at Islington in 1929 their stand was one of the most striking, and a great success.

On 6 May 1925 the capital of H.P. Bulmer and Co. was increased to £200,000 by the creation of 100,000 cumulative preference shares of £1 and a further 30,000 ordinary shares.

In June 1921 Esmond had taken his degree at Cambridge and become a director with a fee of £650, working with Durham; and Bertram, having acquired a good deal of experience of the business during his vacations from King's, graduated in Modern Languages in 1925 and also became a director, with a fee of £500, sharing responsibility for the sales side with Howard. Then Edward ('Teddie') Ball, a cousin of Howard and Esmond, who had graduated with First Class Honours in Natural Sciences at Cambridge (Sidney Sussex College) and had taken his Diploma in Horticulture there, after a year's training at East Malling and experience at Long Ashton (with an Assistant Lectureship in Pomology at Bristol University), came in 1927 to join Durham, and became a director in 1933. (His wife was a cousin of Stanley Baldwin.) Edward Bulmer, the youngest of Percy's sons, having graduated in 1929 at King's College, Cambridge, joined the Board next year. Finally, Fred's youngest son, Becket, after graduating also at King's and spending a year at Wye Agricultural College in Kent, joined the firm in 1936 to work on the farm at Broxwood, of which he became manager next year. So it was still very much a family firm. Even Durham did not become a director until his retirement in 1935.

The laboratory which Edward Ball joined in 1927 was very small – just a narrow room at the end of the packing room where the bottles of Pomagne were washed and decorated. Here the yeasts for pitching the casks of draught cider were cultivated, every batch being carefully checked for purity under the microscope. But soon much roomier premises were allotted upstairs, and it became possible to carry out more extensive tests on the fruit and cider; and the first of what were to be many laboratory assistants was engaged.

ORCHARDING

In the years between the wars a major preoccupation of the expanding cider industry was the supply of cider apples. The main drive was for increasing home production by growing its own apples, and by encouraging farmers to grow more and to manage their trees more efficiently.

We have seen that in the early years of the century Bulmers had acquired 'The Whettons', the 68-acre farm at Broxwood, both in order to supply the works and also to enable experimental research to be conducted on the improvement of old varieties of apple and the introduction of new ones. Further acres had been acquired at the neighbouring farms of Sherrington (80), and Croome House (100). With the expansion of the business Broxwood was no longer sufficient for present, let alone future, requirements.

Cider apple orchards in the western counties were in a shocking state. There had been no large-scale planting for more than 75 years, and their produce was less than one-fifth of what it had been 50 years ago. Farmers were finding that it was more profitable to go over to cooking and eating apples ('pot fruit'). It was estimated in 1923 that 10,000 trees would have to be planted in the district every year to make losses good. At the end of 1932 Professor B.T.P. Barker of Long Ashton reckoned that 30,000 more acres of cider apple and perry pear orchards were still needed. In 1936 the acreage of cider apple trees in the western counties was 67,000, as against an estimated 116,000 in 1894. The fall would have been greater but for the existence of tenancy agreements forbidding the grubbing up of trees, the continuance of an appreciable amount of farm manufacture of cider for domestic consumption, and a slight increase after 1935 in general demand for cider and so for cider apples.

In 1932 Bulmers seized a good opportunity for expanding their nurseries. King's Acre (formerly Cranston's) Nurseries, about two miles out of Hereford on the Brecon Road, established in 1785 and patronised by the Woolhope Club, came up for sale. The firm bought nearly 120 acres. They also bought the entire stock of cider apple trees, some 10,000, in order to keep it in the county. Their object was twofold: to establish a grass cider orchard for their own experimental purposes, and to assist the campaign for giving farmers of mixed farms an incentive to revivify their cider orchards.

Leslie Evans, son of a Herefordshire farmer, recently returned from South America, was put in charge.

First as to experiment. Cider-makers needed early apples, so as to extend the grinding season as far back as possible. But farmers were reluctant to cultivate these, partly because picking them disrupted the busy harvest season, and partly because early blossoming trees risked damage by spring frosts. Bulmers in 1928 introduced six more French varieties of early croppers, and an eight-acre orchard of these was planted in 1931. About the same time a further 18 varieties of later maturing bittersweets highly recommended by various French authorities were imported for trial. To rescue local varieties, growers were invited to send every autumn to a horticultural show held in the Shire Hall at Hereford a basket containing specimens of all the varieties they grew, with the name attached (though different names were often attached to the same variety). A collection was also made of promising Devon, Somerset and other varieties. The criteria for short-listing were: intrinsic quality; resistance to pests and diseases; capacity for interpollination; the needs of various types of soil; provision without excess for coverage of a full grinding season; and a desirable proportion between bittersweets, sweets and bittersharps. Some 30–50 varieties were estimated to be sufficient to allow for all these needs to be covered. Edward Ball, who took over from Durham in 1935, sought to combine the merits of the Foxwhelp, superb in quality but low in cropping capacity, with the resistance to disease and the blossoming habit of the imported Médaille d'Or. The former was available in an orchard at Lower Breinton, the latter at The Whettons. From hundreds of seedlings one was selected, now known as Ball's Bittersweet.

It was reported in 1933 that, of a sample of 728 trees planted, all but 11 were doing well. Another report, of 1938, gave the average yield at Broxwood in the past six years, when spraying had been carried out, as 3.2 tons an acre. (It would have been more if allowance had been made for foreign varieties tested and found wanting.) According to the Ministry of Agriculture crops averaged two tons an acre in a good, one in an ordinary one; but it was hoped that this performance could be doubled. The useful life of a cider-apple tree seemed, from collation of authorities, to be 70–80 years.

The trees favoured by Bulmers were 'standards', partly brought from Broxwood, their stems 7 1/2 feet high, so that the leaves and fruit would be out of reach of farm animals (for often the orchards would be used for grazing). The tree was 'stopped' in the nursery at 7 feet, and ready for planting at the end of the following year, by which time it would have three good branches (six if it were retained for a further year). It was recommended that these trees should be planted at each apex of a 35 foot equilateral triangle: in the pattern thus produced no one tree would touch another.

Pioneering experimentation was also done with 'bush' trees, whose stem was less than 2 1/2 feet (first tried at Adam's Hill). Of these trees 130–200 could be planted to the acre (compared with 40 of standards, the ground between being cultivated). Bulmers planted 90 acres of these in 1932–1933 at King's Acre and elsewhere, transplanting the standard trees to various orchards in the county. Some varieties achieved a crop of as much as 10 tons an acre—'Chisel Jersey' in 1939. But for general adoption standards were still at this time more recommended. The orchards were sprayed throughout in January and February with chemicals to counteract scab, at pressure sufficient to penetrate right into the trees.

The Herefordshire County Council owned about 12,000 acres of farm-land, let out in 300 small-holdings. Bulmers, at the beginning of 1934, presented its Agricultural Education Committee with a large power spraying outfit, to be lent out to farmers for winter spraying at a charge designed to cover only the bare cost of wash, labour and fuel. (In 1939 they contributed £200 towards a new one to replace it.) The expenses of a farmer's using it worked out at no more than 24s an acre or 6d a tree.

Bulmers raised their own apple trees from pips supplied from the works. The seedling trees were later budded with varieties of cider apple which met the required criteria. Young trees were supplied to farmers at low cost, along with materials for their protection from farm animals and vermin. And initially—most important – an advisory staff was established whose services could be hired on contract for guidance in planting, pruning, suckering and spraying. The staff could also help to renovate old orchards by grafting unprofitable varieties of tree with ones of good quality which were also good croppers.

Considerable propaganda was needed to persuade farmers to sink capital in a venture which could not, in the nature of things, produce any return for several years. No one would plant the famous Foxwhelp, which was not a heavy cropper. The National

Association of Cider Makers (of which Fred Bulmer was Chairman in 1930) began to offer prizes for the best new cider orchards, and for the best tendance of established cider orchards, in Herefordshire. The attraction was that for the foreseeable future demand would exceed supply, and in 'hit' years the excess would not be wasted, since big firms like Bulmers now had the storage capacity to cope with the extra cider. Bounties were also offered for the delivery of consignments of certain types at certain contracted dates.

The Bulmer scheme was as follows. Trees were supplied to farmers at the very low price of 3s 9d each, which included necessary protections from damage by farm animals. For a further 1s, a tree could be planted, staked and fitted with those protections. A credit scheme helped farmers who were worried about capital outlay with no initial return. Moreover growers with small quantities of early apples ready for the mills could deliver them in sacks to Leominster station, whence the goods agent would forward them in bulk to Bulmers' siding at Hereford at the low rate of 5s a ton. Nor was there any obligation on growers to sell their apples to the supplier of the trees. Similar schemes were introduced elsewhere, but the Herefordshire one was reckoned (by the *Birmingham Post* at least: 21 August 1933) to be the best, and it was highly praised also in the *Estates Gazette* (20 February 1932).

By 1933 Bulmers, with some 210 acres of nurseries in Herefordshire, had planted 76,000 trees, by the end of 1937, over 200,000. They began sending out trees in 1927, earlier from The Whettons. By 1938 they had distributed 86,000, by 1947, about 150,000.

It may be appropriate here to say something of perry pear trees. In speaking of 'cider' we have generally been subsuming perry. Quantitatively it was a small element: in the first 16 years of Bulmers it accounted for less than 7% of their fruit consumption. But some connoisseurs have had a particularly partiality for it, notably Durham. During the 1920s he carried out a survey of the perry pears of Herefordshire, being the first to explore the great wealth of varieties and try to sort out the confusion resulting from the existence of so many names that were purely local. He was also the first to emphasise the importance of the shape and the habit of growth of a tree for the purpose of recognising identities. His labels made of lead affixed to selected trees are still to be found in good condition in orchards throughout the West Midlands. They are high on the trees because he stood on his saddle to affix them.

Riding around on horseback, he became a familiar figure, visiting farms and often staying at Taynton Court, home of the famous Taynton Squash pear, which gave a liquor not unlike champagne. Following up his field studies, Durham established at the Bulmer nurseries at Broxwood a reference collection of about 40 of the best perry pear varieties, which proved to be of great value to researchers.[6]

Perry made of Longland and Moorcroft pears was said a century ago to be delicately flavoured and perfumed, and better than some foreign sparkling wines. In 1899 a committee set up by the Herefordshire Fruit-growers' Association listed 8 varieties of pear as 'vintage'. Bulmers' perry is made partly from the famous Bareland, Barland or Borland pears (whose bloom has a damask rose colour like that of apples, not other pears). Still perry, perfectly dry and sugarless, has a marked freedom from acidity. Some varieties of pear, such as the Holmer, after a hot summer, yield a juice of extraordinary saccharin density. Perry is reputed to be more stimulating than cider, though still considerably less alcoholic than the champagne it visually resembles. There is a legend of a sheep-shearing supper washed down with perry which was responsible for events that led to five marriages.

IMPORTING

Although the ultimate hope was that all the supplies of cider apples and perry pears needed would be home grown, with the expansion of the industry there was no chance of this happening, except on rare occasions, in the foreseeable future; in all but 'hit' years a proportion would have to be imported. We have seen that in one pre-war year, 1911, the supply had to be topped up at Bulmers by 1,053 tons from France. During the war, in September 1915, five eminent French horticulturalists visited the works to explore the possibility that France might find in peacetime a regular outlet to Britain for its surplus; and in fact this did come about, as the following figures (tons of apples) for imports shows:

Year	From France	Year	From France
1923	2,710	1928	—
1924	6,372	1929	2,818
1925	2,649	1930	2,499

1926	3,144	1931	12,353
1927	2,939	1932	19,120

Owing to the rate of monetary exchange it was sometimes even possible to buy French apples more cheaply than Herefordshire ones. There was some haggling, but the normal availability of French supplies put the English growers, only loosely organised in the National Farmers' Union, in a weak bargaining position. In 1923, for instance, French apples could be bought for £5 10s. a ton delivered to English cider works, as against £6 being asked for local ones. English apples were also unusually scarce; so Fred and Esmond Bulmer and Durham went over in August to France, where they found apples rather scarce in Normandy also but moderately plentiful in another district. As a result ten separate cargoes were arranged to leave French ports for Bristol. In 1924, a year in which the English crop was no more than average but trade was boosted by the removal of the duty on cider, Bulmers' bill for foreign apples was £40,000. In 1925 there was again a poor crop in England, and nearly all Bulmers' top staff crossed the Channel at short notice—Howard, Esmond and Bertram to Honfleur, Durham, accompanied by Edward, to St Malo. Next year, when trade was brisk and overtime was being worked at Ryelands Street, the English crop was even poorer, owing to a cold, wet May, but the French crop was exceptionally good, so the deficiency could easily be made up. In 1930, on the other hand, the French crop was poor: the price to English importers was £7 10s. a ton, so English growers could expect the high price of £6–7. But next year the English crop again failed, and most English cider was made from French apples.

These foreign apples were also not a wholly reliable source. Transport strikes could cause cargoes to go bad. Even the threat of a strike could inhibit the giving of a firm order. In 1931 a Spanish cargo, from Asturias, could not even be loaded owing to a dock strike (fortunately it was sold locally at a loss of only £150). There was also a threat from the fact that, whenever the French apple crop was below average, their cider-makers were liable to press their Government to prohibit exports.[7] This happened, for instance, soon after the Bulmer foray into France in 1925. Again, storms or fog could upset time tables. In November 1923 temporary shortage of apples caused by gales in the Channel obliged Bulmers to suspend cider-making for four crucial days; and in October 1927 three shiploads carefully timed to arrive at five-day intervals arrived all together because of fog.

Concentrated apple juice was also being imported in the 1930s – ten times more was imported in 1932 than in 1931, according to the *Devon Gazette*. Concentration reduced the bulk for transport to about one-seventh. A total of 100,000 gallons from Annapolis Valley in Nova Scotia was imported in 1932, as against 17,000 in 1931. From Canada as a whole 300,000 gallons were shipped in that year. This was due to the disastrous failure of the English cider apple crop. None of this juice came from cider apples, which did not grow in Canada. Bulmers imported for experimental purposes 37,000 gallons of concentrated apple juice in 1933, nearly 20,000 in 1934, at an average cost of about 3s 9d a gallon; but the amounts fluctuated considerably—5,033 in 1935, only 42 in the 'hit' year 1936, none in 1937,12,321 in 1938, and 100,345 in 1945 (imported as a precaution when war appeared imminent).

Cider as a finished product was also imported into England, mainly from France, but also from Spain and Canada. Some of it was sold under the foreign maker's own label, but most was imported by the leading cider-makers for blending purposes. Nearly 3,000,000 gallons were said by the *Hereford Times* to have been imported from France in 1925. Official figures quoted in Parliament gave 1,950,239 gallons as the amount imported in the nine months January–September 1932.

Annual national imports of cider and perry combined in the early 1930s were as follows (in gallons):

1930	738,377	1935	717
1931	366,454	1936	220
1932	2,275,176	1937	41,007
1933	664,180	1938	65,496
1934	1,166	1939	132,264

But in these years Bulmers had to import cider only in the one highly exceptional year 1932, after a disastrous crop failure, when they imported a total of 534,455 gallons (490,360 from France and 44,095 from Spain) at a cost (including carriage, freight and duty) of £26,840. In that year, Parliament was told, probably about half the cider in England was derived from foreign apples. By contrast the 1933 English crop was not only unusually heavy owing to September rainfall, but unusually high in sugar content and therefore 'vintage', owing to abundant summer sunshine—better than any year since 1921. It replenished the storage vats for three years.

In 1928 the Board of Trade introduced a 'National Mark' scheme for a number of products, in the interests of quality and uniformity. With the onset of the slump it became part of the 'Buy British' campaign. In May 1931 it was extended to cider, with the additional object of encouraging English growers of apples, especially bittersweets, and of establishing standards for their produce. There were two grades: 'Select Cider' (black and white label) and 'Select Cider, Champagne Process' (gold and white label). The criteria, agreed between the National Association of Cider Makers and the National Farmers' Union, with advice from Long Ashton, were as follows:

(1)   The cider must be made from apples grown in England and Wales.
(2)   The finished product must be made from (a) pure fruit juice or (b) pure fruit juice to which not more than 25% of a syrup made from pure beet and cane sugar had been added. The original gravity of the finished product must be not less than 1.04 at 60 degrees Fahrenheit.
(3)   It must be absolutely free from concentrated apple juice and other fruit juices, from artificial bouquets and essences, and from the recognised signs of inferior cider—'ropiness', 'sickness' and excess of acetic acid.

To make inspection manageable, the Mark was made available only to producers of 3,000 gallons a year (of cider of any kind). By June 1933 64 firms, 2 associations of farm cider-makers and 25 firms authorised to bottle approved brands with their own label had qualified. Bulmers used the gold and white label for their Pomagne cider, being the only firm entitled to do so. But the scheme was immediately crippled by the unfortunate failure of the English crop, which made the wide use of imported fruit, juice and cider unavoidable; it never really caught on, and died a natural death in the Second World War.

The policy of Empire Preference adopted by the National Government elected in the autumn of 1931 caused temporary anxiety. It was proposed at the Ottawa Conference of October 1932 that Canadian and Australian apples imported for the cider industry should be freed from duty, while foreign apples would be subject to a duty of £4 10s a ton. But those Commonwealth apples were not really suitable for making cider, though so-called cider was made from them.[8] The measure would have been disastrous, because the price of the essential French supply—and how essential it was, 1932 was even then demonstrating in spectacular fashion—would have been prohibitive. Fred Bulmer, holidaying on the Continent with some of his family, was summoned post-haste to Ottawa to explain this to Baldwin and the crisis was averted: foreign apples sent direct to English cider-makers were exempted so long as the supply of home-grown apples was not sufficient. Meanwhile the cider-makers reassured the English growers by guaranteeing that the price paid to them for apples would not fall below £4 a ton in the next 5 years. (In a normal year it would be £5–6. In 1932 Bulmers were paying £6 5s. for bittersweets, £5 for other cider apples and for perry pears. For Foxwhelp or Kingston Black they would give £7 5s.) Naturally there was annual haggling, but at the end of that period the *Hereford Times*, remarking that the quinquennium had included two 'hit' years in one of which, but for the guarantee, glut prices would have fallen as low as £2, adjudged that the agreement had worked well and creditably. For the subsequent quinquennium the growers acquiesed in a minimum price of £3 10s.

EXPORTING

It might be thought that exporting would give great opportunities for expanding the sale of cider, especially to countries with a hot climate or at least a hot summer. We have seen that even in their earliest years Bulmers exported some cider overseas. By the beginning of the interwar period they were supplying agents in Egypt, Nyasaland, India, Malay, Indo-China, North China, Argentina and elsewhere. But there were limiting factors. Canada's seasons other than summer were cold, and it was in any case no doubt satisfied with the sort of cider it was used to. Australia and New Zealand, before the advent of air transport, were very far away. The obvious market should have been the United States, and indeed until well into the First World War Bulmers did a good deal of business there.[9] But even before it 19 of the States were 'dry', and large parts of the rest were dry by local option. In 1917 Congress adopted Prohibition as a Federal war-time measure for food control, and by the Volstead Act of 1919 it was written into the Constitution by the Eighteenth Amendment. Respectable cider-makers could hardly enter into the ensuing bootlegging racket.

It was not until 7 April 1933 that Congress voted that the United States should go wet again, with effect from 7 November. Large prospects for exporting cider there seemed to be opening up again. In the autumn of that year Bertram Bulmer (accompanied by his newly married wife Christine, at his father's personal expense) made a three-month tour of the States. He soon decided that it would be better to have regional agents rather than rely solely on a major agency in New York; so agents were also appointed in Boston and in Minnesota, Louisiana and California. Everywhere the couple were well received, and much interest was shown in Pomagne. The first shipment was of 6,000 cases to the Cresca Company of New York, their representative in the Eastern States. Repeat orders were considerable. In ten months in 1934–35 £13,000 worth of cider was exported by Bulmers to the U.S.A. But unfortunately the Federal Government later on decided to tax Pomagne cider as if it were champagne, and it could not compete on those terms with the sparkling wines.[10]

A possible field for expansion nearer home was offered by Ireland, where cider was still drunk but manufacture, active between 1870 and 1914, had sadly declined. The old orchards of Waterford County, with their 'Blackwater' cider, had been outstanding, according to an article in the *Cork Examiner* for 24 December 1932. Writing to congratulate the paper on it, Fred Bulmer recalled how, on a visit to S.W. Ireland many years ago, he had thought that he had never seen a district more suitable for cider apple trees. Hitherto the Irish duty on cider had been low, and Bulmers sent a good deal of it to Eire, to private customers and to wholesalers of whom the most important was Findlaters of Dublin. But Dermot Findlater told Bertram that, at the instigation of a manufacturer called W. Magner of Clonmel in County Tipperary who was a personal friend of De Valera, the latter had clapped a penal import duty of 1s a gallon on cider. On Findlater's advice, following the principle 'If you can't beat 'em, join 'em', Bulmers did a deal in March 1937 by which the cider part of Magner's business was turned into a separate company in which they had a 50% interest. It was hoped to plant 4,000 trees in the region in the first 3–4 years and more after that. The arrangement promised well, and at one time the firm of Bulmer, Magner & Co. was selling 2,000,000 gallons a year of cider and Cidona. But by then war had intervened; and in any case the future of the venture belongs to a later chapter.

In 1919 sales were still largely to private customers. Stanley Baldwin, even as Prime Minister, always ordered his cider in his own copperplate handwriting, in 20-gallon casks of draught. The Labour ministers Sir Charles Trevelyan and J.R. Clynes were also customers. In the early 1920s reliance on such private customers seemed satisfactory enough, but there was a danger of complacency in view of the rise of competitors. While Bulmers were dominant in the Midlands and Wales, Whiteways were so in London and the South, and Gaymers in the East and North (including Scotland and Ireland). Howard, reinforced by Edward from 1929, spent a lot of time making contacts with brewers and wholesalers throughout the country. Two men from outside were recruited on the sales side, with a salary, not merely on commission as previous agents had been: in 1923 Capt L.W. Lewis and in 1926 Capt (later Colonel) Alan Williams, who were in due course to become respectively London and Manchester managers for the firm. But there was still much to be done. Cider was little known outside the West Country. A salesman who had a beat extending to Cheltenham and Peterborough often had to explain to publicans what it was. The area contained only half-a-dozen trade customers, mostly hotels selling the bottled variety only. In 1928 an important step was taken with the appointment of Harold Robinson, a friend of Howard's who had been engaged since the War in selling insurance, as Sales Manager. Universally popular and incurably optimistic, 'Robbie' was very successful in building up the sales side. He was made a director in 1944. One of Howard's great contributions to the firm in the time of its expansion was his ability to pick good men; and his wartime experience had brought him into contact with a wider range of people than those, admirable though they were, whom Fred was able to enlist from his Shrewsbury and Cambridge circles.

Publicity was of two kinds. The first was for the unsophisticated public. It may be typified by the slogan (1936), 'A for Apples, B for Bulmers, C for Cider', and by a ubiquitous placard depicting a young countrywoman with rosy cheeks pouring an abundance of rosy apples from a cornucopial sack. But there was also, for those who aspired to sophistication, a kind intended to make the point that cider, a drink for many decades associated only with rustics, had now become, since Bulmers launched Pomagne, a drink once more for high society. We have seen that in 1911 the firm was granted the Royal Appointment and any association with the Court was naturally exploited indirectly. Advertisements in magazines now showed a couple dining tête-à-tête in evening dress at a restaurant, the man recommending cider to the woman in the presence of an approving waiter. The idea that cider was a ladylike drink (by implied contrast with beer) was sedulously inculcated; and 'Every woman knows that mineral salts in apples keep the complexion clear'. A new medium was brought into play when, on 24 November 1932, Fred Bulmer gave a radio talk on 'The Art and Craft of Making Cider', with appropriate background noises, for the B.B.C., still less than ten years old.

When the National Government was formed in 1931 Philip Snowden's supplementary budget raised the duty on beer by 31s per standard barrel, which meant a penny on the pint for the consumer. The brewers protested that cider, at least as alcoholic as beer, was not touched; but in reply to pressure from them Hore-Belisha explained in January 1933, first that the proceeds of a tax on cider would be swallowed up by the expense of collecting it, and secondly, that it would blight the campaign for orchard-planting and so deprive the farmer of a profitable crop. The net effect was, that at a time of economic depression when people had to count their pennies, a pint of cider cost 4d and a pint of beer 6d. Wider markets were also opened up by the introduction in the mid-thirties of the first really effective screw-top flagon. Bulmers' 40-ounce glass flagons were a convenient size for the patrons of the off-licences, and inexpensive at 9½d or 10d a flagon for Woodpecker.

Fred Bulmer secured an arrangement with Flowers' Brewery of Stratford-on-Avon that their houses should stock only Bulmers' cider. This proved lasting, and was the first of many such arrangements.

Already in 1932 the Press began to talk again of a revival in cider-drinking. It was said to be a favourite lunch-time drink in London restaurants. According to the *Daily Mail*, the output of British-made cider was up 11% on 1924 and the average selling price a gallon up from 2s 1d to 2s 3d. The *Fruit-grower* estimated that in the West cider-drinking was at 4–5 times its pre-war level (but that surely cannot have included farm labourers). At the Lewis Arms at Pentyrch, near Whitchurch, 50 gallons were sold in 1932,570 in 1933. At the annual Cider Tasting Day at Long Ashton that year (an event founded in 1905 and now attracting 2,000 farmers a year) it was estimated that 20,000,000 gallons a year were being drunk, as against about 6,000,000 twenty years before. But of course the sale was still only a small fraction of that of beer: the paper which said that cider was becoming 'the great national drink' was talking nonsense.

The 1934 crop of cider apples was a 'hit' everywhere, in Herefordshire the best for 25 years. The *Sunday Times* reported that the cider boom was providing hundreds of extra temporary jobs for the unemployed. At one time Bulmers had 300 extra hands working, to cope with supplies from 2,000 growers. By December they had bought 19,000 tons of apples from Herefordshire alone. All the county's supplies were bought up, for the guaranteed minimum of £4 a ton, with bonuses for growers who entered into contracts to supply within a given time. Winter sales enabled the firm to make room for the juice of 1,000 tons of apples a month, and to go on making cider for as long as apples were available. By 1938 the total was 168 vessels holding 5,758,449 gallons. More than half of these were still made of oak, but there were 22 concrete ones holding 100,000 gallons each. They had storage facilities, described by the *Hereford Times* as 'one of the sights of the world', for 5,000,000 gallons.

NEW PERSONALITIES

Harold Robinson was only one of several characters imported from outside during this period to join the members of the Bulmer family in key positions. The most remarkable was Alan Hudson-Davies, who had been with Esmond and Bertram at King's College, Cambridge, and had achieved First Class Honours in Natural Sciences. He had had four years with the National Institute of Industrial Psychology and five with I.C.I. when he came in 1933, after Esmond's death, to succeed him as Works Manager (he became a director in 1936, and remained on the Board until 1946). He was a man of exceptional charm as well as ability who easily fell into the firm's tradition of good understanding between executives and workers. Calm and deliberate in making decisions, he gave people clear instructions and then left them to get on with it. An uncle of his had been one of the firm's first lorry drivers. He shared Fred Bulmer's leftish sympathies and, inspired by him with enthusiasm for the same causes, served on the Hereford City Council, specialising in education, housing and health. (He left in 1941 to be wartime chairman of Birmingham Manpower Board, and in 1946 became Managing Director of Fibreglass, of which he was chairman from 1964, being also a very active director of its parent company, Pilkington's. His second wife was a daughter of the famous Russian singer Chaliapin. He was knighted in 1975, a year before his death.)

Vernon Beach Thomas ('Beach') joined the firm about the same time. He had been for some years a Development Department engineer in Europe and Canada, and had acquired an expertise which ranged from structures through hydraulics to electricity and electronics. (One of his jobs had been improving the design of the Snowmobile and testing it in Arctic conditions.) His retirement and return to England coincided with the slump of 1932. Bulmers snapped him up, as they had snapped up Durham. He was a brilliant and ingenious man with a remarkable ability to appreciate new techniques without training. (Indeed one of his few drawbacks was a passion for taking new machines to pieces: if there was anything wrong with them, the makers or suppliers were glad to be able to say that he was responsible for it, and it was hard to prove the contrary.) He set about reorganising the mechanical side of the works, and was to play a great part in their future development. One of his few rules for running electric motors was characteristic: 'If it's too hot to sit on, don't use it'. He had already become a legend in the firm by the time he retired in 1966.

Also in 1933 came Adam Cochrane. He was transferred in 1937 to the London Office, and returned there, after being severely wounded in the war, as manager. But soon, after Robinson's untimely death in 1946, he was brought back to Hereford, and he was Sales Director there for nearly 20 years.

Richard McBride, who had had sales experience in the North, was introduced by Hudson-Davies to be Assistant Secretary to Reginald Phillips, on whose death in 1938 he succeeded him as Secretary to the company.

When James Guest retired from managing the farms and orchards at Broxwood in 1937, he was succeeded by Leslie Evans. Becket Bulmer started working there in 1936, but as a Territorial officer he was called up as soon as war broke out, and in the last stages of it in Europe he was killed, three months after Edward.

MECHANICAL PROGRESS

The basic processes in the production of cider outlined in Chapter VIII were developed and refined during the period between the wars and we may now take a look at them as they were towards the end of that period (first warning off readers who are not mechanically minded).[11]

Apples were delivered in bags, either by rail or by road and were weighed on entry to the factory. They were tipped out on to concrete platforms in which were small graded channels to convey them by means of water to a collecting pit at the foot of an elevator fitted with buckets which dipped into the pit. The buckets were perforated to allow the water to drain away from the apples. As the water drained out of the pit it passed through a moving screen which removed grass, leaves, etc.

The juice was pressed out in two press houses, one of them a recent addition, in the following way. After being ground to a pulp in mills the crushed apple pulp was spread on cloths made of manilla or sisal which were folded over, and each packed layer of apple pulp, about 16 to a 'cheese' (the name used for layers of apple pulp prepared for pressing), was pressed by hydraulic rams, which compressed the cheese so that the juice ran out through the cloths and was collected in trays at the bottom of the press. From there it ran into tanks or pits from which it was pumped into the storage vats. Each press had two points at which the cheese could be prepared so that one was being pressed while the other was being prepared. The residue, known as wet apple pomace, was dried, after which it was pressed for the extraction of pectin, used in jam-making for causing the fruit to set.

As soon as the juice had been pressed out it was pumped into vats, where it began to ferment because of the yeast which had previously been on the skin of the apple. The fermentation depended upon the temperature and after about three weeks it normally contained about 5% of alcohol. After it had been allowed to stand and most of the yeast had settled to the bottom, it was then racked off and then filtered through cotton pulp, and, if necessary, filtered a second time. It was then ready to be bottled or pumped into small casks for use as draught cider in public houses. In the latter case it had some more yeast added to it to keep it fresh and sparkling during the time it was on tap. In each hour 300 casks of varying sizes could be filled.

Cider required for bottling was generally chilled and bottled at a temperature just above freezing-point, having had some carbon dioxide gas added to it. It was also sent out to bottlers in barrels for them to fill themselves. When bottled by the firm the cider was carbonated and bottled on a 36-head rotary filling machine, after which the bottles were stoppered and packed ready for despatch. The only operation which had still not been automated was the very delicate one of wrapping foil round the neck of the bottle.

The Pomagne cider process unique to Bulmers has already been described. A word should be added here about the highly important process of bottle washing. Most bottles were returnable, that is to say that the customer sent them back after they had been emptied. The bottles were washed on an automatic machine which submerged them into a caustic soda solution, then soaked and brushed them inside and out. Finally they were rinsed with clean water before being filled.

Casks were also carefully cleansed before use by being flushed out with hot water under high pressure. They were then inspected and if they were not thoroughly clean, the head was taken out and they were scrubbed.

PECTIN

Perhaps the most important innovation at Bulmers between the wars was the manufacture of pectin. Much jam is made of fruit which does not facilitate setting. The long boiling required for this purpose involves loss of flavour and volume as well as expenditure of time and fuel. This can be saved by the use of pectin (at first only in liquid form), a product of certain fruits, including apples. (It is also used to coagulate jelly sweets such as Turkish Delight.) Extraction of it from pomace is by hydrolysis using an acid solution. We have seen various uses to which the pomace from the cider mills was put. Selling it to pectin factories proved more lucrative. Professor Barker of Long Ashton was in 1933 advising the *average* cider-maker to sell his pomace rather than try to extract the pectin himself (prices varied considerably – from 5s to 20s – a ton for wet, from £5 to £12 for dry). But he added that *big* cider-makers could afford to have their own dryers.

Bulmers had had a dryer of their own ever since Percy's fruitful visit to Germany. They now perceived a chance of a lucrative side-line. The price offered by the English firm making pectin was progressively sinking. At Bertram's instigation Bulmers began in 1936 to extract pectin themselves instead of sending their pomace to pectin factories, employing the hydraulic presses used in autumn for cider-making. There was the added advantage that this would help to keep the works busy all the year round: the seasonal nature of cider-making had always been a major drawback. By 1937 they had two large machines capable of drying every 24 hours the pomace left after the pressing of 500–600 tons of apples; 45 tons of liquid pectin were produced in 1937,96 in 1938 and 297 in 1939. In 1939 a pectin factory, designed by Beach Thomas, experimental and quite primitive, was built at the end of the vat-house on the Ryelands site, to operate outside the cider-making season.

The residue of the pomace could still be redried and sold for cattle-food, either incorporated in some balanced cattle-feed or mixed with molasses and compressed into cubes.

LOOKING BACK AND FORWARD—MOORFIELDS

The 1920s and 1930s together would have formed a suitable period for a chapter to comprise even if we had not now come to regard them in retrospect as 'The period between the wars'. They spanned the years during which Fred Bulmer was the pre-eminent leader, though with increasing help from members of the family and other executives, culminating in the Jubilee celebrations of autumn 1937, which were followed by his retirement from active participation early in 1938. It was a period of expansion and development rather than of great innovation. Lorries gradually took over from drays for local transport, and to some extent from railways for longer journeys. To ease the transport problem depots were also established in London, Birmingham, Manchester, Derby, Northampton, Bristol and elsewhere. Arthur Ratley, Northern Division Area Manager, can recall the time when the Manchester depot consisted of a railway arch, and horse-drawn carts still delivered the cider. All opportunities had to be taken of pushing sales. These included attending licensees' funerals, which were always a good source of new contacts, since those attending adjourned afterwards to a neighbouring pub.

The London depot was established in 1935, on a 1½-acre site at Perivale which cost £2,560. The cost of building was £8,044. To tide over bad cropping seasons for apples there were now 150 storage vats at Hereford, which by the end were sufficient to hold more than 6,000,000 gallons of cider. There were 1,500,000 bottles of Pomagne cider in the cellars. By 1919 the firm had become the largest cider business in the world. Then it employed 200 people; by 1938 the figure was 800. In 1919 it used 4,228 tons of apples; in 1938 it used 22,277. On 25 April 1938 the nominal share capital of the company, £70,000 in 1919, was increased by £100,000 to £300,000, made up from 200,000 Ordinary Shares and 100,000 Preference Shares of £1 each. Directors were now receiving, in salaries and fees, an average of about £6,000 a year. In the 1930s the taxfree dividend on preference shares was 7%, while on ordinary shares it varied from 5% to 7½%.

Meanwhile a step decisive for the future had been taken, with the purchase in 1936 from Mr William Bowers for £900 of 0.9 acres of slum property on the Moorfields estate, with frontage on Whitecross Road. To this was added in 1939 4.6 acres of it, bought for £2,000 from the London, Midland and Scottish Railway, and a further 1.4 acres of land beyond the Yazor Brook, adjoining Wragg's timber yard, also bought from the railway, for £400. The Moorfields estate lies on the north side of Whitecross Road (the Brecon Road), opposite the end of Ryelands Street and thus conveniently near the old site. Its immediate use was prevented by the war, but it assured the possibility of massive expansion; and the area of the firm's Moorfields site was eventually increased until it far exceeded that of the Ryelands site.

[1]One forward-looking step Fred was advocating as early as March 1919: he urged the County Council, both for commercial and for educational reasons, to support the earliest possible introduction of the decimal system.
[2] In 1937 we hear of the brewers being divided as to whether they should press the Chancellor of the Exchequer to reintroduce the duty on cider.
[3] The composer Gerald Finzi, inspecting the works during the Three Choirs Festival, put his head inside one of these vats at the instigation of Edward Ball and sang a scale with dramatic effect. Oak vats continued to be erected by Bulmers down to 1957, and bought from elsewhere down to 1960. Up to 1933 wooden casks were made for the company's use at its cooperage. After that the latter confined itself to repairs, mainly of sizes under 30 gallons.
[4] Wooden vats contract slowly with age. To keep them tight the hoops have to be driven farther and farther down the sides, until finally the bottom one is forced off, and after suitable reduction is put back as the top one.
[5] In October 1930 the Ely Brewery Co. had to apologise for having sold as Bulmer's Cider a mixture of Bulmers' with other cider.

[6] On all this see *Perry Pears*, ed. L.C. Luckwill and A. Pollard (1963), pp.10–11.

[7] Correspondingly, we find the Hereford Branch of the National Farmers' Union in January 1926 pressing for import duties on cider apples and cider.

[8] Cider made experimentally from Canadian apples at Long Ashton in 1933 was adjudged passable but no match for English cider.

[9] There was an odd episode in December 1917. The New York Customs refused to recognise the claim of any cider to be naturally sparkling: at the advertised price it must have been carbonated. Bulmers invited them to send representatives to see their cider being made. They came, they saw, and they relented.

[10] This decision was eventually revised in 1977, as a result of continuous representations by Bulmers, backed by the National Cider Makers' Association and the British Government. The new rate of duty was low enough to revive old hopes.

[11] They are described in a Bulmer brochure 'The Wine of England', reprinted from an article which appeared in *Food* in January and February 1936.

CHAPTER TWELVE

THE SECOND WORLD WAR

In the Second World War, as in the First, the Government allowed, and even encouraged, cider-making, as being good for morale. The making of pectin was also encouraged, to save shipping-space and dollars. Of course major building on the Moorfields site had to be postponed, but a new crate factory was opened there in 1941. In February 1941 a new 35-ton boiler, measuring 30ft by 9ft 3in, was delivered. When the roofs of the pectin building and the boilerhouse were gaping, the Air Raid Precaution Service stepped in to ensure that the Ministry of Supply made materials for repair rapidly available. There was much improvisation. Thus Beach Thomas imported as a prop for the conveyor, itself made of scrap metal, a fir tree from The Whettons. (It was so green that it sprouted next year.) One permanent feature of the firm which originated in those days, no doubt owing to the rationing of food in the shops, and which has become extremely important, was the establishment of a works canteen. A sum of £545 was spent on this in 1941, and the £2,300 spent in 1946 was an indication that it was realised that the canteen had come to stay.

Apart from one or two bombs directed at the munitions works none fell on or near Hereford. The war came nearest to home one Sunday in the summer of 1940 when trainloads of soldiers arrived at Hereford Station straight from the beaches of Dunkirk. To tide over the period of sorting out they were distributed, by Bulmers' lorries, to homes in the neighbourhood of a certain size with gardens to match. Thus Adam's Hill catered for 100 of them. Sophie Bulmer did much work throughout the war for the care of refugee children.

In March 1941 Fred Bulmer, Durham and Todd resigned from the Board, and on 2 September Fred died, his work accomplished. He had been succeeded as Chairman a few months before by his nephew Howard.

Of the pre-war workforce of about 800 the Forces claimed 180 and Civil Defence 4. More women workers were now recruited, many of them straight from school. For the cider-making season the firm continued to advertise for extra help—women aged 17 and over, men aged 18–21 or over 35. On one occasion when Bertram

Bulmer had struggled first in French and then in German to explain to 90 Polish refugees what their work would be, Arthur Evans, appearing suddenly on the scene, put it across to them forcibly in a mixture of sign language and bad language. One recruit was an Austrian refugee from the Nazis, L.E. Seibold ('Sib'), who was released from internment, and found work by the kindly foreman Harry Jones in the new crate factory. He became a charge hand, and remained so until his death in 1964. Members of the sales force not called up for service could also be drafted to Hereford for that season, continuing for the rest of the year to run the depots. One of them, Harold Robinson, took over as Acting Works Manager in 1941, when Alan Hudson-Davies was appointed wartime Chairman of the Birmingham Manpower Board, and became a director in 1944. The quality of the auxiliaries traditionally recruited from South Wales inevitably fell, but there were other good casual sources. Thus an airforce corporal formerly employed by the firm, who happened to be stationed in the neighbourhood, came with some of his colleagues to lend a hand on Sundays and started a useful tradition at his base. Working girls gave help at the orchard farms after hours as members of the emergency Land Corps; buses full of Bulmer girls often left for them twice a week. The Government, in view of the importance of the cider apple crop, lifted the ban on agricultural workers applying for jobs in the works, provided they were otherwise unemployed. Pay for auxiliaries for a 48-hour week was £2 8s a week for men, £1 12s for women, but increased steadily as the War went on. In the pectin plant in 1942 women were getting £2 10s to £3 for shift work.[1]

There were however factors which limited the production of cider and put up its price. One was the rationing of sugar. Another was shortage of containers and machinery. Another was scarcity of apples, which therefore became very expensive, partly owing to shortage of harvesters, partly to the cessation of imports from France. A *maximum* price for cider apples had eventually to be fixed by the Government. In 1941 and 1942 it was £18 12s 4d a ton,[2] three times the *minimum* agreed for 1940; in 1943–46 it was £14. Foreign apples being unobtainable, the acreage of cider orchards in England, 63,000 (one-third of the total of apple orchards), was insufficient. Windfalls and 'cull' fruit (cooking and eating apples) had to be used to an extent unacceptable in peacetime. (Even so the cider-makers were worried by the number of firms which were being prosecuted for using cider as a basis for concoctions purporting to be table wines, etc., and sold at exorbitant prices. They were harming the genuine cider trade.) In 1942, however, Bulmers were able to make about three-quarters of the average pre-war amount—enough, it was hoped, to fill the vats and keep business going till the end of the war, with a surplus to give the salesmen a good send-off when competition returned again. It was fortunate that the 1944 cider crop in the western counties was very heavy, since the 1945 one was to be poor, in some places disastrous, owing to a late frost. One result of labour and petrol shortage was that Bulmers were obliged to sell their Broxwood farms as being too distant, with the object of planting further orchards at King's Acre.

Another result of petrol rationing was, that salesmen took to bicycles for shorter journeys. But sales promotion continued. (A mug of appalling vulgarity made in the shape of Hitler's face bore a rhyme advertising Bulmer's cider.) Shortage of petrol, however, led in 1944 to zoning as between the chief cider-makers. Bulmers lost their footing in the south from Cornwall to Hampshire (the traditional Whiteway country), and in the East from Essex to Lincolnshire (the traditional Gaymer country), but made compensatory gains in the West.

An economy measure of a different kind was the imposition by law of deposit charges on bottles and crates. Customers were thus encouraged to return bottles, but these had to be complete. '*You* can replace the stopper, *we* can't,' ran a Bulmers advertisement in the national press. The supply of bottles for cider was also maintained by the withdrawal for the duration of their new non-alcoholic beverage Cidona (presumably this drink was not considered capable of boosting morale). It had been launched in 1939 with an advertising campaign that cost more than £50,000. As for pectin, most of the skilled workers were absent. In 1942 the plant was temporarily closed for the installation of new filters, but after that production was at a higher level.

During the war the firm managed to recover any ground initially lost. Annual dividends (after deduction of Income Tax) were 7% on preference shares (total £3,500) and 7% on ordinary shares (total £7,000). Directors' salaries varied from £5,500 to £4,025, and their fees from £800 to £388. Production was as follows:

	Cider (gallons)	Pectin (tons)
1940	5,206,300	971
1941	3,719,500	2,419
1942	3,148,800	2,624
1943	4,034,300	3,383
1944	4,283,400	3,306
1945	5,092,400	3,455

In 1945 it was possible to raise the dividend on ordinary shares to 12 1/2%.

In June 1943 the old question was raised again in Parliament: why, when the tax on beer had gone up (from 80s per standard barrel in 1939 to 281s), did cider remain untaxed? It received the old answer: the amount of cider consumed (it had been 12,500,000 gallons in 1940) was a mere drop compared with the ocean of beer – not enough to repay the cost and trouble of collecting tax.

From 1942 onwards the firm kept in touch with its employees by means of a news letter circulated every few months. It was largely filled with information about individuals, both serving and remaining; but it also contained information of lasting value about what was happening in the business. Of the 180 who were serving with the Armed Forces 9 were killed. This was a comparatively light proportion, but it included Esmond and Becket Bulmer, to add to the loss of Fred in 1941. About 50 of the employees were expected to return to the firm.

[1] In October 1944 the Agricultural Wages Board turned down, as inflationary, an application from the Agricultural Workers Union to increase the minimum agricultural wage for men from £3 5s to £4 10s a week. They said that the present wage compared favourably with pay in comparable industries. The claim had been made against the better judgement of the Union's leaders, whose figure of £4 had been rejected by vote of the rank and file.

[2] Cf the £20 fixed by the Government for the climactic war year 1918.

CHAPTER THIRTEEN

FURTHER DEVELOPMENTS: 1945–1965

The period between the end of the War in Europe and the end of 1965, when Howard Bulmer and Edward Ball retired and the Board was reconstructed to bring in new blood from outside, seems sufficiently homogeneous to form the subject of a single, if long, chapter. Within this, however, various aspects of the business will be treated separately, as in Chapter Eleven, because to deal with everything in chronological order would produce a confused impression with no clear outlines.

After surveying the general fortunes of the company, now beginning to be a group, we shall take stock of its management, and incidentally of the regrouping of the other leading cider companies. We shall then survey the background to this—the development of the Moorfields estate, the new plant installed there and at Ryelands Street, the maintenance of the fruit supply to feed this and the increasing importance of pectin; then the various products and their marketing; and, last but not least, the employees, on whom the growing prosperity of the firm ultimately depended.

RECOVERY, DIFFICULTIES AND PROGRESS

The early years after the War were naturally taken up with renovation and reconstruction. For instance, large numbers of bottles had to be bought. Of the new bottles many burst because they were not properly sealed; but they did make the exploitation of new outlets possible. Bertram Bulmer toured France, Switzerland and Belgium to inspect new machinery, and paid several visits to America. As to building, renewal of bombed housing and premises had to have priority nationally for the resources of the construction industry. Shortages of numerous commodities and consequent rationing continued. When Bulmers bought the Hereford Transport Company it was largely for the sake of taking over its petrol ration (they sold it again in 1953, after petrol rationing ended, at a capital profit of £13,857). Shortage of bottles compelled restrictions on the production of non-alcoholic apple drinks until 1947, and in fact Bulmers only went back to them eight years after that. Even with exporting still prohibited, cider-makers had themselves to go on rationing their customers, not only because of shortage of bottles, but more because of shortage of fruit and sugar.

With the importing of apples also still prohibited as a wartime measure until 1948 the English orchards could not supply enough. As for sugar, for reasons of currency conservation rather than lack of potential sources, the Government rationed its supply to the cider industry annually on the basis of a percentage of pre-war consumption. In September 1950 Bulmers had to announce that, while they had already purchased the same quantity of cider fruit from their regular suppliers of past years, as in 1949, their ability to purchase still more depended on their being granted more sugar by the Ministry of Food. In the event their request for 500 tons more was turned down because all the available supply had been allotted to other food industries. Although in some years the ration reached 90% of pre-war consumption, in 1951, for instance, it was barely more than two-thirds of it. Such restrictions prevented cider-makers from profiting more from the post-war shortage of beer.

Nor were the early 1950s easy in other ways. The year 1952 was particularly difficult. Though sales of cider had increased, the profit on these had been offset by increases in costs, and the only price increase deemed feasible was a small one on flagon cider. It was becoming increasingly difficult to afford to expand and modernise the factory and to keep the machinery efficient and up-to-date. The year 1953 was again a difficult one, through very bad weather in July; and when economies and lower costs of some raw materials had nevertheless enabled profits to continue to be made, 1954 came up with one of the coldest summers in living memory, when there was little call for thirst-quenching drink. Though by contrast the summer of 1955 was one of the warmest, occasioning record sales of cider, in 1956 the weather was dismal from June to September.

Trade then looked up. In 1957 sales of every brand of cider at Bulmers surpassed even those of 1955, and so did those in 1958, despite poor summer weather in both years; and in 1959, a warm dry summer, with an apple crop which, though not large, was exceptional in quality and sugar content, maintained the impetus, sales approaching the records of 1957. Though the spring Budget of that year effectively lowered the price of beer by 2d a pint, to the detriment of all Bulmers' sales, a rise in the price of it in summer 1960 boosted those of draught cider in particular and enabled the firm to raise the price of its bottled brands in October. Meanwhile, to meet competition, and the demands of popular taste, Bulmers in April 1956 had marketed an extra sweet cider, which went rather against their inclinations but produced some additional business.

Sales of cider depended very much, as we have seen, on the vagaries of summer weather; but in the late 1950s we begin to hear of excellent sales, especially of Pomagne in connection with Christmas and New Year celebrations. Sales of this doubled in 1955–58 and in 1959 about 15,000 dozen bottles of it were sold in special Christmas packs, almost all of it additional to previous sales for the period. Packaging was very important. One-gallon jars, introduced in 1960 for draught cider and for the new line, Strongbow, proved popular, especially for home consumption.

The background of all this was the steady expansion of the factory on the Moorfields site, with the major introduction of new presses and bottling lines, shortly to be described. On a royal visit to the Hereford Cattle Market in 1957 Howard Bulmer presented a Wedgwood cider mug each to the Queen and Prince Philip on behalf of the Herefordshire cider-makers. The Prince having said he would like to see cider made, a visit to Bulmers was arranged for him and took place on 12 November 1958, lasting more than four hours. First he inspected a collection of over 100 varieties of cider apples and perry pears assembled by Edward Ball, and then he toured the works, lunching in the Board Room. Mrs Bertram Bulmer supervised the preparation of the lunch by the staff. A special Hereford edition of *The Citizen* was printed to mark the occasion.

The Budget of 1962 imposed purchase tax of 15%, which cost the firm £300,000 for the period May–December. This, together with other rising costs and wages, necessitated increases in retail prices of cider from July 1963; but although sales fell, profits still increased. This was partly due to economies: considerable sums had been spent on schemes for modernisation and cost-cutting. The whole question of project profitability was now kept more strictly under review. A report of 1964 estimated that projects in view would involve capital expenditure of £857,000.

One form of economy, recommended by consultants employed by the firm, was reduction in the number of depots, and this may be as good a place as any to say something of these important if not very newsworthy adjuncts. We become more conscious of them after 1962, when the *Woodpecker News* was started, a landmark in the history of the firm. There are photographs of parties from depots being entertained on visits to Hereford, and news items about individual members of their staffs, such as that the administrative staff at Perivale consisted of an Englishman, a Scotsman, an Irishman and a Welshman—and it worked. There was, from 1955, a fine central garage and repair workshop at Hereford. Very little cider now went by rail to customers, though some was still so supplied to depots. Most went by road in large lorries and was distributed to customers in smaller ones. In 1962 there were 18 tankers of 1,000–3,000 gallon capacity, used chiefly for pectin. In all there were 151 vehicles (besides many others that were hired), and 151 drivers with 92 mates; and these numbers rose steadily in subsequent years. The driver would deposit his loaded trailer at the depot and return to Hereford with a trailer full of empties. All the depots were near motorways, and all kept heavily stocked. But in view of improvements in conditions of road transport the consultants advised in 1964 that the number of depots should be reduced from 21 to 9, and this subsequently took place.

COMPANY AND GROUP

The three decades after 1945 saw the gradual absorption of most of the other cider-making companies into two large groups of brewers, while the output from farms steadily diminished. Coates (1956), Gaymers and Whiteways (1961) were acquired by Showerings and renamed 'Coates Gaymers' and Showerings in turn were taken over by Allied Breweries (1968); and the Taunton Cider Co., having swallowed up some smaller cider companies, was eventually taken over by a consortium of breweries, largely at the instigation of Courage. This was later joined by Bass and other brewers and finally in 1971 Guinness also joined the consortium. There were occasional disadvantages in this development for Bulmers, who now controlled practically all the rest of the industry and something like half—sometimes more than half—the market. The concentration of licensed premises in fewer hands tended to squeeze prices and profits. It was increasingly difficult for Bulmers to get the brewers to accept new lines of cider in their tied houses, as they were already swamped by ones brought to them through mergers and take-overs. In 1959 the brewers in many cases rised the price of draught cider to their tenants, to the benefit of their own profits but to the detriment of sales.

Strong competition in sales and advertising naturally put pressure on Bulmers' financial resources. But with national consumption of beer something like 50 times that of cider, and with marketing arrangements so interlocked, the brewers were (and still are) for the most part content to continue their tolerant policy towards cider-makers. The opening of their tied houses to cider helped to increase overall sales. They made trading arrangements, for instance, to sell Bulmers' keg cider in these, which thus became the house brand of cider in various brewers' houses. Trading relations, despite an occasional confrontation, were generally friendly. In this respect Howard Bulmer played an important part; and well into the 1980s Bertram has regularly entertained parties of brewers.

We saw in Chapter Eleven how the Bulmer-Magner Company was established at Clonmel in County Tipperary as a separate company in which H.P. Bulmer & Co. had a 50% share. It flourished, and at one time was selling about 2,000,000 gallons of cider and Cidona a year. In 1946 Bulmers Hereford acquired the remaining 50% of the shares from Mr Magner; but since Irish law at that time did not allow a British company to own a majority of shares in an Irish concern, Irish nationals had to be found to fit the bill. A Mr. Thomas Jackson and a friend of his were introduced, and they thus controlled the company, which embraced Bulmers Ltd Clonmel, Pectin Ltd Clonmel and Apple Products Ltd Clonmel.

But troubles arose. In 1956 the British Government decided that they could no long allow very strong cider and perry to be sold without duty in competition with beer and wine, which were heavily taxed, and imposed a high duty on any of those products which contained more than 8 1/2% by volume of alcohol. Most of the firms that had been producing high alcohol products reduced the strength to below the level at which duty became payable, and Bulmers now felt that it would pay them to compete in the market for strong perry. The most popular brand was made by Showerings in Somerset and sold initially as 'Champagne de la Pomme' but from 1950 as 'Babycham', with enormous success. Bulmers, advised by their advertising agents, decided to market a rival product under the name of 'Chamlet', which they duly registered as their trade mark. Showerings belatedly decided to challenge this in the courts, briefing G. Aldous, Q.C., and a bizarre case ensued. Showerings alleged that the name 'Babycham' referred to a baby chamois which had indeed from 1953 appeared on their labels and in their literature; and further, that it was meant to suggest the fact that the perry was the *champ*ion of baby bottle products; but pressed by Bulmers' counsel, Sir Lionel Heald, Q.C., Mr. Showering conceded that they may have had champagne in mind as well. They also maintained that, since many customers in bars called for it by the abbreviation 'Cham', these would be liable to get Chamlet instead of what they wanted. For Bulmers Sir Lionel stated that they had decided on 'Chamlet' after long consideration. It was not an invented word but a famous old English word whose meaning had been the subject of considerable argument among experts.[1] It had no relation to the character of the goods, and therefore could legitimately be offered as a trademark. After five days of argument at this level, very expensive to both parties, Bulmers lost the case, and had to scrap all their labels, stocks and advertising material at further considerable costs.[2]

Bulmers then tried to continue the contest by marketing 'Godwin's Champagne Perry', named from the firm whose goodwill and title they had taken over in 1948 (see above), embellishing the name later with the prefix 'Golden'; but Golden Godwin Perry proved expensive to promote and never seriously competed with the well-established Babycham, so they soon withdrew from this field.

The rivalry with Showerings extended to Eire, with complicated legal and other repercussions. The upshot was, that Bulmers sold their interest in the branch at Clonmel to Mr Jackson for £27,000. This was a sad outcome in particular for Bertram Bulmer, who had been largely responsible for fostering the Clonmel enterprise. The final irony was that Jackson, shaken by a car accident and doubtful of his ability to carry on without the help of Bulmer expertise, sold the business to a consortium of Guinness and Allied Breweries. Allied Breweries, who owned Showerings, thus acquired Bulmers' Irish trademark; so that 'Bulmer's Cider' was produced in Eire by Showerings (Ireland) Limited, and Showerings incidentally led a cut in the price of cider in Britain to the detriment of Bulmers.

Meanwhile the company of Bulmers had begun, in 1948, itself to become a group, with the taking over of the Herefordshire company of Godwin's Cider Ltd and (temporarily) Hereford Transport Ltd. The name of the former was changed in February 1956 to Henry Godwin Ltd. When Godwin's went into voluntary liquidation there was a distribution to Bulmers of £28,375. (Its trademarks were retained, but its premises at Holmer were, for reasons of economy, used after 1960 only for storage.) In 1959 Bulmers acquired a majority shareholding in the Gloucestershire Cider Co. at Wickwar (formerly owned by Cheltenham Breweries), because this firm was about to amalgamate with Stroud Breweries by arrangement with Whitbreads, who were also taking a financial interest. Had Bulmers not been able to effect this arrangement their cider would have been excluded from most licensed premises within 30 or 40 miles of Hereford. Through it they also obtained an interest in the Creed Valley Cider Co., which increased their business in Somerset and Devon. Then, in the summer of 1960, the firm bought from Webbs (Aberbeeg) Ltd the goodwill of William Evans & Co. of Hereford, makers of 'Golden Pippin' cider and 'Elpex' pectin.[3] Of its premises only the vat house was taken over (eventually sold in 1967 for £12,000 to the Saunders Valve Co.). The result was that Bulmers' cider would be on sale at all Webbs' licensed premises. They enlarged their own pectin factory at Ryelands Street to provide for the business in this product previously done by Evans, their only competitor in Britain.

In the 1960s the policy of take-overs was stepped up, still chiefly within the ambit of the drink trade. In 1965 the firm bought all the issued share capital of the Tewkesbury Cider Co. Ltd, which gave it access to all the licensed properties of Ansell's Brewery. It also went into the wine business, at a time when the drinking of wine was becoming more popular in Britain. In September 1964 the firm of H. Parrot & Co. (London) Ltd. was divided into two companies trading separately under a parent company. H. Parrot & Co. (1964) Ltd. was to remain the agent in Britain for Veuve Cliquot champagne; Parrot (Wines and Spirits) Ltd, in association with H.P. Bulmer & Co., was to be agent for Liger-Belair Burgundy, Fonseca's Port Wines and P.F. Heering's Liqueurs. Adam Cochrane and Peter Heering were to be on the Board.[4]

Mary Bulmer had been right when she said that drink was one of the things that did not go out of fashion; but there was always the chance that a particular kind of drink might do so. Clearly the time had now come when some diversification would be prudent. In 1962 Bulmers established, for long-term purposes, two development companies, Ryelands (Hereford) Developments Ltd and Ryelands (Hereford) Properties Ltd. The former aimed at capital profit, the latter at income from rent (they were kept distinct for reasons concerning taxation). Next year the firm began discussions with several other firms with a view to acquiring products with a proven market.

Naturally one of their first investments was in hotels and public houses, and their earliest acquisition was most rewarding. The Red Lion is a half-timbered 14thC inn at Weobley, ten miles north-west of Hereford, characteristic of that most picturesque village. It was bought for £17,500, with garden, bowling green and outhouses (including a medieval 'cruck' cottage of considerable historical interest), looking down towards the tall, graceful church spire. It was restored and enlarged so as to be able to accommodate 80 for dinner or 150 for parties, and its cuisine so enhanced as to attract gourmets from far and wide. The firm used it extensively for purposes of entertainment, and it had bedrooms sufficient to accommodate guests for shooting parties, for instance. Bulmers produced in 1963 a 20-page booklet, *The Inns of Herefordshire*.

The resignation of Alan Hudson-Davies in 1945 and the death of Harold Robinson in 1946 left only three directors—Howard and Bertram Bulmer and Howard's cousin Edward Ball. Howard, besides being Chairman, was ultimately responsible for the sales side, Edward for the scientific and orcharding side, Bertram for everything else. At the beginning of 1947 they were joined by Adam Cochrane as Sales Director. In 1959 John McWhirter came as Sales Manager. Under him were Divisional Managers for the three Divisions Hereford, Northern and London, with nine areas under them and a total of 51 teams for the United Kingdom.

Harold James, who joined the company in March 1949 as Assistant Development Engineer, contributes vivid recollections of other principals at that time. Richard McBride was still company Secretary, 'a man of sterling silver' who had come from West Hartlepool in 1934. He instigated most of the improvements in the office, and was responsible for bringing into effect a pension scheme which compared favourably with those in most leading firms. He was of medium height, dapper and neat, with a toothbrush moustache and rather large cool-looking brown eyes; cautious, discreet, a late-marrier. He guarded with his life such secrets as who was paid what. Bertie Potts, who had joined a year before him, was Transport Manager, tall, well-built, smartly dressed, with gold-rimmed spectacles. Even on the rare occasions when he conformed to the democratic garb of the directors – sports coat and grey flannel trousers—he kept up his image by wearing an expensive-looking tie and shirt with cuff-links. His thinning brown hair was sleekly brushed back from a high-domed, balding pate. His demeanour was bustling. These recruits were now joined, in 1946, by Duncan MacCalman, an honours graduate in engineering, brought in from I.C.I. West Hartlepool as Works Manager; and he introduced from the same source Hans Barrow as Works Engineer and Bert Simmons as Foreman Engineer. Mac-Calman was a proud Highlander, implacable in his prejudices as he was firm in his loyalties. He was tall, pale and handsome, with a shock of grey hair. This team released Beach Thomas for the formidable task of putting into effect the company's ambitious schemes for Moorfields. MacCalman, Potts and McBride occupied as offices the three first-floor rooms looking out over Ryelands Street to what was then the garage for lorry maintenance (later the Advertising and Printing Departments). Harold James has mental images of locomotion at that time: Howard Bulmer in a modest Rover, Bertram in an Austin, MacCalman scorching in a Hillman, Potts in one of the first Volvos in Hereford, McBride on a bicycle.

Not all the memorable characters were so exalted. MacCalman was once looking out of a window with a colleague when he saw an attractive typist come into the yard. Four men there immediately stopped work and she went over to talk to them. MacCalman was about to remonstrate when his companion commented: 'That girl is responsible for more of our men not deserting to Wiggins than anyone else in the firm.' There was a man who looked after the store of barrels. He knew his barrels as a shepherd knows his sheep, and used to talk to them, saying to one, for instance: 'You haven't had an outing for some time; I think I'll allow you a trip now.'

James remembers the directors meeting every day in the panelled Board Room downstairs at Ryelands Street from 9.00 to 9.45 to go through the post, already sorted by the office staff. This meant that they kept their fingers on the pulse, even if there was some delay in the mail's reaching executives and relevant drawings sometimes got detached and went astray. It was an unobtrusive way of monitoring performance. If some firm, for instance, had had to send a reminder of a bill to be paid, Howard or Bertram would want to know why. The directors also inspected copies of every letter sent out by the firm.

McBride became a director in 1961. So did MacCalman, but he

died six months later. Richard Ankerson, whom Bertram Bulmer had recruited for the London Depot, came to Hereford after the War and was made Works Manager in 1962.

With the 1960s a younger generation began to be recruited to the Board. (James) Esmond and David, the two elder sons of Edward and grandsons of Percy Bulmer, were elected, in 1962 and 1964. Esmond, after schooling at Rugby and National Service with a commission in the Scots Guards, had graduated at King's College, Cambridge, with an Upper Second in both parts of the Historical Tripos. He also studied for a spell at the Gregorian University in Rome and the Sorbonne in Paris, and spent a year with Whitbreads and with the London Press Exchange, Bulmers' advertising agents. David, likewise educated at Rugby, after National Service with the King's Shropshire Light Infantry which took him to Kenya, was seconded to Schweppes for a time, and in 1962 had six months in America gaining experience in breweries and studying marketing and advertising methods. Bertram's second son, Giles, a few years younger than his cousins, joined the firm in 1962, after graduating with Honours in Natural Sciences at King's College, Cambridge.

Between 1948 and 1960 the turnover of H.P. Bulmer Limited increased steadily, with only three very slight hiccoughs, from £1,604,000 to £3,008,000. The net book value of fixed assets rose from £387,000 to £1,342,000. Pre-tax profits varied between £412,000 (1953) and £204,000 (1958), the average being about £336,000; but the gross ordinary dividend (as percentage of nominal share values) rose steadily from 20 to 35. Annual retained profits transferred to reserves varied from £68,000 (1958) to £183,000 (1955), the average being about £140,000.

From 1961 to 1965 the figures given were now for the whole group. Average turnover was £3,672,000 (maximum £4,190,000 in 1965); average value of fixed assets £1,628,000 (maximum £2,134,000 in 1965); average pre-tax profits £444,000 (maximum £590,000 in 1964). The ordinary dividend rose from 42 1/2 to 55. Average retained profits were £210,000 (maximum £292,000 in 1965).

The business was now so much larger and more complicated that in 1963 a budgeting control system was introduced, with the assistance of a firm of consultants, Binder, Hamlyn, Fry & Co. This helped to control costs and effect economies in all departments.

In November 1964 a further, far-reaching step was taken with the appointment of Peter J. Prior as Financial Director of the company, for not less than five years from the beginning of 1965. Turnover was now such that the company needed expert financial guidance brought in from the world of big business. Prior, aged 45, was recommended by the firm's London accountants. He had been educated at Wycombe High School and had graduated in economics at London University. During the War he had been commissioned in the Infantry and later in the Intelligence Corps, and had won the Croix de Guerre. He gave his recreations in *Who's Who* as free-fall parachuting, picture restoration, music, motor-cycling and steam locomotives. He was a Chartered Accountant, a Council Member of the British Institute of Management and an Associate of the Institute of Production Engineers. Among other activities, he had been seconded by the management consultants Urwick Orr and Partners to reorganise United Nations Refugee Camps, and had introduced planned maintenance for 60 overhead cranes in a boiler works. His present position was Financial Director of British Aluminium; but he would be glad to escape from London and commuting conditions and from functional to general management. His message to *Woodpecker News* was: 'Systems alone do not solve problems—only people can do that. Human relations are what really matter in business'; and he remarked of his new environment, 'There seems to be a family feeling about the place.'

At the end of 1965 Howard Bulmer retired as Chairman after 47 years with the Company, 24 of them as Chairman, though he remained on the Board until the end of 1967. He was presented on its behalf with a solid silver cider mug of 1766 magnificently embossed with a representation of apple picking (illustrated in *Woodpecker News* no. 11), by his oldest surviving fellow-worker, Len Bishop, who accounted for 47 of the 214 years devoted to its service by his family. Edward Ball retired simultaneously but consented to continue to give the company the benefit of his exceptional knowledge of orcharding, from which it had profited for 38 years. He had been a Governor of Long Ashton for several years, and from time to time a judge of cider at the chief shows, including the Royal. (He also served on the Hereford Diocesan Advisory Committee for 20 years and was a Trustee from its inception of the Herefordshire Historic Churches Trust, for some years its Honorary Treasurer). Adam Cochrane remained as Sales Director until December 1966. He had seen the sales force increase from about 40 to over 90, and sales multiply by a factor of more than eight, from one-third to nearly two-thirds of the national total.

In his speech on Howard's retirement from being Chairman Bertram took occasion to survey the changes that had occurred since Howard joined the firm in 1919, at a time when the end of Ryelands Street was still a place of apple trees.[5] Sales were at that time largely to private customers, and as to draught cider confined almost entirely to South Wales, Herefordshire and Worcestershire. Howard organised the sales force, and established friendly relations with brewers and other members of the trade. The value of Bulmers' sales was now 65 times what it had been then. Then there were two travellers; now there were 70 managers and representatives. Then there were two or three horse drays, taking cider to local customers and to the railway; now there were 250 lorries and cars working from 17 depots. Under his chairmanship the Moorfields site had been enlarged from 5 1/2 to 90 acres, and 500 more acres of land had recently been bought for cider orchards. The company had grown into a group formed by the inclusion of various other holdings.

Howard himself had been President of the firm's Sports Club for more than 20 years, and had always taken a special interest in the welfare of present and past employees. (This interest was to continue long after his retirement.) He had been appointed High Sheriff in 1940. In 1963 he had been elected Chief Steward of Hereford, an office going back at least as far as 1617, the qualification for which was defined in 1835 as to be 'an illustrious and discreet man'. He died at Longmeadow on 8 March 1985.

MOORFIELDS: EXTENSION AND PLANT

By far the most important activity of the firm in this period was the extension of the Moorfields site and its development. We have seen that before the outbreak of war in 1939 it had acquired about 7 acres in this area. In 1942 5.3 acres of land adjoining the Yazor Brook were bought from a Mr Howells for £1,625, and in 1943 about 2.6 acres on Plough Lane for £978 from a Miss Hopton and others. Plough Lane, which starts from the Plough Inn, Whitecross Road, about 200 yards west of the exit from Ryelands Street on the other side of that road, and runs N.N.E. towards Yazor Brook, was to become the main access road to the new works. Then in 1948 a 2.7 acre field adjoining the old Hereford and Brecon Railway line was bought from the Ecclesiastical Commissioners for £2,400. The firm had thus acquired a total of about 17 1/2 acres; but the estate remained, and remains, partially penetrated by the residential Mostyn Street, which runs parallel for 200 yards with Plough Lane and then makes a right-angle turn to run E.S.E. for a further 60 yards.

In 1945 the firm had submitted plans for the development of this estate to the City Council. In Town Map No.1 this area had been scheduled for residential use with open spaces, and permission had to be obtained for it to be rescheduled for industrial purposes. The general strategy that emerged was that most of the production of cider should be progressively transferred to the Moorfields site. There the production process should flow from the north end of the site, where the empties would be stored, to the south, where full cases of bottles would be stored, loaded and despatched.

In the post-war period, when it was not yet possible to obtain a licence to put up a new industrial building, it was nevertheless permissible to put up a second-hand one. Here the Scottish connections of the Works Manager, Duncan MacCalman, proved valuable. A redundant seaplane hangar at Greenock on the Clyde, measuring no less than 340 by 120 feet and 35 feet high to the eaves, was bought. Dismantled, it was transported to Hereford by Dawnays of Swansea, and re-erected lengthwise between Plough Lane and Mostyn Street as a storehouse for filled bottles. The total cost of the operation was £16,000. The proximity of houses at the corner of Mostyn Street was a problem, involving 'ancient lights' of the nearest house. But MacCalman had overcome this by agreeing to move Bulmers' fence back a yard from it, thus enabling the lady who lived there to drive a small car round and use a shed as a garage. This, and no doubt his charm and powers of persuasion, sufficed to avert a serious crisis. But when planning permission came, it was found that the City Surveyor made it subject to the provision that the black bitumen-painted iron walls should be repainted in green. Painting the 80,000 square feet of surface would have cost about £3,600, more than half what had been paid for the building itself, quite apart from the expense of renewal when the bitumen inevitably began to show through. The company appealed. The Government Planning Inspector appointed to adjudicate was taken by Bertram Bulmer to a good viewpoint. There he formed the opinion that black was the colour that would keep the building least conspicuous, and green would be sure to clash with nature's green, if not initially, when it faded. So another serious crisis was averted.

When the Government was able to permit new building, the immediate and most essential need was for a new mill and press house. This was designed, in association with the Hereford architects Powell and James, by Beach Thomas, who proved in retrospect to have been remarkably far-sighted.[6] Begun in 1948, it was completed by the end of of 1950. It was a square building about 100 yards from Whitecross Road, in line with Ryelands Street. It could be approached either from there through what is now the car park where the woodpecker sculpture stands or laterally from the north-west by Greenland Road, which leads from Mostyn Street.

Every consignment of apples was discharged on arrival into one of three trough-shaped canals, each with three compartments, let into the ground to facilitate unloading and charged with water by lateral flumes. Thence the apples were conveyed by water to one of two elevators, which raised them so that they could be dropped into a rotary drum for washing and then into the mills. The resultant pomace was pumped up into hoppers over the presses. There were eight presses with two press-beds each, arranged round a central axis. One tray was available for building up the pulp in cloths for pressing while the other tray-load was being pressed. After pressing the residue of pomace was passed by conveyor to six other presses for a second pressing. The resultant juice was then pumped through settling-vats in the adjoining vat-house to six concrete vessels housed there, each with a capacity of 80,000 gallons, named after famous cider apples such as 'Foxwhelp' and 'Kingston Black'. From there it was pumped through bitumen-lined mains, laid by Harold James, passing under Whitecross Road to the main vat-house on the old Ryelands site some 400 yards away, or to other vats on the Moorfields site. The residual pomace, after being dried, went to make pectin, and the pips to the orchards to grow seedlings and so complete the circle.

The new mill was capable of processing, with shift-work, 1,000 tons of apples in 24 hours, to produce 175,000 gallons of apple juice. The machinery it contained was claimed to be as great an advance in cider-making as the hydraulic press and power mill had been over the hand press and stone mill. One very beneficial effect was the reduction of the seasonal long queue of lorries in

Whitecross Road and Ryelands Street, through the speeding up in the reception of apples from the growers. By the 'permit' system the grower intimated when he was ready and the cider-maker told him when he might deliver. The underground mains meanwhile took tankers off the streets. One of the old presses at Ryelands Street was now allocated to pears, being used for apples at peak periods only. The other was converted for various purposes.

At 9.30 p.m. on 15 December 1950, a few days after the opening of the new mill, a schoolboy saw smoke rising and raised a fire alarm. Sacks of pomace were found to be ignited, and the fire brigades of Hereford, Leominster and Ross were summoned. Firemen had to crawl, wearing breathing apparatus, along the 80-foot high roofridge to uncover sections and allow the smoke to escape. A pall of acrid smoke then drifted over the north-east area of the city. Water which was being played from hoses on to the exterior froze in the winter air. It had in any case to be applied with selective care, for fear the pomace would swell and the floors collapse under the weight. Sacks of pomace had to be thrown out, and many of the singed ones burst into flame when lifted. Lorries queued up by floodlight to salvage the ejected pomace. Another section of the building, similar in size, had to be insulated with protective sheeting. It took 11 days more to clear away the smouldering sacks of pomace, about 10,000 of them, weighing 400 tons in all. However, when it was all over, the damage to the building proved to be limited, for the most part, to the holes the firemen had had to make.

In 1952 Canon Moor Farm, which lay beyond the north end of Plough Lane and the Yazor Brook and was let by the Ecclesiastical Commissioners to a Mr Raymond, was bought by Bulmers for £5,250. (It was commonly known as 'The Prairie', and is now traversed from north-east to south-west by Prairie Road.) This added 6.5 acres to the site, bring the total up to about 24 acres. To avoid flooding by the Yazor Brook the ground level had to be raised by several feet; 4,000 tons of earth and hardcore fill were put down, and consolidated by a vibratory machine. This meant considerable delay before the land could be used for building. On the land beyond Prairie Road between Widemarsh Brook and the footpath leading to Widemarsh Common were erected two large buildings for the bulk storage of pomace, each measuring 42 by 20 yards and capable of storing 1,200 tons.

In 1954 the first steel storage tank for cider was erected, made possible by the discovery of how such containers could be protected by wax. It was round, like a small gasholder or oil refinery tank, 45 feet high and 56 feet in diameter, and was believed to be the largest vessel in the world for the storage of any potable liquor, holding 550,000 gallons.[7] Designed basically by the company and constructed by Motherwell Bridge and Engineering Company, it took nearly six months to complete. It was then, after testing with water,[8] filled with cider at the rate of 8,000 gallons an hour. Two others followed in the winter of 1955-56, and by 1960 there were seven of these white giants, named after planets, in two groups ranged along the near side of the old railway line.[9] (An eighth, added in 1969, was named Apollo XI, after the American space-traveller, the planet Uranus being excluded for reasons which can only be guessed, and a ninth, named 'Taurus'.)

A word may be said here about relations between the company and the City Council. These could be amicable enough, as was shown by a Ceremony on 25 April 1955, when an Avery weighbridge, capable of weighing laden lorries of up to 30 tons, was installed on the north-east side of the new press house. The 573rd Mayor of Hereford, Mr T.W. Grimmer, was weighed against cider and registered 124 pints, and the combined county councillors of Herefordshire and Worcestershire were also weighed. Toasts were drunk in Pomagne, and also in Cidona to mark its reappearance after 16 years of interruption caused by the War. But ever since the hangar affair there had been some tension with the planning authority, who could be 'chivvied' up by the submission of an appeal whenever it failed to decide on any application within the statutory period of two months. There was also a section of the Council, sometimes a majority, which was obstructive of the company's plans for expansion. Some were not yet reconciled to the effects of the re-zoning of the Moorfields estate for industrial development. They were exercised about securing a playgound for the children of Mostyn Street (numbering about 20) and open spaces in general. Some allotments at the end of Mostyn Street were badly needed by the company for building in the heart of their site, next to the hangar. They were demonstrably under-used, but a *quid pro quo* was exacted, and can be seen today in the public plantation of trees beside Plough Lane to the south of the company's offices.[10]

There was controversy also about footpaths which would have to be diverted to fit the company's plans, and about danger to children using them at points where they were crossed by new roads. The footpaths were diverted, and footbridges were built at the company's expense. But obstruction had become so harassing that in March 1955 the company felt it had to force the issue. Bertram Bulmer requested a meeting with the planning committees of Leominster and Ross to discuss possible sites for industrial expansion. The prospect of potential jobs and wealth being diverted from Hereford elsewhere was too much for the opposition to face. To some extent personal feuds may have underlain the controversy, including even schism in a Scottish Dancing Club which Mac-Calman was involved with. But it would be unfair to discount genuine environmental concern.

The status of Plough Lane was now regulated by an agreement made between the Corporation and Bulmers on 27 January 1957. The Corporation could at any time move the company's fence from its present position to an agreed one. It would execute such street works as were necessary to extend the lane, free of charge to the company, and thereafter maintain it as a highway repairable by the inhabitants at large. The use of Plough Lane for industrial traffic would relieve the residential Mostyn Street.

The next major building required was a bottling plant to deal with the expanding sales of cider and Cidona and to provide for the new 'baby'-sized bottles. Bottling machinery is on a similar line throughout the drink industry, but Bulmers' new line claimed to be the largest and most advanced in the world. It was erected in 1957, at the end of Plough Lane on the right just short of the Yazor Brook, part of which was now covered over. A processing department contained the whole chilling, carbonating and filtration plant. There was an administrative block, extensive stores, and a new heating chamber to house two boilers. The electrical work was all carried out by the works staff. The whole complex cost about £100,000. By the end of the year it was in use, enabling most bottling operations to be transferred from Ryelands Street to Moorfields.

The bottling plant dealt primarily with returned bottles. It had two lines, capable of dealing, for 24 hours a day, with 800 dozen flagons of Woodpecker cider, and 2,000 baby bottles of Golden Godwin Sparkling Perry an hour. The cider was pumped

400 yards from the main storage vessels, still at Ryelands Street, through bitumen-lined mains into 6,000- gallon receiving vats lined with Prodor-Glas. The depalletising of crates was manual. This was followed by automatic removal of bottles from the crates, cap removal, label removal, washing, filling with cider, recapping, cap tightening, capsuling (if required) and recrating. Finally, the crated bottles were passed by conveyor to the 'fulls' store (the hangar). To take stress off the refrigerator, very cold water was supplied, at the rate of 10,000 gallons an hour, from a newly sunk well near by, which also supplied the condenser unit in summer.[11]

The ratio of building area to open space on the Moorfields site was satisfactory; but anxiety about overcrowding and room for expansion was vastly relieved in October 1959 by the acquisition from Mr J.W. Matthews for £34,500 of Red Barn Farm. It had been clear for some time that the company would require some 26 more acres of land. New land was urgently needed to accommodate the cider business which was being taken over in 1960 from William Evans, whose existing factory, covering 11 acres, was unsuitable for integration. Negotiations were protracted. The owner had intended to use the land for developing a housing estate. The City Council wanted to acquire it for development into an industrial estate, to provide a school, etc. Discussions proved abortive, and Bulmers finally bought the whole farm, of about 66 acres, from under the nose of the Council, which had intimated to Mr. Matthews that it intended compulsory purchase. The southern part of it, between the Yazor and Widemarsh Brooks and adjoining the Yazor Brook at the westward end of the site, consisted of low-lying fields liable to flooding which could not be used for building without very great cost and delay. It had to be regarded as a long-term reserve. In 1969 the company owned 82.4 acres at Moorfields, of which 29.25 had been developed. An area of 11.25 acres was designated to be released as site for a school; so 41.9 acres remained for long-term development by the company.

At the beginning of the same year, 1959, the company had bought from P. Bolt & Son, for £4,600, 2.4 acres of land on the east side of Plough Lane, south of the hangar, between it and Briggs' tyre factory on Whitecross Road. This land had been zoned on the original Town Map partly as a shopping area, partly as an open space, and it was only after some resistance from the City Council that it was re-zoned for industrial purposes. Meanwhile another claim on space had emerged in the firm. One symptom of the increased prosperity of the workforce was the proliferation of the number of car owners amongst its members. In 1946 the number had been 8. It rose gradually from 31 in 1947 to 64 in 1958. There was adequate parking space for these; but by February 1959 the number had increased to 111, and by November 1960 to 183. At a Works Advisory Committee meeting complaint was made of the inadequacy of the parking space provided. In the neighbourhood outside the factory gates there was room for about 65, and accommodation was needed also for visitors, who totalled about 3,000 a year. The council gave permission in 1962 for just over an acre of this newly acquired land to be allocated to car parking. This provided space for 220 cars, an absolute minimum – indeed already inadequate. A park for lorries was also urgently required. Space for this was found on the Canon Moor Farm site, beyond the end of Plough Lane and the Yazor Brook. A central main garage for works vehicles, designed by Harold James and Bertie Potts, was established in 1955 between the two rows of storage tanks. Enlarged and equipped with modern plant, it was greatly admired.

An area of Red Barn Farm further to the west was designated for the production of apple juice drink. In 1963 a new oil-fired drier for pomace was installed on the north-west side of the press-house. The dried pomace was blown by a pneumatic pipe-line for a distance of 60 yards directly into the stores, with a substantial saving of labour, bags and transport gear. At the same time a new boiler, also oil-fired, was installed near the north-east side of the hangar, with a steaming capacity of 10,000 lb an hour (twice that of the existing one) for the present and future needs of the bottling plant.

By 1962 storage capacity had increased to 11,500,000 gallons. This included 558,000 in Ebon-lined concrete tanks at the Widemarsh vat cellar taken over with William Evans and Co.

In June 1963 there was a heat wave. This and news of a forthcoming price increase tested to the utmost the capacity of the new bottling plant. But buffer stock, stored mainly in the hangar but also in space normally used for pomace, was at its highest: nearly 200,000 bottles were ready for despatch. For the rest, the situation was met by maximum overtime worked by the permanent staff, and by the part-time women in the daytime up to 9.30pm. The new flagon-line broke all records for a day on 20 June, when 6,477 dozen bottles were filled. This represented 98% efficiency; and even the old, smaller lines at Ryelands Street achieved more than 90%. By the end of June buffer stocks were very low, but they held out. The department now handled 18 varieties of liquor in 32 different packs, on 11 production lines.

What was left on the Rylands Street site? Pectin, for one thing. A new two-storey department for it was erected over the old cooper's shop. The plant, enlarged to take over the Elpex business acquired from William Evans & Co. in 1960, was one of the largest pectin plants in Europe, capable of producing 25,000 tons of liquid pectin a year. A new evaporator, of stainless steel, was installed there in 1962, capable of concentrating over 1,000,000 gallons of apple juice each season and available during the rest of the year for processing pectin. Apart from storage of pomace, all the process took place at Ryelands Street. This department replaced the Engineering Stores, which in turn took over the premises of the Heavy Engineering Section. The latter moved to an area of Moorfields between the press house and the Yazor Brook—a step towards concentrating all the engineering trades there. There were still storage vats at Ryelands Street, and Pomagne,[12] perry and the non-alcoholic drinks were made there; and various operations such as filling and despatch of cider in wooden casks and 'polycasks' still took place there. Easily separated units such as the laboratory and the drawing office remained there; but the general offices moved to the main site at Moorfields, providing a site eventually for the Cider Museum. The laboratories, much expanded in size and staff since Durham's day, monitored products at all stages and tried to improve them, tested new materials for possible use, eliminated waste and gave technical advice to customers when required. During this period, according to Dr W.W. Beech of Long Ashton, cider research dealt initially with juice composition, then with changes taking place during fermentation, and latterly with factors controlling flavour formation. The future of the cider industry depended on a complete understanding of the chemistry, micro-biology and biochemistry concerned. Bulmers were fortunate in having a tradition from Durham maintained by scientists such as Ball and Nelson. At the end of this period there were 20 scientists working in seven laboratories each with its own task, under F.J. Buckle, a Cambridge Ph.D. who had joined in 1948.

FRUIT

As soon as the war in Europe was over, Bulmers were able to resuscitate their scheme for producing cider apple trees and distributing them to growers. Some 17,000 were planted in 1945. But the national situation as regards such trees was more parlous than ever. In 1945 the Ministry of Agriculture estimated that, while there were 265,000 cider apple trees in the United Kingdom under nine years of age, there were 1,925,000, more than seven times as many, which were over that age, a large proportion of them probably by now barren.[13] To produce the anticipated output of cider for 1947 (20,000,000 gallons, nearly 50% more than before the war) the industry would need 100,000–125,000 tons of cider apples (the average for 1923–36 had been 66,250), plus a certain proportion of cull apples. Planting of new orchards had been failing to keep pace with expected requirements even before the war-time suspension. Such young trees as there now were had not reached the transplanting age, and it took 4–5 years to produce a tree suitable for transplanting into a grass orchard.

On 2–3 October 1947, the first major conference on cider fruit production to be held in England took place at Hereford. There was an exhibition of cider fruit at the Shire Hall and an inspection of the County Trial Orchard at Burghill. It was generally recognised that in Herefordshire, as elsewhere, the acreage of farm cider orchards was falling and the remainder deteriorating, while the consumption of cider was increasing and demand far exceeded the local supply of fruit. Professor B.T.P. Barker of Long Ashton made an authoritative speech on 'The Future of the Cider Industry and Cider Apple Production'. He warned that if farmers did not co-operate with their customers in improving the marketability of their products, specialist orchards would have to be established; and indeed some cider-makers were already establishing such orchards for themselves. Mr A.E. Baldwin, M.P. for Leominster, pointed out that it was no good for landlords to plant trees if their tenants would not care for them properly; on the other hand they should not feel justified in raising their rents immediately on the plea of having planted trees, when these would not bear an appreciable crop for about 10 years.

Bulmers' contribution to the conference included a demonstration by Bertram of their King's Acre orchards, a talk by George Wood on 'Orchard Lay-out and Planning' and an important paper by Edward Ball on 'Nursery of Cider Apple Varieties'. Bulmers had planted about 60 acres of bush type trees at King's Acre. (These consisted mostly of imported *Médaille d'Or* bittersweet: it blossomed late, in June, and so escaped frost damage; it was self-fertilising; and being resistant against aphis and caterpillar it needed no spraying; but it was vulnerable to apple-blossom weevil, and its branches were brittle.)

Bush trees have already been described. Barker spoke of them as being still at the experimental stage, and recommended them, but not for ordinary farmers, for whom he considered they required too much skill and attention: they were for specialists. But commercial growers should learn about them. They produced five tons or more of apples to the acre after 7-10 years, when their quality was already as good as that of apples from 'standards' aged 40-50 years.[14] Actually, of 2,358 trees sold by Bulmers to growers in 1947-48,560 already were 'bush', and of 3,132 sold in 1949-50 no less than 2,142 were 'bush'. (Some of these went to Bulmer Clonmel.) As a result of the cider-makers' efforts the tonnage of apples to the acre began to increase.

In a paper on 'Cider Orchard Restoration in Herefordshire; 1923-1947', published in 1947 in the *Journal of the Ministry of Agriculture*, Edward Ball made a forecast about planting needs for the next 25-30 years, on the premise that trees planted before the beginning of the firm's scheme in 1927 would disappear in about 40 years' time from now. Up to the present less than one-third of the trees needed had been planted. Rather more than 5,000 trees a year would have to be planted in 1947-51 if supplies of apples were to be adequate for the period 1966-81. The scheme would be completed by 1966, but a renewal scheme would have to begin about 1985. In the event, by 1960 Bulmers were selling between 5,000 and 10,000 trees a year at very low prices to farmers in the area. The cumulative total of trees they had sold by 1970 was about 300,000 (260,000 standard and 40,000 bush).

In 1951 the acreage order of the leading cider-orchard counties was Devon, Somerset, Hereford. Ten years later it had been reversed, Hereford accounting for a third and the other two for a quarter each of national output; and by 1970 Hereford accounted for three-sevenths. According to the *Financial Times* for 10 November 1965, it was the only county in which planting policy seemed to be making good. But what Barker had foretold in 1947 was gradually coming to pass: cider orcharding was generally becoming concentrated in the hands of fewer, specialised growers, who could hope to make it pay.

Bulmers in 1965 took more than four-fifths of the West Midlands cider apple production. Nevertheless, according to *The Times* for 5 December 1966, the 3,200 growers in Herefordshire were anxiously considering how they could treble the productivity of their trees. It was estimated that only six of the growers achieved 3 1/2 tons of apples an acre, while more than 3,100 achieved less than 37 cwt. Bulmers on the other hand claimed that on a test plot their trees had been producing more than 10 tons an acre over a seven-year period.

They were now appointing an Orchard Manager (A.R.B. Neame), and were hoping to plant up 1,500 acres more in the next few years. In 1965 they acquired Monnington Court Farm, of 465 acres, at Monnington-on-Wye, between Hereford and Hay, most of which was to be used for orchards of required varieties of apple grown from budded seedlings.[15] In October 1965 they also bought the Moorhampton Farm House estate of 68 acres in the parish of Yazor on the Hereford–Weobley road. An outside firm of consultants was employed to survey their orchards in 1966. The object was, not to displace farmers, but to obviate the necessity of relying in some years on imports from France; and in fact it had orders in hand from farmers for 3,000–4,000 trees.

One question raised at the 1947 conference presaged dissensions ahead. At the beginning of the century English cider apples fetched about £1 10s a ton. By the outbreak of the First World War Bulmers were paying £2 (£4 if delivered to the factory). In 1919 the price was £3 15s and it varied about that figure between the wars. We have seen that during the Second World War the Government stepped in, setting the maximum price at £18 3s 4d a ton in 1941–42 and £14 in 1943–46. Growers had now come to expect some such return, and with the prospect of emergency government control being lifted they began to press for a guaranteed minimum price. The cider-makers' spokesman, Mr Bufton, replied that they had been offered one for the next 5–10 years, but the National Farmers' Union had rejected it. The cider-makers urged that comparison should be made with pre-war prices, not with emergency prices imposed in conditions of scarcity. The only card the growers had in their hand was the threat of ceasing to grow cider apples unless they could be made more profitable and either going over to 'cull' apples or grubbing up their orchards altogether (a process actually subsidised by the Government in the interests of growing more food). But this card was trumped in 1948 by the removal of the ban on importing. (Bulmers imported 3,521 tons in that year out of a national total of 6,335, though at a cost, after transport expenses, of more than £19 a ton.)

In the event, after the removal of Government price control in 1948, a gentleman's agreement between the National Farmers' Union and the National Cider Makers' Association fixed the price at £14 again, but for 1949 only. 1950 proved a disastrous year for the growers; for after a big crop in 1949 a record one in 1950 filled the cider-makers' vats and left the growers with 20,000 tons of apples wasted out of about 55,000. At the same time conditions were difficult in the cider industry. Money was tighter. Sales were down, and it was not thought feasible to increase them by lowering retail prices. So negotiations broke down, and contracts were made with individual growers, at about £10 a ton. The price offered for 1952 by the N.C.M.A. was a minimum of £10 for five years, as against £14 demanded by the N.F.U. But this was for mixed apples. For genuine cider apples Bulmers offered £12 10s *if delivered to the factory*.

In 1953, when the crop was large and of good quality, Bulmers received a record quantity of apples for any one week, 4,680 tons, all from Herefordshire and adjoining counties. That October Bertram spoke reassuringly to the Herefordshire branch of the County Landowners' Association. Consumption of cider had altered little in the past 40 years, he said.[16] Cider apple prices were unlikely to fall because then growers would lose interest: falls would have to be very drastic before they decided to grub up their orchards. There were no signs of over-production. At present Bulmers were short of storage space, but they would soon have new vats. Before the War they had imported half their fruit. Now imports were much lower, and could be further reduced. As things turned out, the average price paid for cider apples in the period 1950–1966 remained about £12 50s (for perry pears the figure was a little over £10).

As for the importing of apples, the Minister of Food stated in Parliament in August 1950 that there had been none since May 1949. The regulation of 1931 arising out of Fred Bulmer's intervention behind the scenes at the Ottawa Conference was still in force, by which imports were only exempt from a heavy duty in years when sufficient home-grown apples were not available to cider-makers. The English crop was good in 1949, still better in 1950, and a record in 1951, and Bulmers imported no apples from 1949 to 1953. But in 1957 the crop failed over nearly all Europe, and French apples had to be bought at more than double the usual price in the autumn of 1958 when stocks of cider in English vats were running low. But in 1959–61 and 1963 there were again no imports. Variations in the English crop from year to year were considerable. Thus while in 1960 it was the lowest for many years, in 1962 it was a record. By exceptional exertions continuing into the New Year all the local crop of that year was absorbed, and all the storage vats filled with good cider. The total tonnage of fruit delivered to the works ranged from 17,510 in 1948 and 19,307 in 1957, to 39,378 in 1952 and 47,910 in 1962. In a good season like 1952 Herefordshire farmers could get about £500,000 for their cider apples. The 25-year-old planting scheme was paying off.

In the speech already cited the Minister mentioned that some cider had been imported for blending. In fact 1,833,243 gallons had been imported in 1949,1, 048,227 of this total going to Bulmers. Cider production in France was 20 times that of England, but exports were limited by the high level of consumption there, and by palatal differences. Nevertheless between 1949 and 1958 Bulmers imported from France for blending purposes amounts varying from 585,287 gallons in 1951 (costing £19,137) to 1,760,124 in 1953 (costing £72,881).

Concentrated apple juice was also imported, to relieve pressure on storage space.[17] Amounts had been small until 1939, when 100,345 gallons were bought in for precautionary stocking up in anticipation of war, and they were negligible during the war; but they reached nearly 400,000 gallons in 1948, to meet the demand for cider that followed the end of rationing. After that none was imported until 1956, but by 1959 the amount had risen again to over 300,000 gallons, and similar figures were recorded in several years of the 1960s, the cost being then about 12s a gallon.

PRODUCTS AND MARKETING

This may be the place to review the products of the firm as they were in the early 1960s. First the alcoholic drinks.

[18] The medium-sweet WOOD-PECKER was claimed to be the most popular cider in the world. Carbonated, it was sold in flagons (imperial quart, 40oz.) and half-flagons, with internal screw stopper and rubber ring; also in half-pint bottles with crinkly metal crown cork and in cans. In still form, it was sold in flasks, jars and two-gallon 'polyjars' (jars of polythene). It was also sold in litre bottles (35.2oz) with an aluminium cap. These bottles were not returnable, because the supermarkets they were produced for were not prepared to handle empties, and supermarkets now accounted for an increasing proportion of the trade.

DRY CIDER, less sweet than Woodpecker, was also available, and No.7, a very dry, still cider with no remaining sugar content, was sold in 'smalls' and was particularly recommended for diabetics. Popular taste still demanded the traditional light medium-sweet cider: the dry and more strongly flavoured was an acquired taste, which was perhaps ultimately more constant for that.

POMAGNE, sweet or dry, made of carefully selected vintage fruit, remained the favourite Cider de Luxe, as a table drink or for celebratory occasions, with a faithful clientele.[19] It was sold in what looked like champagne bottles, displaying the year of vintage like superior wines, with protruding corks secured with wire. Pomagne was also bottled from 1955 in 'baby' bottles, in the attempt to compete with Showerings' Babycham; but sales proved disappointing, and advertising of it was soon confined to certain not unpromising areas. German Panzer troops stationed in 1962 at Castlemartin in Carmarthenshire were said to have taken a great liking for Pomagne.

STRONGBOW, a strong dry cider, sold in the same sort of bottles as Woodpecker, was launched in 1960. Its name was a happy inspiration, and it soon established itself. Supported by heavy advertising, it proved a great and lasting success.

DRAUGHT cider (dry, medium dry or sweet) was sold in casks of 6–10 gallons if it was still, of 6–30 if it was 'conditioned', i.e. given briskness by the addition of a small quantity of yeast to impart a slight fermentation in the cask. The unit could deal with 2,000 casks a day. Still draught cider was also sold in half-gallon 'flasks', in one-gallon jars or in two-gallon polythene jars. In

1965 6,500,000 gallons of draught cider were made in Britain to 13,900,000 of bottled, and the gap was to widen dramatically after that.

Bottling cider, blended and sweetened to meet customers' needs, was also delivered in bulk to bottlers, who carried out their own bottling using Bulmers labels overprinted with their own name and address or coded for identification.

PERRY was sold in flagons. The attempts to exploit 'Golden Godwin Sparkling Perry' in 'baby' bottles as a rival to Babycham proved short-lived. So did LIMELIGHT, a lime-flavoured sparkling perry sold in baby bottles which was introduced in 1960 with considerable advertising expenditure.

The chief non-alcoholic drink from apples was the sparkling CIDONA, carbonated at 2 1/2 volumes with carbon dioxide and sweetened with sugar and saccharin. Almost strangled at birth by the war, it was revived in 1955. The cheaper CIDAKIN, a legacy from Godwin's, was also marketed then, a sparkling apple drink, one part apple concentrate and six parts carbonated water, delivered to bottlers to bottle under their own label. A large contract for this was made with Messrs Thomas & Evans. By 1959 Bulmers were getting an ever-increasing share of the expanding market for such products, but they had to compete not only with similar apple drinks but with the more thirst-quenching citrus fruit drinks; and when in 1961 sales failed to respond to a warm summer it was decided that, while continuance with the lines was still worthwhile, intensive advertising and sales promotion of them was not.

Simple apple juice has long been a popular drink in Germany, Switzerland, France and Canada. Production of it from dessert apples at Bulmers began in 1936, and by 1939 over 200,000 gallons had been produced. Then war came, and the Ministry of Food barred production till 1947 (apples were needed to make jam for the Forces). The background in England was not encouraging, but in 1960 Bulmers began marketing pure bottled apple juice, each bottle the produce of 1 1/2 lb of apples, with no sugar or preservatives but enriched with Vitamin C, under the name of APPLE JOY. A special drive for it was made in south coast towns, but progress was slow. Enough fruit was available for foreseeable demand, but demand would be the dominant factor, not just chance occurrence of surplus apples.

Concentrated apple juice, reduced by a factor of nine, was also marketed.

Of other products PECTIN was by far the most important. Production, which had reached 971 tons in 1939, leapt forward to 2,419 in 1941 and by 1948 had reached 8,186. Powdered pectin came in after the Second World War, and was much in demand for confectionary; also for export, since its concentration greatly reduced weight and bulk. It was 30 times as strong as the liquid pectin supplied in barrels. In 1958 the firm was spending large sums on research to improve its quality, reduce costs and find new uses for it. It now became profitable to use imported citrus peel, already dried, as well as the residue of cider apples. The best source of pectin is lime peel, and competition for this was fierce, since lime trees grow only in a quite narrow belt of latitude. In 1962 Bulmers made an agreement with L. Rose & Co., the well-known manufacturers of Lime Juice (a subsidiary of Schweppes). Lime peel, which had previously been treated as waste, was dried and shipped from Ghana to Hereford; and an oil-fired rotary dryer like those at Hereford was installed by Bulmers out there at Asebu in the Central Region for their company, Rombeluse Limited. With a monopoly in Britain after William Evans was taken over, pectin was accounting in 1965 for £494,000, or 11.3% of the company's sales.

PECTA PUREE for stabilising and thickening sauces was also made. And finally, the residue of the pomace after the pectin had been extracted was sold in cube form for cattle-feed. Giles Bulmer visited the West Indies and parts of the United States and Central America in 1965 in connection with pectin, to study methods of processing citrus fruit for its manufacture.

Odd indications of favour for Bulmers' cider crop up in news items. We hear of its being the only cider carried by the Royal Yacht *Britannia*. Six casks of sweet cider are ordered for the Harvest Supper at St Martin's in the Fields. The Admiral commanding the American Sixth Fleet was a customer for Pomagne.

Which? magazine for December 1964 (pp. 365-7) investigated cider and perry, of which about 20,000,000 gallons a year were at that time drunk in England. It set out to examine for alcoholic content drinks so described and tested 46 bottled or canned varieties. Bulmers' ranged from Woodpecker Special Quality at 4.0%, costing 1s 3 3/4d a pint, to sparkling Pomagne Cider de Luxe at 8.1%, costing 5s 4 3/4d a pint. Showerings' 'Babycham' (dry) rated 8.2% at 7s 6d a pint.

Purchase tax and increased costs and wages had caused prices to be increased from July 1963, but for some years after that, though costs rose steeply in 1967 and purchase tax was increased by 20%, the price of Woodpecker, accounting for about half of Bulmers' sales, was kept unaltered.

Advertising of major products became more intensive and more imaginative in this period. Some of it concentrated as before on simply plugging the name. Many spectators of football matches, a vast number when these are televised, take in consciously or subconsciously the word 'Strongbow', staring at them in huge letters from the barrier behind the thrower-in on the touchline. Sometimes the name was attached to a picture suggesting ideas to be associated with it. A girl shown in the *News of the World* in 1953, neatly but not expensively dressed, had the simple caption, 'Say Bulmers for Cider'. There was some competitive aggression. On 10 June 1955 the *Hereford Times* carried an outrageous instance: 'In Hereford everyone is asking for Whiteways.' Bulmers could only counter a week later with a picture of an attractive girl with a 'pom' dog and the caption, 'The smartest girls in Hereford are asking for Baby-Pom' (Pomagne in 'baby' bottles).

When Cidona was reintroduced in 1955 salesmen were instructed that they should not take the initiative in 'knocking' competitors, but that there was no harm in saying that Cidona should appeal, for instance, because it was sweeter than Cydrax, or that if Corona claimed to be a good drink for children, Cidona was a drink that *all* the family could enjoy together. It was associated with a particular character, 'The Cidona Boy', shown not only as a member of a family but cruising on a bicycle or roller-skates, or sitting on a horse or wall, with the caption, 'Sweet sparkling apple drink that all the family could enjoy'.[20]

The drive to persuade the public that cider was not just a drink for yokels but a table or party drink suitable for all occasions, ages and classes, had made considerable progress. The suggestion that it was a more lady-like drink than beer was now followed by the suggestion that strong, dry cider was a drink for he-men. It was with publicity on these lines that Strongbow was launched in 1960; and special attention was paid to the 18–26 age-group, which was now earning higher wages than before, in many cases not yet absorbed by the expenses of matrimony. Motorcyling clubs adopted it, such as branches of what were later to call themselves 'Hell's Angels'.

In October 1953 B.B.C. cameras came to film at Bulmers, to make a documentary entitled 'Cider Apples Go to Press' for the 'Television Newsreel' programme, with Godfrey Baseley as commentator—not strictly advertising, which was barred, but all the more effective. Two years later a new era in advertising began, with Independent Television, financed by 'commercials'. Bulmers were quick to seize the opportunity. A very popular trio, The Beverley Sisters, were engaged to put across with all their blandishments the following song:

Bring out the Bulmers' cider,
    That's the cider I adore.
Bring out the Bulmers' cider:
    I couldn't ask for more.
See how it sparkles like my eyes.
    Pour me the cider I idolise.
Bring out the Bulmers' cider,
    The cider that satisfies.
(First six lines repeated).
Bring out the Bulmers' cider,
    It makes me feel so bright,
Bring out the Bulmers' cider,
    We'll have a ball tonight.

'Whetting your whistle with Woodpecker cider' was the theme of another song.

The opening of Bulmers' new bottling plant at the end of 1957 was proclaimed to all the regions by the equally famous actress Diana Dors. A photograph in the *Hereford Times* for 11 April 1958 showed her at her home being presented by David Bulmer with a huge silver-lined Easter egg full of 'baby' bottles of sparkling Golden Godwin Perry, for her part in the firm's new television series begun a week before.

Another form of promotion was the offering of rewards for collecting of Bulmers' labels. A bizarre example, claimed (not surprisingly) to be a 'world first', was The Bulmers Do-it-yourself Comedian's Kit, launched at the Carlton Towers Hotel in London in October 1963, and fully described both in B.B.C. 'Woman's Hour' and on Southern and Border Television, and referred to by Robert Robinson in 'Points of View'. It was widely reported in the British Press, and even noticed by *Combat Paris* (which, however, predictably, indeed pardonably, got the whole thing wrong). The account in *Punch* ran as follows: 'For the usual collected labels and a small sum in cash purchasers of a currently advertised commodity also get a gramophone record full of jokes by a name comic in which the pay-off line is missing; with the disc, a script with the pay-off. You just read out the last line of each joke and – hey presto!—YOU are a star comedian.' The disc, scripted by Bob Monkhouse and Denis Goodwin, played for 12 minutes, including built-in laughs. The stooge who fed the material to the owner was Monkhouse.

Packaging was also important. As the *Financial Times* said (10 November 1965): 'Bulmers in particular have been experimenting with new types of packaging, to break down cider's image as a cheap drink suitable only for bucolic rustics or, in the gassy bottled form, as an escape-route for beer-haters in the saloon bar.'

A film 'The Cider Story' was made for showing to visitors to the works and for letting out by Film Libraries to schools, youth clubs, etc. In the B.B.C. Television quiz 'What's My Line?' Bulmers' Nursery Manager, Geoffrey Potter, survived eight questions before being run to earth by Isobel Barnett and identified as a Cider Apple Grower.

Following consumer research an intensive advertising campaign was launched in 1964. Radio Luxembourg played a prominent part because its popular music attracted a large audience of young people, and commending cider to the young was an important element of the strategy. Television in the south-east of England was another chosen medium, it being known that cider, perhaps for climatic reasons, had more appeal to the south than to the north.

There was a national press campaign throughout the summer of 1964 which was designed to emphasise that the new but now established Strongbow came from the same place as the long popular Woodpecker. It was hoped that if their different virtues were compared, even in competition, by a sort of 'dialectical' synthesis a higher image of Bulmers would emerge. So a test called 'Operation Oxford' was mounted, centring on an election in which 2,000 members of the public attended a Free Tasting at the Town Hall and registered their votes. The campaign opened with a Cider Parade on 9 May through the centre of Oxford. This was led by 'The Baton-Hi Girls', who were followed by a luxury launch float, which was to be the first prize in a competition. During the whole period Oxford buses carried a long banner with the words 'It's quicker by boat—Win one from Bulmers'. Just what the competition involved is not clear, but the launch was duly handed over at Salter's Boatyard by Esmond Bulmer to the winner, a N.A.A.F.I. furniture fitter. There was also a Best Talent Competition, won by King Cobra and the Rattlesnakes. Top seals from Woodpecker or Strongbow bottles were used as tickets for a raffle with 20 prizes entitled 'Win with Oxford United'. 38 off-licences had window displays on Bulmer products. July 1 was Strongbow Day, when in almost all public houses twenty half-pints of Strongbow were offered free (with the result, it was claimed, that the public house sales of Strongbow were doubled in Oxford).

The intensive advertising campaign of 1964 in the national press and on television in the south-east was considered to have justified itself by results, and the firm decided to continue it in 1965, with more colour advertising, notably full pages in the *Sunday Times, Reader's Digest* and *Weekend*. For the television campaign opening in March there was a new commercial, made at the hotel at Boulter's Lock on the Thames in the previous September—made not without difficulty, as the week chosen proved to be the only really wet one in the summer, and the 50 people involved had to be paid to wait until the sun shone, though some useful shots were taken inside the hotel.

Let us now turn to exports. In 1947 the wartime ban on exporting cider was lifted, and four years later Bulmers' exports were the highest since the war. In 1956 they were again a record, and more than double what they had been in 1938. So far, so good. But were they as large as they might have been? Prospects in the United States were still frustrated by the classification of British cider with wines for purposes of excise. But a report in the *Western Daily News* for 11 November 1952 gave a bullish account of exports of *Devon* cider, claiming that in the West Indies it competed with American Coca-Cola, that it was increasingly popular in East and West Africa, and that several Middle Eastern countries were acquiring a cider palate. (Which? Not Moslem ones presumably.) Bulmers had agents at least in the West Indies – in Barbados, Dominica, St Kitts, Grenada and St Lucia, islands described in an article in *Woodpecker News* for September 1963; also, for instance, in Bahrein and Portuguese Guinea. An order for canned cider was received from St Helena. Cidona in concentrated form was exported 12,000 miles by sea to Fiji. But there remains the question: were Bulmers ever as successful overseas as they might have been?

In 1963 Esmond Bulmer, recently appointed a director, gave an account in *Woodpecker News* of a visit to Moscow. He reported that, while it was hard to do business with such slippery customers, there was undoubtedly a market behind the Iron Curtain for pectin, and perhaps for Pomagne, at least if Bulmers were prepared in return to market Vodka and some other Russian products. (In fact Britain's first export order for powdered pectin for Europe was secured in 1966, when Bulmers shipped to Gdynia for Poland 10 tons of it, for which they received £8,000. This order was obtained in competition with the United States, France, Italy and Denmark.)

EMPLOYEES

Let us try to see Bulmers' workforce in local perspective, in the light of the situation in 1957 as reviewed by a County Council inquiry of 1960. The population of the city was 33,000, expected to rise to 45,000 by 1971. It was not intended that it should become primarily a manufacturing city. When local employers were asked how much extra land they were likely to require for future industrial purposes, most replied 'none', but Bulmers replied, '30 acres'. Of the total of insured employees in 1957 only 28.7% were engaged in manufacture, and even with some new metal industry the figure was unlikely to rise above 35%, as against a national average of 41.7%. Nearly 10% were engaged in the manufacture of food and drink.

Bulmers employed between 1,000 and 1,200 at Hereford in the cider-making season. To these must be added several hundred employed at the depots, as lorry-drivers or as agents. Arthur Morris, the Personnel Manager, told the Rotary Club in 1959 that, with the installation of new machinery the firm had been able recently to draw for seasonal workers on purely local sources. A year later, however, we hear of 23 workers being brought over from Waterford in Ireland, for night-shift work only. (Previously such workers had stayed at the Hillside Hostel, but accommodation was now scarce, and Bulmers had to arrange the billeting themselves.) The canteen at Ryelands Street, started in 1941, provided a meeting place for some of Bulmers' workers, and there was later a smaller one at Moorfields in the Bottling Department.

In October 1960 a custom was instituted of presenting to every employee who had served for 25 years or more an inscribed gold wristwatch and a cheque (at this time for £25). There were 101 initial recipients, with a total of 3,049 years to their credit. F.W. Bradley, Records Office Manager, who had served for 50 years, was given a silver rose-bowl as well. Pensioners who had qualified also received a cheque. An annual lunch party for pensioners and their spouses was instituted. Participation in the success of the firm was encouraged by monetary prizes available to any employee who made a suggestion for an improvement which was adopted. One went to someone who had been with the company for less than a year. There were also small bonuses for productivity and for such things as alertness in the tedious work of spotting on the conveyor bottles which should be rejected. There were bonuses also for lorry-drivers who won awards from the Royal Society for the Prevention of Accidents. Of 91 drivers entered for these in 1965 no fewer than 61 gained an award.

In a business in which much of the work was necessarily of a routine and humdrum nature it was particularly important to give the employees good reason to feel that their efforts were worthwhile, to let them see how the cogs fitted into the wheel, and the wheel into the machine. The success of the firm was patent to all, and the accessibility of the directors, in the tradition established by Percy and Fred, induced a feeling of loyalty, as is testified by the absence of serious unrest, let alone strikes, and by the general impression of goodwill. In the words of the engineer Harold James: 'If a workman had any complaint, he would probably voice it in person to one of the directors doing his daily round, to whom he would as likely as not be known by his Christian name or a nickname—a fact which incidentally inhibited any foreman tempted to bully.' But as the workforce grew something more than that was needed. There was no strong movement for unionisation, but in the late 1950s a Works Advisory Committee was set up. This consisted of about 15 representatives elected by departments, the Personnel Manager, a departmental manager, and the Works Manager as Chairman. It met once a month. Its scope was limited. To begin with, only factory workers, not office or distribution ones, were represented. Also, in a private company which did not publish its accounts, information was restricted. Discussion of wage rates was excluded. In theory it was otherwise unlimited but in practice it tended to concentrate on internal factory administration. This may seem minimal representation by modern standards: but in practice the committee was extremely useful as a safety valve, and for bringing home to the management problems such as that of car parking already mentioned.

Despite Fred Bulmer's experience, care was now taken to move workers round as far as possible, so as to relieve them from monotony and give them an idea of the manufacturing process as a whole. John McWhirter, who came from the grocery business to be Sales Manager and stayed till 1964, made his chief mark by circulating to his Sales Force of 70 a manual (by J. Haworth) entitled 'Your company', setting out the whole background of their work. But there was still much to be done. We have seen that during the Second World War a newssheet was circulated to employees in the Services telling them about the doings of other employees and what was going on in the business. With the growth of the workforce there was now a crying need for something of this nature on a far more elaborate scale. This was at last provided in 1962 by the founding of the *Woodpecker News*, under the editorship of W.A. Matthews, to appear thrice yearly. Attractively got up it was to contain accounts, some historical, some topical, of the various departments,[21] occasional articles of general interest, and an abundance of personalia about employees, with plenty of photographs, and accounts of the activities of the sporting clubs of the firm. A diagram on page 2 of *Woodpecker News* No. 6 (1964) gave the factory employees a guide to the organisation of the works; and an account of the work of the Bulk Department in No. 7 began with a full description of how cider is made.

Some of the sporting personalities transcended local fame. Charles Walters, who represented the firm for 30 years in Oxfordshire, had previously played football for Tottenham Hotspur, and in this capacity held a F.A. Cupwinners' Medal for 1921, besides coaching the Oxford University Cricket Club for many years. David Haywood ('Dai the Ball'), a representative of the firm in South Wales, was captain of Cardiff at Rugby Football in his day, and won several Welsh caps. Glan Williams, South Wales Area Manager, had captained Pontypridd at Rugger for a number of years, and was Chairman of the Members' Committee of the Glamorgan County Cricket Club. Horace Moore, who became

Regional Sales Manager at Manchester, had several English Amateur Football caps.

Even the youngest could achieve a mention, with photograph: one of them, aged 18, won a national open award for typewriting – good punctuation and accuracy with a speed of 57 words a minute. An unusual short-term visitor also earned a mention with photograph: he was a Ghanaian maintenance engineer from Asebu, where the citrus peel for pectin came from, who spent six weeks in 1965 working in the pomace-drying plant and with the Works Engineering Staff. He looks as if he thoroughly enjoyed the experience, and we can well believe the statement that he was very popular with all.

The *Woodpecker News* also serves as a reminder of the otherwise too easily forgotten work of the depots and branches. It describes and illustrates, for instance, the entertainment at Hereford in April 1963 of the divisional and area managers (and their wives, for once). They dined at the City Arms and next morning, after being shown the film 'Cider Story', toured the works and lunched at the Green Dragon.

There was odd space, too, for anecdotes. One told how a dissatisfied customer wrote that he was returning a cask by rail half-full. The railways siding checker notified the office of the arrival of a half-empty cask. Whereupon he received a query from the accounts clerk: was the cask half-empty or half-full?

---

[1] The *Oxford English Dictionary* says it is an obsolete form of Middle English 'camlet' which denotes a certain costly eastern fabric.

[2] The use of the word 'Champagne' continued to be controversial.

In 1975 Showerings, warned by the experience of Goldwell Ltd., wished to forestall a possible writ by the Champagne Houses designed to prevent their using the word 'champagne' to describe anything other than wine made in the Champagne district of France. Bulmers, feeling that the term was less essential to them (for describing Pomagne), only agreed to join in if they should be liable for no more than one-third costs, with a maximum of £3,000. The Champagne Houses counterclaimed, and after a 22-day hearing won an injunction. Bulmers then declined to join Showerings in appealing.

The total costs of the actions were so high that Bulmers were glad to have let themselves in for no more then £3,000. They may, in fact, have gained on balance from the publicity. A B.B.C. team went out into the streets to stop passers-by and ask them to choose between a glass of Pomagne and a glass of champagne, neither being identified. Of the six people who tried five preferred the Pomagne. The sixth would only reply: 'You can't fool me: I know which is champagne.'

[3] This firm had been founded in 1850, at the corner of Widemarsh and Blueschool Streets. It was bought in 1884 by William Chave, a retired pharmaceutical chemist who used his scientific knowledge to improve cider, and moved to better premises on Widemarsh Common. They were pioneers in the extraction of pectin from apple pomace. The firm began to manufacture it, in addition to cider, in 1917, in response to wartime requirements.

[4] Peter Heering was sole proprietor of the firm of P.F. Heering, a family concern established at Copenhagen in 1818. Its brands included Cherry Heering, the world's leading cherry brandy, and Kahlua Coffee Liqueur.

[5] On the lorry trailer from which he spoke sat their mothers, Mildred and Sophie, widows of the founders, with a combined age of 185.

[6] It is described in detail in *The Bottle and Packer* XXV, No. 5.

[7] Fermentation vats, however, rarely exceed a capacity of 100,000 gallons, because of the problem of controlling the temperature of fermenting liquid. Storage vats are subject to no such limitation.

[8] Not without an alarming contretemps. The tank had a domed top, and the pressure of the liquid on the underside of this produced an uplift (equal to the difference in the weight of liquid which would have been held by a cylindrical vat of the same diameter and height). The sides lifted by 3–4 inches, pulling the bottom plate so that it was off the foundation for about two feet in. The difficulty was overcome by digging a ditch round the vat, putting in a heavy concrete ring, welding lugs on to the bottom of the vat, and fitting bolts from this down into the concrete.

[9] In 1956 an agreement was made about the use of the junction and siding at Moorfields Goods Yard.

[10] The Mayor and Town Clerk, visiting the site, saw a tenant in a garden opposite and asked him if he would approve of sale to Bulmers. 'It's the best thing that could happen', he replied. 'If we are working here our wives can see if we are not working hard enough. If we moved to Plough Lane we could sit down and smoke unobserved.'

[11] In 1963, in view of increases in public water charges, the firm decided to sink a new well and use a softening plant. There was also a considerable rise in the charge for disposal of effluent water, and this the firm could not avoid.

[12] After the 1950s Pomagne was no longer fermented in bottles and 'disgorged'. It was fermented now in tanks. Four of 4,000 gallons were installed in 1956. The changeover was complete by 1965.

[13] Official cider orchard calculations did not begin to be made by acreage until the 1950s; but an unofficial estimate of 1940 was that 190,000 acres in Britain were under apples, 63,000 or one-third of them being cider apples. By the

mid-sixties the acreage of cider-apple trees in England had fallen to 23,000, but scientific cultivation had increased the tonnage of apples to the acre.

[14] The *Financial Times* for 30 April 1955 reckoned that 'standard' trees took about 25 years to reach a remunerative yield, 'bush' trees about half of that (but with no benefit of produce growing between them).

[15] One-third consisted of low-lying land liable to flooding which had to be let off as grassland.

[16] The Ministry of Agriculture figures suggest an appreciable increase. Nationally consumption rose after 1935, but was stable in 1948–60 at about 18,000,000 gallons, increasing thereafter at the rate of about 8% a year.

[17] In France the juice is heated, and the 'esters' (evaporating volatile aromas) are collected, condensed, concentrated, cooled and stored. The remaining juice is boiled down in a vacuum to about one-sixth of the original volume, and stored separately at a temperature 0 C under a blanket of nitrogen or carbon dioxide. When it is required for fermentation the two components are diluted and reunited.

[18] The alcoholic strength of cider varies between about 3% and 8 1/2% by volume. In this it is comparable with beer, whereas that of wine ranges from 7% to 14%. There is no legal limit in Britain, but a 'wine-made' duty levied on anything over 8.7% effectively imposes a maximum. (H.M. Customs and Excise notice 1631 of 1976.) In France use of sugar in making cider was illegal. Sweet cider could only be produced by checking fermentation, which kept it very weak, or by mixing in concentrated apple juice. 'Cidre doux' might not contain more than 3% of alcohol.

[19] The term 'vintage' was applied to cider made from vintage quality fruit, having a higher than average alcoholic strength. The term 'champagne' was perforce not used of cider after 1975.

[20] It was advertised in 1956 in the *Radio Times*, the greatest advertising medium in the world, with a weekly circulation of 8,832,579, and in the *Daily Mirror*, with the largest daily circulation in the world of 4,725,122.

[21] For instance, few readers can have known anything before about the cooperage. Up to 1932 new hand-made casks were produced here for the company's use. Since then only repairing was being undertaken, and that mainly of casks of capacity below 30 gallons; but R.B. Carpenter and his staff were still repairing some 9,000 casks a year. So much was explained by Edward Ball in *Woodpecker News* No. 4.

181

CHAPTER FOURTEEN

NEW MANAGEMENT

The final period of our main subject covers only five years, 1966 to 1970 inclusive, but they were years of remarkable intensification. Whereas in 1945–65 emphasis was all on new development and plant, especially on the Moorfields site, in these years, with the arrival of Peter Prior, the emphasis was on promotion and publicity, which will be dealt with first after description of the new management. As to the fruit supply, it was again a question of pursuing more intensively policies previously established. There was further diversification and financial enterprise, and care was taken to find out the feelings of the enlarged workforce. The firm's operations were now so much bigger that the problem of financing them became crucial; and this led to the company's going public at the end of 1970. That date seemed suitable for the closing of this history, though a short epilogue will bring it up to date.

BOARD AND EXECUTIVES

On 29 December 1964, three days before Peter Prior was due to take over as Financial Director of the company, an Extraordinary General Meeting altered the provisions of its Memorandum of Association. The maximum number of directors was raised to 10. Directors and ex-directors were made eligible for pensions like other employees. The Board was authorised to appoint any of their body as a Managing Director, Chairman, Vice-Chairman or director with special functions. Anyone so appointed was not to be affected by the rules for rotational retirement of Directors and he was eligible for various forms of remuneration. The Board might also appoint any employee of the company to be a departmental director. These provisions anticipated changes planned to take place after the retirements at the end of 1965 already dealt with. They heralded a considerable devolution of responsibilities, and the establishment of a staff of executives with prospects of a permanent career.

At the beginning of 1966 the Board was radically reconstructed. Bertram Bulmer succeeded Howard as Chairman. Peter Prior became Managing Director with far-reaching discretion. Esmond Bulmer took over from Bertram as Chairman of Ryelands Properties and Ryelands Developments and soon after also from Adam Cochrane as Chairman of the subsidiary company of Parrot (Wines and Spirits) Limited. His brother David became Distribution Director. Bertram's son Giles became a director and was put in charge of the Pectin and the Industrial Products Division, now producing over one-fifth of the profits. (In 1969, after 16 weeks at Harvard Business School, where he graduated in management development, he returned to be Development Director, responsible for new methods of research development and supply from world-wide sources.)

On 5 December 1969 the *Sunday Telegraph* Colour Supplement devoted an illustrated article, by Theo Richmond, to the Bulmer members of the Board. Bertram, Giles, Esmond and David are seen grouped in the original orchard of Credenhill Rectory, now inhabited by Giles. Esmond, soon to be Conservative M.P. for Kidderminster, is shown with his family at their elegant home near Leominster amid their antique furniture and eighteenth-century oil-paintings. Giles is busy with his hobby of hot-air balloons, on which he is an expert. Bertram is guiding a tour of the new orchards, which have little gates in the fencing that badgers can push open with their snouts (otherwise they will tunnel underneath and so admit rabbits in their wake). He is credited with 'a sense of humour drier than the driest cider' and 'a donnish chuckle'. Any worries the newcomers may have anticipated about the possibility of finding 'passenger' Bulmers entrenched were soon dispelled.

The continued presence of G. Brian Nelson, generally approved, was reassuring to both old-stagers and newcomers. Yet another alumnus of King's College, Cambridge, he had been recruited for the Laboratory in 1952 after graduating with First Class Honours in Natural Sciences. Having shown there promise going far beyond the purely scientific, he had been appointed Production Director in April 1965. He was destined to become Managing Director in 1970 of the Cider Division and in 1975 of the whole group.

Other executives were brought in from outside. Giles R.C. Shepherd, a director of Charrington's Breweries introduced by Esmond Bulmer, had been appointed a director of the company at the same time as Nelson. He was now made Managing Director of the subsidiary company Parrot's, and in due course also took over control of the other wine interests acquired by the company; and he was made responsible for the growing concern of Bulmers' Hotel Assets. (He resigned in 1970 and later became Managing Director of the Savoy Hotel.) Keith Jamieson, who had launched Gerber Baby Foods for Brown and Polson, was introduced in the hope of promoting home sales from off-licences to offset loss of public house trade resulting from the takeover of the Taunton Cider Company by the brewers Courage, Charrington and Watney Mann. Another importation was D. Christopher Sowry as Advertising Manager.

Turnover had been growing fast, with sales increasing by 45% over the past five years. As Doina Thomas wrote:[1] 'In a fascinating traditional business new management has provided an intriguing modern case of transformation springing, not out of the usual failure, but out of success.' It was felt, however, that there was capacity for further growth. The business had been getting too big for the old arrangement by which Howard and Bertram Bulmer had run everything, ably backed by a few others. Prior wished to rebuild the management structure radically, in co-operation with the family. His object was to divide the company into units 'capable of being managed, not on a centralised functional basis, but on the basis of profit-accountable units'. He wanted to recruit managers who could be 'left to get on with it'. Each executive was to be given a clear description of his duties, and to know who had to report to him. Within his sphere he was to have a good deal of scope. (There was some danger here: departments began to feel isolated from each other.) In order to attract first-class people to manage the major subdivisions London rates of salary were offered at Hereford. There would be a performance review every six months.

Prior now began to imprint his mark on the firm by the appointments he made from outside. In particular, when he became Group Managing Director in 1966, he appointed to succeed him as Financial Director Richard R.G. Hollis, an ally of his from collaboration within other companies, who had most recently been Group Chief Accountant of Venesta Limited. In May 1967 Richard McBride retired as company Secretary, leaving as the chief memorial to his tenure the Pension Fund structure. He was succeeded by N.G.U. Morris, who joined in 1969. Other directors introduced from outside included Robin O. Graham, who came from Ansell's Breweries as Director of Development and was appointed in 1968 to be Commercial Director, having George Murray under him, with responsibility as Division Director for negotiations with major national breweries; Peter W. Green, a chartered accountant previously with Urwick, Orr and Partners, who took over from David Bulmer as Distribution Director; and in October 1970 a member of a prominent Herefordshire landowning family, Sir Humphrey Mynors, Bt., of Treago, St. Weonards, who had retired from being Deputy Governor of the Bank of England. (He was later succeeded as director by his brother David.) To run the orchards came Rex Neame, hitherto farm manager to his family brewing and farming firm of Shepherd Neame Ltd., of Faversham, Kent.

It was obviously no easy matter for Peter Prior to establish him- self in the consciousness of a workforce of about 1,500 with strong traditional ties. One method he chose was, to use his own words, 'sporadic bursts of eccentricity'. 'Occasions' were contrived, which incidentally served to break the monotony inevitable in much of the manufacturing work, at which he could be on show. Such an occasion was the arrival of steam locomotives for the Bulmers' Railway Centre, which was largely his brainchild. Others were the flying of a large red flag with hammer and sickle for two visits in autumn 1967 of a Russian Trade Mission; the ceremonial arrival at the works of the millionth ton of apples; and the demolition on 9 September 1966 of the 120 foot brick chimney, made redundant by the new oil-fired boilers, which had stood on the Ryelands Street site since 1939. This took place before the cameras of the B.B.C. programme 'The Midlands Today' (two new chimneys made of steel took its place till they in turn became redundant). The workforce naturally took time to get used to an influx of new executives, especially as these were put in above, and paid more than, employees with long service; but when it became clear that nothing essential had altered, they may well have been relieved on balance to feel that, now that the group was so much larger and more complex, its finances were in the hands of professional experts with experience of other large business concerns; and their financial ability was soon to become evident when the company's balance sheets started to be published.

At the end of 1966 the name of the group was shortened from H.P. Bulmer and Company to H.P. Bulmer Limited. This was an obvious convenience, but there was one abstention when the vote was carried on the Board. The 'and Company' had been the only residual acknowledgement of Fred Bulmer's participation in the original venture. By 1968 the group consisted of H.P. Bulmer plus five subsidiaries—two property companies, another cider company, a wine and spirit agency, and a citrus-peel processing plant in Ghana.

Hollis inherited no external debts and plenty of good assets. But the family, though eager enough for growth, was not so impatient for immediate results as a professional Financial Director would be, especially when he came to be responsible to anonymous stockholders. The return on capital from all operations was 17% in 1967. He hoped to raise it to 20% in five years. In fact financial progress was remarkable. Between 1965 and 1968 inclusive turnover rose from £4,190,000 to £8,157,000, pretax profit from £450,000 to £687,000, fixed assets from £2,134,000 to £4,309,000, and ordinary dividend from 55 to 65%. Less of profits, however, was transferred to reserves, apart from a record sum of £317,000 in 1967.[2]

PROMOTION AND PUBLICITY

The chief movement of Bulmers in the period 1966–70 was intensification of the already active drive for promotion and publicity. Already in 1966 theirs accounted for 83% of the total expenditure of the cider industry on advertising. In 1967 they spent £480,000 (as against £255,000 in 1964) and a further steep rise was expected. As a preliminary the new management commissioned in 1966 a report from a firm of advertising consultants on Attitudes towards Cider, which was updated in 1970. It produced some large generalisations about the psychological disposition towards cider of men and women respectively, and of young people. The one tangible result was the identification of lager beer as the chief rival. The advice as to how the younger generation might be 'conned' into preferring cider was not such as a responsible firm would be likely to accept.

On 10 April 1967 the firm held a national sales conference at the Skyways Hotel, London Airport. Introducing it, Keith Jamieson emphasized that times were changing. Customers were now better off and more sophisticated, more prepared to try new things, indeed inclined to demand novelty. Again, whereas a few years before there had been only a handful of supermarkets in Britain, there were now some 20,000; and it was estimated that about 6,000 off-licences had been modernised. The concentration of cider-making in the hands of fewer companies had led to more professionalism in the industry. Bulmers must meet these challenges, indeed lead the way.

The conference inaugurated an advertising campaign from 11 April to 31 August entitled 'Swing through summer with Bulmers'. This included what was claimed to be the biggest premium offer ever made in the licensed trade. For an order accompanied by a top-strap or capsule from a Woodpecker or Strongbow flagon a substantial reduction was made in the price of a particular brand of bath towel ('extra-large, gorgeously coloured'), an insulated bag, a sleeping-bag or a folding table. This was followed by a winter campaign on how to give a cider party. It was conducted through off-licences, with the backing of advertisments in the press and leading journals, particularly the *Radio Times*, *T/V Times* and *T/V World*. Anyone submitting three top-straps from Woodpecker or Strongbow flagons received a 128-page paperback book on party puzzles and games for all ages, and a leaflet with coloured photographs to illustrate ideas for a cider party cup and cocktails, such as Strongbow Orange Punch, with hints on how to run parties.

Television commercials continued to be important, and had to be planned with research and particular care, since six minutes cost £67,000. There was some criticism that the words were letting down the visuals. The company's 'Woodpecker Winter' commercial television film won a diploma in 1968 in the alcoholic drinks category at the Venice International Film Festival. For ordinary press advertisements the chief popular media were now the *Daily Mirror* (circulation 5,000,000), the *Radio Times* (4,250,000) and the *Television Times* (2,250,000). Full pages were also taken in camping magazines. A prestige colour advertisement of 1966 showing a 200-year-old cider glass appeared in the colour supplements of the quality Sunday papers, *Country Life*, the *Illustrated London News* and *Punch*.

Minor promotional exercises included a national competition for a poem on Herefordshire cider. The prize, won by a chemistry student, was £50. He was also conveyed to Hereford, with a friend of his choice, in a chauffeur-driven limousine, shown round the works, and entertained to dinner at the Red Lion, Weobley, by David Bulmer. It must also be mentioned, with reluctance, that in the autumn of 1968 the firm was offering free to anyone sending certain Bulmers' bottle seals an 'authoritative' guide to the Zodiac entitled *Astrology and Horoscopes*!

Sponsorship as a form of advertisement was far less common in those days than it became later. In September 1968 Bulmers sponsored a new national air race, the Strongbow Air Race, as the main event of the annual air display at Shobdon Airfield, near Leominster. They provided a trophy (worth £200), and cash prizes of £250, £100 and £50 for the first three home, which made it the richest air race in British light aviation. It was to be a handicap race over 80 miles. It attracted 33 entries, and was won by Bill and Victoria Todd in a Jodel aircraft, at an average speed of 121.75mph Bertram Bulmer, as President of the Day, was flown in by helicopter. Giles Bulmer, possessor of no. 9 British ballooning licence, was pilot-in-charge of the 'Bristol Belle', 50 feet in diameter, Britain's first modern hot-air balloon, in which he had a sixth share. (Unfortunately adverse weather conditions prevented more than a short flight.) The race became annual, attracting about 30 aircraft, and in 1969 it was nominated as the final qualifying event for the British Air Racing Championship. Weather compelled a three-week postponement, but there were nevertheless 12,500 spectators. Giles went up again in the 'Bristol Belle', with Bertram (at a few minutes notice) as an apprehensive passenger, to the tune of 'Up, up and away!' One competitor who turned up in 1970 (though weather again compelled postponement of the race) was Sheila Scott, fresh from another record-breaking flight round the world.

The success of the air race prompted the company to sponsor a motorcycle race. The competition for the Strongbow Trophy, open to machines of up to 1000cc, was first held at Croft Aerodrome, Darlington, in 1970. There were 40 finalists from 94 entrants, and Peter Prior, who started the race, was among those who completed the ten-lap course. The average speed of the winner, Frank Moss, was 74mph.

A particularly ambitious and imaginative promotional enterprise was initiated in 1968, Bulmers' Railway Centre. Adjoining the works was the remaining portion of the Midland Railway Moorfields Depot, in the angle between Red Hill and Barons Court Junction. This suggested the formation of such a centre, to attract the numerous people all over the country who have a passion for railways and in particular for steam locomotives, one of the hobbies of Peter Prior. Its operation was entrusted to Steam in Hereford Limited (the 6000 Locomotive Association), The Merchant Navy Loco. Pres. Soc. Ltd., and the Princess Elizabeth Loco. Soc. Ltd. A short arc of track laid across the angle outside the perimeter completed a triangle of track, giving the centre invaluable facilities for turning locomotives and complete trains. An indicator board (as a signpost), a station bookstall (as a sales stall) and some signals were procured as genuine railway museum pieces.

A Cider Train was the main exhibit. It consists of five Pullman cars (bought for £3,600) from the prestigious old 'Golden Arrow' and 'Bournemouth Belle' trains. It was repainted in the Bulmer house colours—red, green and white—and embellished with the Royal Arms (sanctioned by the grant of 1911) and those of the city of Hereford. Four of the coaches were renamed after the wives of Executive Directors of the firm, Bertram and Esmond Bulmer, Peter Prior and Brian Nelson. They are respectively 'Christine', a dining-car holding 42 for use at the works and on tour, 'Morella', a cinema seating 44 for showing company films, 'Prinia', an exhibition, museum and shop coach and 'Eve', a product display coach. The fifth coach, 'Aquila', was too famous to have its name changed. Built for the Festival of Britain in 1951, it was the supreme Pullman car, often used in its day by Royal families and visiting Heads of State, Kosygin among them. Re-equipped, it became a dining saloon for distinguished visitors, thus saving the cost, estimated at £20,000, of a special building for this purpose.

The first locomotive to be acquired, in 1967 for £250, was a shunting engine, a very early (1937 vintage) diesel. The Mayor of Hereford, Mr Bert Evans, being a BR express driver by profession, wearing his mayoral chain over his overalls, broke a bottle of sparkling cider over it in naming it 'Woodpecker' and drove it on its first working journey. Other Awdryesque engines were added. In November 1968 Miss Kitty Gordon, star of the company's television commercials for Woodpecker, performed a similar ceremony in naming one of them 'Cider Queen'. She herself was crowned 'Cider Queen' for the day. This was a prelude to the great occasion, the arrival on 13 November, played in by the band of R.A.F. Credenhill and driven by Mr Evans, of 6000 'King George V'. This had been the pioneer of the Great Western Railway's King Class. Completed in 1937 and immediately sent on show to America, where it was much admired, it was always the 'flagship' of the G.W.R. until, after covering over 2,000,000 miles, it was withdrawn in 1962 and became the property of the Swindon Corporation. Bulmers undertook in 1968 to restore it, on condition it could be exhibited and steamed at Hereford, and housed it in a special shed.[3] A parcel of 1 1/2 acres of land with sidings from the old Hereford-Eardisley line had been bought from British Rail in 1967, and nearly 4 acres more with sidings were added in 1969.

In the first six months 20,000 people came to see the train. It was then decided that it should go on a 450-mile sales tour on March 2–27, embracing Liverpool, Manchester, Nottingham, Birmingham, London and Reading, to give an opportunity for sales executives to meet trade contacts; and in fact 1,500 of these were met. At Kensington Olympia, where it was stationed for six days, it was seen by 60,000 people attending the Ideal Homes Exhibition. Then in 1971 it featured in the Royal Command film performance of the NCB film 'King George V', made at Hereford.

Part of the promotional campaign was devoted to catching or pleasing the eye. Thus store-displays were designed for self-service stores which should catch the eye and incidentally be able to hold up five dozen bottles without collapsing when a customer helped himself. And in general there was a move to smarten things up. After prolonged deliberation with the firm's advertising agency (The London Press Exchange) and its consultants (Conran Design Group), the Advertising Department introduced in 1967 a new Bulmer livery: new colours—green, red and dark brown; a new symbol—a capital B with a cider apple inset; and a specially designed lettering, to be used on all vehicles, signs, stationery and (where appropriate) labels.

The arrival at the works on 20 October 1966 of the millionth ton of apples was made into a celebratory occasion, recorded by a special souvenir supplement of the *Woodpecker News*. The consignment was pulled in by Trooper, a 20-year-old shire horse, in an antique four-wheeled wagon. A basket of apples from the cradle of the firm, Credenhill Rectory orchard, was added, and pressing began. The Mayor of Hereford, Alderman Peter Carter, was then installed on one side of a silver-painted scales, and Bertram Bulmer began to pour cider into a barrel on the other side. At 16 1/2 gallons the Mayor began to rise, and a glass of Strongbow was handed to him to complete the balance. The City Council and officials were then added to the Mayor's side, and finally his 20-stone officer, Mr

Kidd. This brought the total on the other side up to 330 gallons – worth a cheque for £121, which was then given by the company to the Mayor's Charity fund.

One thing the works lacked was an imposing entrance. This was remedied to some extent in 1969 by the erection at the Moorfields entrance, nearly opposite the end of Ryelands Street, of a remarkable piece of sculpture which catches the eye of anyone entering or leaving Hereford by the Hay and Brecon Road. It was commissioned from Mr Walenty Pytel, a specialist in bird and animal sculpture in metal, who fortunately lived—and still lives—in Herefordshire, at Woolhope, but had a reputation far transcending the local. It is a representation in steel of a woodpecker, seven feet high and weighing half a ton, clinging to the trunk of a 19-foot tree made of eight sections of mild steel welded together. The whole weighs two tons, and is bolted to a plinth on a stone pier. It was unveiled on July by the famous ornithologist Peter Scott, who hailed it as a 'magnificent work of art': and very striking it certainly is.

FRUIT

The scheme for encouraging growers to plant the right amount of cider apple trees of the right kinds described by Edward Ball to the conference of 1947 was due to be completed in 1966; but when that time came there was need to extend and intensify it. In 1967 Bulmers added to the recently acquired Monnington and Moorhampton estates The Field, a 240-acre estate at Hampton Bishop, three miles E.S.E. of Hereford. The breeding and propagation of young trees was transferred there from King's Acre, which had supplied 270,000 trees to local farmers since 1927. To encourage farmers to embark on long-term extensive cultivation, they offered in 1967 15-year contracts, extended to 20-year in 1969. Loans and interest were to be repaid only from the time when the trees began to bear fruit, at the rate of 50% of crop proceeds. They also put up the price they would pay for apples by 30s, to £15 a ton, in 1967, and to £16 a ton in 1969. But in an inflationary situation, it soon became clear that this was not incentive enough, and in 1970 the price was £16.75 a ton for the best cider apples. Production of these was now a really profitable proposition, not merely a matter of pin-money for the farmer's wife. Incidentally, elderly people anxious to minimise death duties could invest in trees as an asset less heavily penalised than stocks and shares.

As a further incentive, Bulmers inaugurated in 1968 a cider apple and perry pear competition, with £1,000 in prizes, for their 3,000 regular growers (some 2,000 of whom were known personally to George Wood, the Orchard Adviser). The first prize was a nine-carat golden cider apple. It was won by Mr Philip Davis of Claston, Dormington, whose manager received a silver tankard. The judges' comments were made available to competitors, and prize-winners were given free access to the firm's Advisory Service.

The production of cider apples in England was still falling short of demand. This was partly because the consumption of cider, after remaining level for some years at about 18,000,000 gallons, rose steadily from 1965, no doubt owing to greatly increased advertising, and in 1970 topped 30,000,000 for the first time. That year produced a record crop of cider apples, but half the quantity needed for making cider had still to be imported from Normandy. In 1967, for instance, 37,000 tons had been imported, of which Bulmers, with about 64% of the trade, accounted for 26,000. This was a dangerous situation; for in Normandy, though apples were cheap, there was no general policy for renewal of orchards, so that the surplus available for export might dramatically decline.

Bulmers required about 50,000 tons of apples a year. Their policy now was to increase annually the proportion of these grown in their own orchards, but not so as to supersede in the foreseeable future the total coverage (English plus French), for that would be uneconomic. They calculated that for at least 20 years they would be able to take from farmers the average of what they had taken in 1959–65. King's Acre was in future to be devoted entirely to growing fruit for the company. Hocking's Farm, of 184 acres, at Martley, near Worcester, was acquired in 1968, their first orchard estate outside the county of Hereford. They hoped to bring the acreage bought for this purpose up to 4,000 acres in the next ten years, and by 1970 they had 1,500. Trees were to be bush trees planted at 160 an acre, and it was expected that after seven years the yield would be 10 tons an acre.

The Orcharding Division under Rex Neame was productive of new ideas. It produced an ingenious device which involved fitting on either side of a tractor an adjustable arm carrying a miniature ploughshare. This enabled a man to mark out a field for planting cider apple trees in half the time it previously took three men to do the job. But it was one thing to mark out the field, another to plant. In 1969, at the end of our period, members of the staff invented a revolutionary tree-planting machine based on one formerly used for forestry planting. They knew that in the ensuing winter 95,000 trees would have to be planted to establish intensive orchards on land bought by the company. Previously a gang of eight men could plant, in good weather conditions, six acres a day. With two of these new machines mounted on tractors, even in bad weather, eight men could now plant twelve acres. Each machine could plant a tree every 11.5 seconds. Five were made, and they planted 3,000 acres.

FURTHER DEVELOPMENTS

On 21 April 1967 a new citrus-pectin processing plant on the Ryelands site was opened by Lord Walston, who, besides being Parliamentary Secretary to the Board of Trade in the Labour Government and a pioneering farmer in Cambridgeshire, was an old friend of the Bulmer family. Among those present were R.H. McDowell, who in 1935 had been in charge of the research work which led to the construction of the firm's original plant, and Vernon Beach Thomas, who besides designing that had, in association with the Plant Manager, H.W. Holmes, designed a pilot plant for processing citrus peel. The new plant, with the boiler-house required for the steam to operate it, cost £300,000; but the firm hoped to achieve in the first twelve months exports to 30 countries worth more than half that sum, in addition to supplying the entire home market of about £650,000, with corresponding saving of imports. The plant could produce 400 tons of citrus powder pectin a year. Bulmers now accounted for one-seventh of the world production of pectin. They were planning an £80,000 extension of the division, to allow for a 25% increase in capacity and greater laboratory control. In 1969 pectin accounted for more than a quarter of Bulmers' post-tax profits of £320,000. It was in sufficient demand to absorb the extra amount of pomace produced by increasing cider production.

At Moorfields an access road from the new Yazor Road, running along the course of the northern sewer and providing entry for vehicles approaching Hereford from the west, was approved in June 1967, subject to a contribution from the firm towards the cost of construction. The chief additions to the buildings were new bottling lines and the still larger storage tank Apollo XI. A bottling line brought into commission in 1966 established a record by operating at 97% efficiency throughout a shift of 7 hours 50 minutes. An even more remarkable one was commissioned in 1970. It was constructed by Vickers with Richard Ankerson, the Works Manager, as chairman of the planning committee. It was designed to deal with bottles of six sizes with many variations as to the stoppers, decoration, labelling and package envisaged. Costing more than £300,000, it was the most up-to-date flagon-bottling line in the country. It required only 21 operators to deal with 1,000 dozen bottles in an hour, as against 29 to deal with 800 dozen in its predecessor, besides being mercifully less noisy.

There were innovations about 1967 in the sphere of packaging. The firm was using over 1 1/2 million crates, and would need many more. Wooden crates were costly to inspect, repair and replace. So new moulded plastic crates in Bulmer green were being introduced. These were half the weight of wooden ones, cleaner and more easily handled. Research revealed that there was a demand for lightweight bottles, and both Woodpecker and Strongbow were now made available in cluster-packs of four non-returnable half pint bottles.

A sign of the times was the introduction in 1967 of a small IBM computer, Model 20 in the new 360s series. Its first job was to produce invoices for goods sold and to record dates and payments for the purpose of issuing monthly statements. An important by-product was analyses of sales in different parts of the country, in order to monitor, for instance, the effectiveness of the advertising allotted to the various local television services.

Another notable machine was the brainchild of Fred Bennett, Manager of the Bulk Department. It was a modified version of the Pontifex 36-head flagon-filling machine, and could automatically fill 240 five-gallon cider casks an hour, an increase of 50% over manual achievement. Plastic containers of this size for draught cider were rapidly increasing in popularity.

Meanwhile the policy of acquiring hotels and public houses, inaugurated with the Red Lion at Weobley, went ahead. The Maesllwch Arms Hotel (usually pronounced 'Maiseluck') at Glasbury-on-Wye was bought for £15,000 in 1966. It was essentially a fishing hotel, but the beauty of the surroundings attracted potentially thirsty walkers also. After improvements had secured its up-grading to two stars it was sold four years later for £22,000. In 1967 the firm bought the Cider House at Wootton, near Bridgnorth, a small cottage which for many years had been licensed only to sell cider and which now boasted one of the highest cider sales in the country. On New Year's Day 1969 it took over The Blue Bell at Waring's Green, Hockley, in Warwickshire, thereby reducing from three to two the number of public houses in England still brewing their own beer. The beer, being sugar-free, had commended itself to diabetics, but Bulmers could offer these their No.7 cider instead. Fronting on the Stratford-on-Avon canal, it was ripe for development to attract inland waterway boaters. The Stag's Head at Watford Gap in Northamptonshire, bought for £16,000 in 1969, was another canal pub, with a long frontage on the Grand Union, which also happened to adjoin the Blue Boar Service Station on the M1 motorway. In 1970 the firm acquired The Hampstall Cider House, on the Severn near Stourport, and venturing further afield, the timbered Ram Cider House at Godalming, the only cider house in Surrey. In addition to these 'managed houses' the firm had tenants in The Swan at Abergavenny and The Lord Nelson at Pontlottyn in the Rhymney Valley.

In the early 1960s it looked as if the wine trade was entering on a boom period in England. For Bulmers, looking round for diversification, this seemed an obvious field. We have seen how in 1964 they acquired part of H. Parrot & Co. In 1966 they acquired the share capital of Dent & Reuss Ltd., an agency house established in 1858. Parrot (Wines and Spirits) Ltd. was now merged with this, to trade under the name of the former. The new firm so composed would have one of the best portfolios in the trade, including as it did, besides the Parrot brands, Pol Roger Champagne, Hine Cognac, Kindermann German Wines, Louis Latour Burgundies and Ingham Whitaker Marsala. Esmond Bulmer and Giles Shepherd were appointed to represent Bulmers on its Board.

There was an element of sentiment in the further acquisition, in 1968, for more than £1,000,000, of Findlater Mackie Todd, founded in 1823. Bulmers had been connected with them for 56 years (Mr J.H. Todd, it will be remembered, was one of the original directors when the company was formed in 1918). This enriched the portfolio with other well-known brands, such as Dry

Fly Sherry and Landrost South African Sherry. But within two years it was sold off, to Beechams, for £1,422,128, certain of its agencies being retained by Bulmers.

One product that claimed to be new dates from this period. Though sales of Apple Joy had continued to rise, these were not a sufficiently large slice of the expanding market for pure apple juice. Its bottle carried a deposit, which inhibited its sale through supermarkets, and in comparison with its rivals its presentation was too unsophisticated. The juice itself also lacked finesse. So the Product Research and Development Group was turned on to the problem, and a year later a new brand was launched under the name of 'Pure Apple Juice by Bulmers'. First reports from the supermarkets were encouraging; and there was a free advertising bonus in a rumour that Prince Charles was drinking it regularly at Cambridge.

Efforts continued to be made to sell Bulmers' cider abroad. In 1966 the *Board of Trade Journal*, reporting on the Pacific Fine Foods and Beverages Fair held at Los Angeles, stated that at a beverage-tasting party the best results were achieved by Bulmers' cider (along with Whitbread ales), and that as a result many American stores were anxious to arrange special Bulmer promotions. Portuguese Guinea was the latest country in which they had established an agency. By 1968 the firm was selling cider in some 80 countries, and pectin in 30.

The next venture was in manufacturing cider abroad. In 1967 Bertram and David Bulmer went out to prospect in Australia, where most people did not even know that cider was an alcoholic drink. As a result a subsidiary company was founded there. David was appointed International Director in July 1968. The staff out there, besides himself, consisted of Pat O'Brien and two process operators; and in 1970 an Australian from Sydney, Noel Haviland, was appointed General Manager. Work started in 1969 on building a factory at Campbelltown, 35 miles south-west of Sydney, and Fred Bennett, the production manager at Hereford, went out to supervise the final stages. The initial unit had a production capacity of 250,000 gallons a year, and allowance was made for expansion over 25 years. During the first years, while the market was being tested, Australian bottlers would be used; but if the venture was successful, bottling plant would be installed. Concentrated juice of English cider apples would be sent out, to be blended with a modicum of juice of Australian apples. The new product, a Strongbow type, was to be launched in January 1970, at the height of the Australian summer; and sure enough, on 22 January, with the temperature at 120o, the first bottle left Campbelltown, after promotion at a press conference and on television and radio. One club put in seven repeat orders in the first week.

Woodpecker was also manufactured under franchise for H.P. Bulmer S.A. Limited by Applethwaite Farm Processing Limited at Elgin in the Western Cape district of South Africa.

EMPLOYEES

The workforce at Hereford now numbered 1,500, and there were 300 more at the depots. Nelson's policy was to have a key task analysis system right through the Production Division, with schedules of responsibility worked out together with job definitions and with a performance review every six months. The review carried right down to charge hands. Information about production costing was now passed far down the line. Employees were given access to quite confidential information: they would know the monetary effects of their individual jobs. As far as possible workers were paid a weekly wage rather than an hourly rate, but merit rates were still applied to those paid by the hour. The girls on the bottling and canning lines continued to receive bonuses on performance. In the 12 months up to April 1967 productivity increased by 9.2% in cider and 10% in pectin. This was attributed largely to the acceptance of new methods and working practices. In September 1967 pay increases were made to 570 employees in recognition of overall increased productivity, and increases in hourly rates to men and women in all production departments of cider and pectin manufacture.

Meanwhile a determined effort was made to diminish 'class distinctions'. In August 1967 Prior announced that Bulmers was joining the select band of organizations which had abolished 'clocking-in': 'We believe that everyone employed by the company is equally important to the success of the operations, and should be accorded the same measure of trust'. ('Equally'? Well, not *quite*, perhaps.) In the sales force of 80 too a personal appraisal system was applied. This included a half-yearly interview between the employee, his immediate boss and the Sales Director. The old sales bonuses were modified so that part went into the salary, part was a direct incentive related to the salesman's performance in relation to the sales promotion programme. He no longer simply booked orders: he was assessed on his ability to help to increase sales. A competition was also introduced, for the title of 'Salesman of the Year', on the basis of set standards to be met within the normal range of duties. Each of the four regions submitted a champion. The winner was rewarded by a fifteen-day Mediterranean cruise for two, £20 of spending money and a silver tankard. The other three were given similar awards on a smaller scale. (There was also a cup engraved with the year, the winner's name and his region, to be held by the region for the ensuing year.) All four were brought to Hereford for a special presentation ceremony, and received a tie signifying their membership of the Golden Apple Club, confined to past winners of these awards.

The lorry fleet now consisted of 170 vehicles, varying from six-ton radial vehicles for local deliveries to 13 twenty-ton (3,000-gallon) tankers, 65 of them being stationed at Hereford. There some 112 drivers and mates reported every morning to be on the road by 8.00am at the latest. Tractors with trailers set out on trunking deliveries to depots on a three-shift basis. A driver leaving Hereford at 6.00pm would arrive at Perivale Depot in London, have a half-hour break while his tractor was being disengaged and hitched to a waiting trailer of empties, and be back in Hereford by 5.30am Bulmers' drivers were covering 4 3/4 million miles a year, and earning a high rate of safety awards. In 1969 Des Stanton of the Wolverhampton depot got into the final of the national 'Driver of the Year' competition, having been first in the class for two-axle vehicles of over 25 feet in length in the elimination round.

The suggestions scheme continued to stimulate and to produce some useful results. Some 135 suggestions were submitted in 1968. F. Perkins in 1967 got the largest award so far, of £50, for a plan for inverting No.2 crowners to put polythene corks into Pomagne bottles. This streamlined the process, saved considerable costs, and reduced accident risks. Brian Nelson called it a 'flash of inspiration'. Next year's awards ranged from £3 to £130. A simple suggestion that a tray should be put under the tabbing board in the bottling department won three guineas. Another, for an improved method of reference to customers by geographical location, won the same amount for someone in the computer department. In a class by itself was the £225 paid to Claude Morgan for an invention already described.

In inheriting a large un-unionised labour force from a successful paternalistic régime the new administration might well feel that there was the danger of inheriting also complacent attitudes to working conditions. At all events, it commissioned Urwick, Orr and Partners in 1968 to conduct an Attitude Survey. A question-naire with 49 questions and guaranteed confidentiality as to the answerers' identity was distributed in July to 1,250 employees at Hereford, all those who were not absent through illness or holidays. Returns were received from 650, or 52%—made up of some 75% of senior and middle management, 50% of the rest. The consultants, after scrutinising the returns, concluded that they were sufficiently representative, with no significant groupings as to age or functions; and further, that 'most people at all levels like working for, and are interested in, the company'.

Nevertheless from those who did reply (naturally consisting mainly of people with some desire for change) substantial criticism of certain features did emerge. It appeared that, while in senior management the majority were happy and felt they 'counted', middle management, though also happy, contained a quarter who did not feel they counted; and at shop floor level more than half of the women and more than a third of the men who replied felt they were 'numbers' (i.e. did not count as individuals). Again, below senior management nearly half, inevitably perhaps, did not feel their job was particularly interesting. More people than might have been expected felt that they did not know enough about the company and wanted to be able to feel more interested in it, though *Woodpecker News*, now half-yearly, did also carry articles about various aspects of the business and Prior had begin to issue News Letters. There was general agreement that there was too lit-tle communication between the various divisions and departments (perhaps this was accentuated by the new streamlined organisation). A majority knew nothing of the Works Council—not surprisingly, as it represented only factory, not office or distribution, workers; and people who worked in departments where bonuses were not on offer replied rather scathingly to questions about benefits they had never heard of. At shop floor level there was a general feeling that, since workers heard so much about the success of the company, they were not paid enough (and the majority would prefer more pay to longer holidays).

The results of an inquiry of this sort must naturally be taken with a grain, indeed a spoonful, of salt. Of the 48% who did not reply, how many were contented, how many just temperamentally apathetic? Some of the human problems were inevitable in a community swollen by success beyond the scope of intimate knowledge. Again, even the average human being is not immune from jealousy, cantankerousness or unreasonableness. Thus, if people say they have not been informed, it may simply mean that they have not taken the trouble to read; or if they are asked whether there are sufficient opportunities for promotion, the majority, not having been promoted, may well say there are not. But there will be a residue of issues which produce sufficient consensus to demand attention—in the case of this survey, for instance, the inferiority of the office accommodation.

The questionnaire also allowed space for additional spontaneous comments, and 441 were submitted. Some were such as might not have occurred to the consultants, or even the company; for instance, 'Help with shoes should be given, as shoes are cut to ribbons on glass'. 'Toilets are too far away for many of us, wasting much time'. 'More vending (drinks) machines should be available in the works'. 'Charge hands and senior men cannot easily be recognised because they all wear the same colour overalls'.

The recent statement that 'clocking-in' had been abolished because of a desire to remove 'class distinctions' came in for some comment here: 'Why do the largely sedentary office staff have parking places reserved for them, whereas people working at the far end of Ryelands Street have far enough to walk anyway without the addition of having to leave their cars at Moorfields?' 'The idea of separate canteens and lavatories is ludicrous. Any gap between management and employees is thereby widened.' 'The office workers seem to think that if you wear overalls you are a worm'. 'The engineers are treated as poor relations.' 'I have to queue for my lunch, whereas other employees are served at a table.'

At the very least the questionnaire provided a safety-valve and quite a lot of steam was blown off. Even such succinct suggestions as 'Sack A...B...' (same name from three answerers) were relayed to the directors. Prior frankly summarised the chief complaints in No.19 of *Woodpecker News* (January 1969) and then made general comments. As to pay, the employees received as much as the group could afford. The company tried to keep a balance between fairness to them and fairness to investors, using annual bonus payments for this purpose. The present difficulty was, that despite exceptional improvements in performance the company was finding it hard to keep up with the cost increases thrust upon it from outside. Increased profit had almost been outweighed by increases in the cost of apples, motor fuel and building, and in taxation on fuel and other materials, also in purchase tax and postage and telephone charges.

After a meeting of about 80 managers and supervisors to consider the survey, the following steps were approved. Programmes would be devised for welcoming and initiating new employees, and new training schemes to ensure that employees had a fair chance of promotion, while an existing scheme for discovering who deserved promotion would be reinvigorated. Opportunities for promotion and appointment would be more widely advertised, and within as well as outside the works; and the responsibilities involved would be more clearly explained. To improve communication and understanding of the business, temporary transfers would be arranged between departments and between divisions at all levels. All charge-hands, foremen, supervisors and managers would have informal conversations with everyone under their control, besides normal working relationships, at least four times a year. The *Woodpecker News* would carry more articles dealing with individual workers on the shop floor and in the offices. For the rest, movements of materials between Ryelands Street and Moorfields would be improved; internal postal deliveries and messenger services would be rationalised; filing systems would be simplified, and paper-work, especially form-filling, reduced.

One concrete development that anticipated requests in the questionnaire was the establishment of a social club, the Woodpecker Club, on the Oaklands site, a central site at the western corner of Ryelands Street and Whitecross Road. The company put up £16,000, and made an interest-free loan of £2,000 for the provision of furniture and equipment. The main feature was a large clubroom with an area of 1,050 square feet. Opening off this were a lounge, a snug and a table tennis room, all served by a central bar. There was also a skittle alley, and a small room for television and cards. The existing Sports and Social Club was merged with the Woodpecker Club, which would be supported by voluntary individual subscriptions. It was opened on 4 July 1969 with more than 600 subscribers on the list. By the spring of 1971 there were 900.

In 1935, a Mr E. Wintour, of 'The Steppes', offered to present to the Hereford Museum the complete cider-making outfit of the late Mrs Glenn. The press was accepted, but not the rest. This led Dr Durham, who had seen the whole outfit, to write on 25 March to the *Hereford Times* regretting that it had not all been accepted. He had thought it an ideal domestic outfit to be exhibited in a museum. Such sets had largely disappeared: one big one which would have been very suitable, e.g., for the South Kensington Museum, had become a garden 'ornament'. Soon after the Second World War Lord Chesterfield presented an old cider mill to the City of Hereford, which was accepted, but not without one councillor alleging that he had only presented it to save himself the cost of having it removed. It was erected in place of a Russian cannon from the Crimean War.

But although the South Kensington Science Muesum was originally founded in 1835, museums for individual industries have only recently become at all common. In October 1966, however, the *Woodpecker News* gave notice that a cider museum was to be established, and that Mr Bill Matthews (the Editor) would be grateful for any relevant information or old pieces of equipment, which he had been appointed to collect and catalogue. In the first six months he received, for instance, a wooden tunpail, a cider drinking-horn, and a bottle of 1929 Pomagne found bricked up in a wall in a Bridlington hotel.

An independent initiative was to lead to a more far-reaching enterprise. In 1969 Bertram Bulmer wrote a letter to every parish priest in Herefordshire asking him to spread the word that a survey was going to be made of old cider mills and presses surviving in the area. The questionnaire that followed elicited 220 replies, and the idea of setting up a Cider Museum in the works was now seriously taken in hand.

As early as 1964, before Peter Prior came on the scene, the Board had told the shareholders in its annual report of the financial difficulties encountered by an expanding private company such as Bulmers. Substantial reserves of ready cash had to be kept for emergencies, whereas a public company had access to abundant finance and was able to spend large sums on market development and on promoting individual products. Matters came to a head in 1968, when on the deaths of Mildred and Sophie Bulmer, at a time when expenditure of some £250,000 on the new bottlings plant had kept profits static though sales were rising, the family had to meet very heavy claims for estate duty and capital gains tax. Since most of Bulmers' profits had been ploughed back into the business, the obvious course was to go public, a move which would also have on-going tax advantages. (Another great private firm, Pilkingtons' glass, was deciding about the same time to go public.) The Bulmer family, however, were to retain at least 65% of the shares, a provision which would continue to stave off take-overs and approaches such as had already often been made. Naturally the change seemed regrettable to Bertram Bulmer in particular, but he too recognised its necessity in the present circumstances, and he himself made the formal proposal, at a meeting on 4 December 1970, 'That the company be converted into a public company'.

The arrangement was, that each of the 200,000 Ordinary £1 shares in the company should be subdivided into four shares of 5s each, and that the authorised capital of the company should be increased by the creation of 11,200,000 additional ordinary 5s shares to £3,100,000 (£100,000 of preference and £3,000,000 of ordinary shares). £2,300,000 was to be capitalised, being part of reserves, and appropriated to the holders of ordinary shares, this sum to be applied to paying up in full 9,200,000 ordinary 5s shares.

The launching of the shares on the market was entrusted to the company's recently appointed merchant bankers J. Henry Schroder Wagg, with broker support from Cazenove. Schroder Wagg were to purchase 3,500,000 ordinary 5s shares at 13s 1 1/2d for sale to the public. They were to apply to the Council of the Stock Exchange for permission to deal in, and quote for, the whole of the 10,000,000 issued ordinary 5s shares. The offer was to be advertised on 7 December 1970.

An explanatory letter was sent by Prior as Group Managing Director to all employees. They would be given first chance to buy a proportion of the shares that were on offer (up to the limit of 10% prescribed by Stock Exchange regulations). It was explained that big concerns such as breweries might be less likely to buy shares because they would not hope to gain control of the company since the Bulmer family would be retaining 65% of the shares. But this latter fact was a guarantee that there would be no violent changes in the way the firm was run. The same people as before would remain as executive directors, no doubt with the addition of a non-executive director from outside, as was customary when firms went public. A personal message from Bertram Bulmer as Chairman explained why, to his regret, he had had to accept that this step had become inevitable in the changed circumstances of the present. He reinforced Prior's assurance that there would be no great change in the way the firm was run.

In 1970, with 60% of the £25,000,000 market, Bulmers were enjoying a bonanza pressing year following one of the heaviest ever crops of cider apples, and were budgeting to sell 20,000,000 gallons of cider in the next year. By the next spring they would have 1,500 acres of their own orchards, capable of producing over 15,000 tons of apples a year when mature. They had one of the most modern flagon-bottling lines in Europe, capable of filling 1,000 dozen bottles an hour.

Though it happened that the stock market was in general depressed in December 1970, more than 5 1/2 applications were received for each share. The 200 Bulmer employees who bought shares had reason to be grateful for the priority they had been given. Offered at 67 1/2p (13s 6d) on 7 December, their value on 3 May 1971 was 93p. An initial 5% interim dividend having been paid to those who were shareholders before the company went public, a final dividend of 7 1/2% was paid in August after little more than eight months.

[1] In a long and valuable article, 'Bulmer's Golden Apples', in *Management Today* for February 1968.

[2] Comparable figures for 1969–70 cannot be given, as the Group changed its annual accounting date from 31 December to 30 April.

[3] It was joined in 1975–76 by two other major locomotives, the ex-Southern Railway 35028 'Clan Line' and the London, Midland and Scottish 6201 'Princess Elizabeth'. Two steam tank engines, reconditioned by the Worcester Locomotive Society, were brought to Bulmers so that they could have an occasional run on a 'Steam Open Day'.

[4] In the same spirit Alan Hudson-Davies, as Chairman of Fibreglass, established a Glass Museum in the new works at St Helens.

EPILOGUE

After the company went public Bertram Bulmer remained as Chairman until 1973 and, thereafter, stayed on the Board as a non-executive director.

During his seven years the business had doubled. Peter Prior then became Chairman until 1982, when the chairmanship passed back into the family in the person of Esmond Bulmer with Brian Nelson as Group Managing Director and Richard Hollis as Financial Director. New directors were added to the Board by internal promotion and in 1980 John Rudgard took over the marketing of all the group drinks as well as becoming Managing Director of Dent & Reuss (the wine company owned by Bulmers).

The period since 1970 has continued to be one of general success, affected by the vagaries of weather and size of apple crops.

The leading brands of cider continued to be Woodpecker, Strongbow and Pomagne, and the company's share of the cider market was about 50 per cent.

In 1976 the Chancellor of the Exchequer put an Excise Tax on cider and perry; none had been levied since 1923. Consequently, the company had to face serious problems which were surmounted largely by good management and the co-operation of the workforce, which was kept constantly informed of the difficulties as well as the successes.

The policy of encouraging farmers to grow the right varieties of cider apples continued, as well as that of producing a fair proportion of the company's needs from its own orchards.

In 1982 a record of 20,000 tonnes came from the company's orchards and on 7 October of that year the mills pressed a record for a day of just over 1,000 tonnes.

Growth necessitated extra accommodation and in 1978 a new office block on the Moorfields site was built to house 300 people, together with a self-service canteen seating 250. New plant in the works included a steel storage vessel named STRONGBOW holding 1,630,000 gallons—the largest vessel in the world for storing alcoholic liquor.

Apart from one US corporation, Bulmers were one of the largest producers of pectin in the world and in 1982 the division won the

Queen's Award for Export Achievement. On behalf of the firm the Chief Scientist, Dr F.J. Buckle, received from the Duke of Edinburgh the 1983 Pollution Abatement Technology Award for the successful development of a new technology for the treatment of effluent.

H.P. Bulmer (Holdings) PLC was formed in 1977 and a profit sharing scheme for full-time members of the company was instituted. A scheme for eliciting suggestions for improvements and inventions continued to produce worthwhile results.

From early times the firm had subscribed by modest covenants to local good causes such as Boy Scouts, Bowling Club and the Choral Society, but only later could substantial donations be made to outside causes, such as the ante-natal clinic at Hereford County Hospital. An unobtrusive plaque on the south side of Hereford Cathedral organ case records that the organ was rebuilt by H.P. Bulmer in 1977.

Hereford Cathedral School, the Diocese of Hereford Community Trust, St Michael's Hospice and the SAS Benevolent Fund (the SAS is based in Hereford) all received substantial grants. The restoration appeal for the famous chapel of King's College, Cambridge, the college which had nurtured so many of the firm's leaders—Fred, Esmond, Bertram, Edward, Becket, James Esmond, Giles, also Dr Durham, Alan Hudson-Davies, Brian Nelson as well as other members of the Bulmer family, was generously supported.

When Bertram Bulmer retired as chairman in 1973 he set about fulfilling a longstanding ambition—to found a Museum of Cider and Cidermaking. A trust was formed with the help of the firm and other wellwishers and the museum was opened in 1981. It records the history of cider apple growing, production and consumption world wide and in 1984 a licence to distil apple brandy (Calvados in France) was granted, the first for 200 years. Oak trees for casks in which to mature the brandy were generously given by Her Majesty The Queen, Prince Charles and various local estate owners and others.

In the earlier part of this book it was seen that relations between the city and company were not always harmonious. It is, therefore, pleasing to be able to quote from a plaque installed in December 1982 in the foyer of the new office block in Plough Lane, 'Presented to the management of H.P. Bulmer Ltd, by the Mayor and Past Mayors of the City of Hereford in appreciation of their kindness and good offices in the past.'

The firm has now become so large that the maintenance of good labour relations, which has always characterised it, called for a more formal framework. A movement to seek recognition by the Transport & General Workers' Union had begun in the late 1960s. In May 1975 there was an agreement made covering the Hereford office and factory departments and the company undertook to encourage its members to join the local branch of TGWU. The union agreed that the interests of its members were best served by the efficient operation of the company.

The Red Lion at Weobley, having fulfilled its purpose, was sold in 1986.

In spite of changes the traditional character has been retained. In the words of Peter Waymark in an article on cider in the *Daily Telegraph* of 27 October 1984, 'It has still the intimacy of a family firm with a Bulmer at its head and its factory, in quiet countryside on the edge of Hereford, is far removed from the satanic mills of industrial England.'

APPENDIX

As briefly noted by Patrick Wilkinson, Flight Lieutenant Edward Bulmer, son of Percy, lost his life in warning villagers at Westcott, near Aylesbury, Buckinghamshire, of an impending explosion when a heavily-laden bomber overshot the runway on take-off and crashed in a field on the other side of the main Bicester road. The cottagers ran to safety and he stopped traffic on the road but he was himself killed. The explosion destroyed the east window of the parish church and in 1953 a new window depicting the same subjects – the Virgin and Child in the centre light flanked by St Michael and St George with the ascended Lord in the tracery above – was placed there in memory of 'the man who gave his life to save a village' as a local newspaper described Edward Bulmer's heroic action in its headline. The window was unveiled by the 10th Duke of Marlborough, patron of the living, whose great-grandfather, the 7th Duke, had paid for the building of the church in 1866. It was dedicated by the Bishop of Buckingham, Dr R. M. Hay, who said, 'We have done something wonderful tonight by the unveiling and dedication of this window, which will bring truth and beauty into the hearts of those who look on it.' The service was conducted by the Rector, Canon G. Dixon. Among those present were Edward Bulmer's widow and two of his sons, Esmond (the present Chairman of the company) and David (a director).

INDEX